GROWING UP WITH JAZZ

GROWING UP WITH JAZZ

Twenty-four Musicians Talk about Their Lives and Careers

W. ROYAL STOKES

OXFORD
UNIVERSITY PRESS

2005

OXFORD
UNIVERSITY PRESS

Oxford University Press, Inc., publishes works that
further Oxford University's objective of excellence
in research, scholarship, and education.

Oxford   New York
Auckland   Cape Town   Dar es Salaam   Hong Kong   Karachi
Kuala Lumpur   Madrid   Melbourne   Mexico City   Nairobi
New Delhi   Shanghai   Taipei   Toronto

With offices in
Argentina   Austria   Brazil   Chile   Czech Republic   France   Greece
Guatemala   Hungary   Italy   Japan   Poland   Portugal   Singapore
South Korea   Switzerland   Thailand   Turkey   Ukraine   Vietnam

Published by Oxford University Press, Inc.
198 Madison Avenue, New York, NY 10016
www.oup.com

Oxford is a registered trademark of Oxford University Press

Library of Congress Cataloging-in-Publication Data
Stokes, W. Royal
Growing up with jazz : twenty-four musicians talk about
their lives and careers / W. Royal Stokes.
p. cm.
Includes index
ISBN-13: 978-0-19-515927-1
ISBN-10: 0-19-515927-6
1. Jazz musicians—Interviews. I. Title.
ML394 .S85 2004
781.65'092'2 B22
2004056815

9 8 7 6 5 4 3 2 1
Printed in the United States of America
on acid-free paper

For Erika

Contents

Introduction

It no doubt is because of my background and training that I have always taken such an interest in the life and career histories of jazz artists. This interest has been reflected in my journalism and books since I left the academic life thirty-five years ago after a decade of teaching at four universities in the United States and Canada and, for two years, in a study-abroad program in Naples, Italy. I was a history major as an undergraduate at the University of Washington in the 1950s, also earning there an M.A. in classics. I was granted a 1965 Ph.D. in classics by Yale University and served as a professor of Greek and Latin languages and literature and ancient history for the decade of the 1960s at the Universities of Pittsburgh and Colorado, Tufts University, and Canada's Brock University.

While now nothing more than a dilettante in my former field of endeavor, I continue to take an interest in things classical and still read Greek and Latin poetry and prose for pleasure. The enormous burden of keeping up with the jazz literature, both in book and periodical form, precludes deeper involvement in the cultures and societies of those two great ancient civilizations, Greece and Rome. But my nearly two-decade-long immersion in them, about equally divided between scholastic preparation and professorial application thereof, has left its mark.

My conversion to the profession of jazz writer and, for fifteen years (1972–87), host of my two weekly jazz programs on public radio has sometimes elicited reactions of puzzlement, even astonishment, but I have seen it as a perfectly natural progression. I had, after all, been closely and fondly observing the jazz scene for better than three decades when I made the change of vocation.

First, let us be clear on one issue that begs to be clarified: how do the two fields of study compare in terms of their importance? My own view is that both are of primary and far-reaching significance vis-à-vis their respective impacts on the greater world and the future. Yes, as Shelley proclaimed of the Western World, "We are all Greeks. Our laws, our literature, our religion, our arts, have their roots in Greece" (and in Rome, I hasten to add), but so are we, globally, all jazzers.

Athens gave birth to democracy, albeit a limited form of it. Jazz, it has been said by Martin Williams and many others, is the very essence of democracy in its ideals of self-expression and collective improvisation among equals. The music that I have devoted myself to—as hobbyist for three decades from my early teens and as professional for another three decades after that—has truly created a worldwide community of jazz followers: fans, casual friends, scholars, students, and both professional and amateur practitioners of the art form.

A quarter of a century ago, being interviewed for a profile, I was asked why I had made the switch from professing Greek and Latin and ancient history to writing and broadcasting on jazz. I simply replied, "I decided to devote myself to another area of classical expression, namely, the art form of jazz."

In defense of the implications of that sentiment, I point to the "popular arts" of the classical Greek world. To cite a most notable example, Greek drama and the festivals in which they were the principal events were public entertainment, just as are our jazz concerts and jazz festivals. Indeed, all of the arts in Greek society—drama, music, dance, architecture, sculpture, painting, and written works— were for public consumption. Aeschylus, Sophocles, and Euripides were not studied in ivory towers; they were performed in open-air theaters for public audiences in the thousands. They constituted only one element of the manifold popular arts of the Greek world. And, yes, scholars in their ivory towers must continue to reexamine these texts as the generations go by. Understanding the past is an avenue to understanding the present.

Several years ago, as the honored guest at a luncheon gathering of young classics scholars presided over by a former student of mine (she is now a much-published scholar, a full professor, and chair of her department at an Ivy League institution), I happened to mention the popular television show *The Simpsons*. The context of my allusion was an amusing reference to a recently published book on the teaching of the classics, *Who Killed Homer?* by classicists Victor Davis Hanson and John Heath. A British native down table from me indicated that he did not know of *The Simpsons* and was informed by the American woman seated across from him that it was "this silly TV cartoon." Jolted by this cavalier dismissal, I nevertheless held my tongue, not wishing to offend.

Occasionally replaying the scenario in my mind, I have concluded that I missed a rare opportunity to give expression to perhaps the fundamental cause of my leaving the academic life, for it was clearly due to the disconnect between the study and teaching of sublime works of art and our contemporary world. The negative assessment of *The Simpsons* was an astonishing display of that disconnect in that it was a failure to recognize that Matt Groening—the creator of *The Simpsons*, a brilliantly comic critique of our society, politics, and culture—is an Aristophanes for our times. For Aristophanes' comedic productions, overflowing with raw wit and biting social, political, and cultural commentary on issues of his day, were aimed at and performed for a public audience, just as is Groening's Sunday night series. Interestingly, *The Simpsons* has already begun receiving scholarly scrutiny.

Indeed, Homer, a blind and illiterate oral poet, presented his epics to public audiences in probably the eighth century before Christ. When I took my initial course in Homer's Greek in the mid-1950s and dug into the supplemental reading assignments, I first learned that the *Iliad* and the *Odyssey* had been composed as oral works. This discovery revealed to me a startling connect with jazz, for Homer did not recite fixed-language poems to those gathered to hear him tell of Achilles, Agamemnon, Helen, Paris, Hector, the ten-year siege of Troy, and Odysseus' journey home after the war's conclusion. He *improvised* his performances, making use of an age-old artistic modus operandi that still exists here and there in our world, a poetic language handed down orally across the generations, a compositional system made up of individual words and verse parts that fit neatly, as needed, into the dactylic hexameters in which the oral poet composes as he perfoms. *Homer was winging it*, just as a jazz musician does. I immediately concluded this on reading the 1930s articles of Milman Parry, the Californian and young Harvard professor who had made the discovery of Homer's oral art by observing, and making recordings of, 1930s Yugoslavian oral poets, one of whom, over a two-week period, performed for him a poem the length of the *Odyssey*. Though I immediately saw the similarity in the way Homer and a jazz musician improvised, I did not pursue the working out of the details. I did choose an aspect of Homer's formulaic language as the subject of my 1965 Yale University doctoral dissertation, but it was left to others to demonstrate that formulaic composition is a significant element in jazz and blues improvisation.

Addressing the Board of Overseers of Harvard College a year-and-a-half before his death at age thirty-three in December 1935, Milman Parry presented a paper titled "The Historical Method in Literary Criticism." In it he expressed convictions very similar to mine regarding the prevailing disconnect between past and present in the field of classics: "I have seen for myself, only too often and too clearly, how, because those who teach and study Greek and Latin literature have lost the sense of its importance for humanity, the study of those literatures has declined, and will decline until they quit their philological isolation and again join in the movement of current human thought."[*]

So is it really all that surprising, much less astonishing, that I found an intellectual and professional home in jazz after twenty years of devotion to the classics?

Silver Spring, Maryland
August 2004

---

[*]*The Making of Homeric Verse: The Collected Papers of Milman Parry*, ed. Adam Parry (Oxford University Press, 1971), 413.

GROWING UP WITH JAZZ

1

Keepers of the Flame

"It was a lot of fun up at Monroe's Uptown House! It was a heck of an experience! You learned a lot of things. It was just so rewarding. Things would be swinging so, you'd get up and you'd scream, because you were so elated and so full of warmth."
Leonard Gaskin

"I saw Lionel Hampton and I was knocked out at the way he put the band across to people. I realized how he communicated to the people, which is something that I've always wanted to do. I've never been into the sort of jazz that doesn't really communicate."
Ray Gelato

"I think a lot of things come through intuition. You *feel* whether something is in good taste or not. Especially, if you listen to artists who have *really* good taste, you're bound not to go wrong when you start to work on a thing by yourself."
Shaunette Hildabrand

I have witnessed the artistry of bass virtuoso Leonard Gaskin on numerous occasions, in several jazz contexts, and hearing him play is always a delight. I had not had that pleasure for a while when, a couple of years ago, I attended the Sunday jazz brunch at New York's Cajun Restaurant. The house quartet was led by Doc Pittman, on cocktail drum and vocals. Carol Sudhalter was on tenor saxophone and flute, Zeke Mullens was at the piano, and Myrna Lake shared the vocals with the leader. And there on bass was Mr. Gaskin. I was in town doing interviews for this book, and it occurred to me while I was enjoying the music and a bowl of artichoke soup that Leonard's life and career would make a wonderful story.

As he is a musician whose professional history covers two-thirds of a century and who began studying music a decade before that, it did not surprise me that an interview covering that span of time would consume the better part of an afternoon. We spent that time in the basement study of his Jamaica, Queens, home, where he lives with his wife, Mary. They married in 1951 and have two children, Poppy and Leonard, Jr.

The room was full of shelves holding many binders of fliers, newspaper and magazine clips, and photographs illustrating his career. There were racks of tapes of concerts and interviews. These constitute the archive of source materials from which Gaskin has culled the information he has contributed to published jazz histories and biographies of jazz greats.

"My father, Haynes Hoguero Gaskin," Leonard began, "left his home town of Trinidad, which was under the control of England. He and his brother left their island because there was no particular advancement for them. My father's ambition was to get to Brazil. Unfortunately he never did but wound up in Belize, a small country in Central America also owned by the British, where he enlisted in the British Expeditionary Force and was sent to Mesopotamia, supposedly to engage the Turks. During his stay there he contracted fever and was sent to a hospital in Alexandria, Egypt, where he recuperated. By this time he was mustered out of the British army. He and my mother, Daisy Leotta Ford, also from Trinidad, had agreed to meet in New York when he was mustered out. They got married in November 1918. A friend, also from the Caribbean, got my father a job in Brooklyn.

"I was born August 25, 1920, in Long Island College Hospital, Brooklyn. I have a sister, Florence Lawrence, who was born in 1923. I remember starting school at P. S. 8 in Brooklyn Heights. Then we moved uptown to St. Felix Street, which is by the Brooklyn Academy of Music. By that time my mother's sister, Lucille, had come to live with us. She bought a piano and she played a little. I still have some of her old sheet music. Most of the Caribbean houses in Brooklyn had pianos in their homes, and it was mandatory that most of us take piano lessons. I started lessons between five and six years of age. I continued that until I was about fifteen or sixteen, at which time we were living in a house in Brooklyn, on Lefferts Place.

"In terms of music, when you learn to play a little on the piano and can read a little, the parents want you to play for aunt so-and-so, or perhaps play for the ladies in the old folks' home. I wanted to be doing something else, out with my friends playing ball, like most youngsters. My father was a very strict disciplinarian and in the event I didn't practice, I would have to get up at 5:00 or 6:00 in the morning and practice. That didn't warm me to the piano.

"We had one of those wind-up Victrolas and my aunt brought in these records, Strauss waltzes and the light classics. I remember listening to Wayne King. My earliest recollection of hearing syncopated music is through piano rolls—Eubie Blake, Luckey Roberts, Willie the Lion Smith. This whetted my appetite for this music.

"We didn't have a radio. Don't forget, this is 1930, and it was very rough. My friend Charlie Drayton was growing up with me and when we were about fifteen we built this crystal set we could use to listen to the remotes from the various hotels throughout the country. There was a tune written by Ed Farley and Mike Riley called 'The Music Goes 'Round and Around.' I'm hearing more of this kind of music, and it's different from the classical music that I've been trying to play.

"I remember something that stuck in my mind through the years, a remote broadcast of Earl Hines coming from the Grand Terrace in Chicago. We'd say, 'Wow, that must be some place!' We envisioned the Grand Terrace as a big wide street, like the boulevards in Paris, and we envisioned this palatial place would be there, and this band would be playing. When I got to see the Grand Terrace, I didn't believe it!" says Leonard, laughing. Ted Weems, Guy Lombardo, and Benny Goodman were other bands he recalls hearing on the crystal set.

"In high school one of our music teachers was an ex-bass player with Ben Bernie. So I started studying bass, and in a little while I was able to play a little and join the school orchestra. We had a very fine school orchestra of a hundred pieces and our director was very strict. We were doing so well that we won third place in a band contest of various high schools.

"I was very determined to learn something about the bass, but I had no instrument. I had some friends that had a little unit with piano and saxophone, and one of them, Ray Abrams, who became one of my best friends, says, 'I bet you fifty cents that you can't get a bass by the time of your seventeenth birthday.' So I bet him. Now I'm going through the process of begging my mother and father. My father was kind of sickly at the time, he wasn't working too steadily, and times were difficult. So I hammered at my mother and hammered and hammered and she in turn must have hammered at my father, and I finally got $75 to buy this bass. I went down to 8th Street to buy this bass and there was a dollar-and-a-half tax and I didn't have it. So I couldn't get the bass and had to come back and hammer some more. Finally, I got the dollar-fifty to get the bass. That was the happiest day of my life. Ray Abrams started writing out little parts for me. So that was the beginning.

"I started studying with Fred Zimmerman, who was first bass player with the New York Philharmonic. The fee was a fortune! Ten dollars a half-hour. I got pretty good at doing what the regimen was at the time. I was on the track team and the music director says, 'You can't serve two masters.' So I had to quit the track team, 'cause I wanted to really learn this instrument.

"By this time I'm learning more about the players that are out there in the street, and I wanted to learn more. We had a ballroom in Brooklyn, the Bedford Ballroom, a facsimile of the Savoy Ballroom, on the second floor of an auto shop. We would go and listen to the Erskine Hawkins band, who was very hot on juke boxes, particularly in the black community. They used primarily territory bands like Andy Kirk, and I remember Willy Bryant brought a band over, and Snookum Russell, and many of those Midwest bands."

Leonard opened a thick ring binder to a flier that read, "Bedford 400 Club presents a Halloween Bargain Dance Featuring 2 Bands—Joe Gordon and His Aces of Swing—Buddy Riser and His Orchestra—Bedford Ballroom—Atlantic and Bedford Avenues—Doors Open 7:30 P.M.— Free checking—Sunday Evening the 31st of October 1937—Admission Ladies 25 cents Gents 40 cents."

"In 1935 or '36, Stuff Smith was playing something called 'I'se a Muggin','" and we'd go over on the subway to 52nd Street and listen to him and Jonah Jones, Cozy Cole, Clyde Hart, and Pete Brown outside of the club doors. They really got to us."

Leonard opened another binder and turned to a flier. "This was my first professional job, with somebody that I didn't know, October 30, 1937. I hardly knew anything about the damn bass, but I could pick out a few notes." The flier announces, "The Full Moon Social Club Invites You to Attend Their Feast of the Ghost and Goblin—In the Main Ballroom of the Beautiful Central Palace—1618 Manhattan Avenue—Brooklyn, New York."

"I'm still going to high school. Here's the little band we formed," says Gaskin, holding up a photograph, "with Ray Abrams and myself, and it became Clarence Berry and his band, because Clarence had a place to rehearse. We chipped in and bought a little 1936 station wagon that we tooled around in and we were quite happy." He recalls the band winning competitions or taking second or third place, sometimes up against far better known bands, even nationally known bands. He laughs. "Isn't that ridiculous? We played all of Brooklyn and Staten Island. So you can get the feeling of the people, how they felt about us, in Brooklyn and surrounding areas and Maspeth and so forth. We were quite the thing. I was very happy doing this, and it kind of whetted my appetite to go further with it. So all of this is part of my introduction to this music."

Leonard Gaskin's mother died in November 1941, and a month later came Pearl Harbor. Both events disrupted life for Leonard, his father, and his sister.

"'What are we gonna do?' I wondered. I had no desire to go into a segregated army. I hadn't had any experience with the South, I hadn't had any form of the flagrant discrimination that existed there. But everything worked out. I took a job as a barge captain. The East River and the Hudson River were full of barges plying the waters, delivering coal, hides, delivering whatever the waterfront needed. Brooklyn had a beautiful waterfront and I often think about it even now. My duties were to know where this barge was at all times and what it was loaded with. I'd be on a gig somewhere and during the night they would move the barge somewhere and I caught the devil trying to find out where it was moved to. But I got paid and it served me very good.

"I was potentially 1-A in the army and every time I'd go down my status would still be 1-A." Because of the barge captaincy and a succession of other defense-connected jobs he subsequently held, including a position at an ordnance depot in Seneca Falls, New York, Leonard was granted deferment from the draft.

"I'm back in New York in early 1943 and I get a job on the docks loading the winch. We had a little club in Brooklyn called the Elks Club and Max Roach was there. He says, 'Man, we're gettin' a little group together at Monroe's, why don't you come up?' So I started going up to Monroe's Uptown in Harlem. The band was run by a nineteen-year-old named Allen Tinney, a pianist who was ambidextrous, a beautiful piano player. We have Max, Ray Abrams, Tinney, a trumpet player that I call one of the first bebop trumpet players, Vic Coulsen, who later went on to work with Coleman Hawkins. Charlie Parker would come up, Dizzy would come up, Hot Lips Page would come up, Roy Eldridge would come up, Coleman Hawkins would come up. All kinds of people would come up, all the white bands from downtown, they would come up to this place and jam.

"The cops kept raiding this place. And somehow or other we wound up in a place called 78th Street Tap Room, which was on 78th Street near Columbus Avenue. Charlie Parker would come in town with Jay McShann; he'd come down there and hang out with us and play, and then Monroe had an offer to go into a club in Harlem, fronting a band at Murrain's at 132nd Street and Seventh Avenue on the site of the old Mimo Club. So we all joined the union at the same time and opened there on June 10th, 1943. We stayed there a couple of months.

"A lot of the guys from the Jimmy Dorsey and Tommy Dorsey bands would come to Monroe's and Minton's. They would come for curiosity, and that would bring some of the other white fellas who were playin' in the hotels and what not. And it was nice! It was always nice. Then you had the piano players from downtown who would be following Art Tatum and Donald Lambert and Willie the Lion Smith and Marlowe Morris. And then there were the serious students of jazz, the devoted fans of the art form, and the 'Carriage Trade,' people who had money and were able to go anywhere and pay for anything."

The several years Gaskin spent as bassist in the house band of Monroe's Uptown House, along with his occasional participation in jam sessions at Minton's Playhouse, were "a lot of fun! You learned a lot of things, and the things that we invented—it was a heck of an experience. It enabled you to really study chord structure and how to alter that chord without changing the melodic structure, and you learned how people were thinking. It was just so rewarding! I remember that things would be swinging so, you'd get up and you'd scream, because you were so elated and so full of warmth, if it could be called that—mental warmth, let's put it that way.

"We got an opportunity now to move down to Kelly's Stables, which was on the next street over from 52nd Street, between Sixth and Seventh Avenue. There were two jazz clubs on that street, the Hickory House and Kelly's Stables. Clark Monroe is fronting this band and we're accompanying the singer Billy Daniels. For a while Thelma Carpenter was the singer. And the feature was Coleman Hawkins. He was playing. Hot dog, was he playing!" Leonard whistled. "Adolf Sax would have been very proud of him, man! He was playing his behind off!

"I'm also working with Herman Chittison." Pianist Chittison's trio had Everett Barksdale on guitar. "We had a radio show on CBS every evening five days a week, from 7:00 to 7:30, and then we did it from 11:00 to 11:30 for the West Coast. We played music for Lanny Ross, and we played Chopin, Tchaikovsky, Paderewski, Grieg. It was quite a thing! On Thursday nights we did a program called *Casey, Crime Photographer*, a mystery. We'd play the background music and the technicians would do the sound effects. All this was radio, so you had to use your imagination."

The succession of musicians and combos that Gaskin worked with over the remainder of the 1940s is truly a roster of jazz greats; for example, Charlie Parker, J. J. Johnson, Coleman Hawkins, Stan Getz, Miles Davis, Don Byas, Dexter Gordon. Thelonious Monk, Errol Garner, Cootie Williams, Eddie South, and Eddie Heywood. He was with Charlie Shavers at the Three Deuces, playing opposite the Art Tatum Trio, and Dizzy Gillespie at the Down Beat Club. In the middle of the decade Leonard made visits to Washington, D.C., appearing at the Casbah with pianist Billy Taylor and at the Brown Derby with Stuff Smith.

"That was actually the beginning of my real career; and then everything went on and on and on, playing with all kinds of bands, all kinds of people. Unlike a lot of people who were in one vein, I was in all kinds of veins, so I was trying to be academic, learn whatever that vein required. It was a very interesting period, and there was so much of it."

Remembering the musicians he encountered during the 1930s, '40s, and '50s, Leonard exuded affection. "They were really joyous people to be around. There wasn't any animosity or any bad feeling. The feeling was one of warmth, one of sharing, one of enjoying themselves. And the camaraderie that existed was just outstanding. You know, back then I'd ask Pops"—that is, Louis Armstrong—"how do you do this? I'd ask Oscar"—Pettiford—"how do you do this? Or Slam"—Stewart—"how do you do this? And they would painstakingly show you how to do the damn thing!"

Some of Leonard Gaskin's other musings on the period are filled with sociological observations.

"We had a lot of outsiders that tried to get in on hanging out with us, particularly on 52nd Street. Now, mind you, this was during the war, and many of the women who came around to the Roxy or Radio City or 52nd Street or anywhere in the neighborhood had loved ones overseas in the Army or Navy or Marines; and they had these characters that would come around and hit on them and make them uncomfortable. A lot of the bad news that was attributed to the musicians was really because of these people. The musicians were into the music. If they chose to smoke or do whatever, that was up to them! That had nothing to do with the people in the streets. All of the bad publicity we got wasn't to our benefit or to our liking. And then also, we had a lot of southern military who resented seeing white and black together, and that created a lot of animosity, a lot of bad news reports, and that was a damn shame."

There were also celebrities who came to 52nd Street bistros. "Frank Sinatra would be there, movie stars would be there. Artur Rubenstein would sit there all night long! It was a mixture of all kinds of things."

In March and April 1945 Gaskin went on the road with a package of Ella Fitzgerald, the Ink Spots, and Cootie Williams's House of Joy big band.

"What an experience that was! We would play cards on the train, and I won considerable money from Ralph Brown and Ella playing quarter tonk, a card game invented in Harlem by the entertainers.

"The second thing I remember about the trip was when we were in the theater in Columbus, Ohio, and the show was over, and Ella says, 'Come on, let's go get something to eat!' So we go into a place and the manager comes running over and says, 'Miss Fitzgerald, my wife and I saw you last night, you were tremendous. You were very outstanding. We enjoyed the show tremendously.' But now here comes the catch. He says, 'Um, it's the policy of this house to not mix the races. I'll make a place for you in the back here somewhere.' We were disturbed, but nevertheless we said, 'Okay.'"

In the 1950s and '60s Leonard's schedule included tours with Louis Armstrong's All Stars and gigs at New York's Metropole with drummer Panama Francis and soprano saxophonist Steve Lacy, rhythm and blues jobs, studio work, a two-month run on Broadway with David Brooks's production of *Trouble in Tahiti*, by Leonard Bernstein, musicals with Lena Horne and others, and *Piano Parade* concerts that featured the trios of Art Tatum and Errol Garner and the Masters of Boogie Woogie, Meade Lux Lewis and Pete Johnson.

In 1956 Gaskin joined Eddie Condon's band.

"I enjoyed that tremendously. We made money, the music was good, it wasn't bebop but it was spirited. And Eddie Condon was one of my favorites, as a person. Had more fun with these guys."

Gaskin holds up a British newspaper and points to a photograph. "It was thirteen hours on a DC-3 to England. So we get on this plane and, naturally, they had the hostesses serving whiskey and we are all drinking and happy Then they decided to go in the men's room and start smokin' pot," he says, laughing. "So the captain comes back and says, 'I'm gonna land this plane in Gander and have you all put in jail.' Eddie, with his charm and bullshit—'cause Eddie was a master conniver and very witty—he and the captain got together and talked, and the captain said, 'Okay, just be cool, I'm gonna cut off the whiskey,' and he went back to his controls. And, naturally, they reach in their carry-on bags and these jugs come out!

"Eddie was sitting on my right in the window seat. When we get to London, the bands are all on the tarmac, three bands on the tarmac. Eddie, by this time, has fallen asleep. So I wake him up, say, 'Come on, Eddie!' He says, 'Where are we?' I said, 'We're in England.' I pull him by his arm and we get to the gangplank and we're going down and the photographers are there and the interviewers and they stick maybe eight or nine microphones in his face. I'm still holding him up. In his stupor, he looks up and he says, 'English pricks!'" Leonard laughs. "All the microphones are on! The press gave us hell! 'Overstuffed, fat, self-indulgent Americans,' something like that.

"We're scheduled to go to various outlying places—Birmingham, Coventry, Bradford, Glasgow, Edinburgh, all those. This is eleven years after the bombing; the war is over, and gas rationing is still on. And there are big craters all over London. Forget about Bristol and all those places. Destroyed! We have this bus—they call it a coach—and in addition to us, we have this young band with us. Humphrey Lyttelton is fronting it. You know his background; he's an Etonian and all that stuff. But these young guys, they drank as much as Bill and Cutty; the young guys are lookin' up to Bill and Cutty as examples, and they could practically outdrink them! So everybody stayed loaded! I mean, loaded to the point of being ridiculous!

"We went to all kinds of country clubs and places, and the people loved it, of course. It was really a beautiful trip." He held up a flier that read, "Eddie Condon, guitar, Wild Bill Davison, cornet, Cutty Cutshall, trombone, Bob Wilber, clarinet, Gene Schroeder, piano, Leonard Gaskin, bass violin, George Wettling, drums, Stole Theatre, London, January 27, 1957."

In the 1970s Leonard spent a lengthy period in Sy Oliver's band in New York's Rainbow Room. "We stayed there so long that we decided, man, let's take a vacation. So we—the rhythm section—would take six or seven weeks off and go to France and Spain and Belgium and Italy, and we made a lot of money. We sold records like hotcakes over there! We performed as a trio or perhaps picked up Guy Lafitte or some other French tenor player, and we used some Americans, some Spanish guys, and some British guys as well."

Gaskin's European jazz festival participation in the 1980s included Nice and Montreux with Earl Hines and the Hague's North Sea Jazz Festival with Panama Francis, a nine-piece band that emulated the Savoy Sultans.

"I haven't recently been working with big name people," said Leonard at the interview's conclusion, "because that requires joining an established outfit and traveling. And I have no desire to travel anywhere. So I work with the local people, whoever has something that suits my pleasure. This way I can have my own trio thing that I do on a Thursday night, and it's two hours so I'm happy with that. And I work with trombonist Eddie Bert every Saturday." He also plays at the Cajun Restaurant for the Sunday brunch session with the quartet that, since the death of Doc Pittman in 2003, is now led by saxophonist and flutist Carol Sudhalter.

A celebration of Leonard's seventieth birthday was a scheduled event at the 1990 Edinburgh Jazz Festival, and in 1994 he was invited to perform at President Bill Clinton's Congressional Ball. Of the many awards he has received, Gaskin is proudest of the citation for his involvement in the community and his commitment to the study of music in the school system. It was presented to him by the President of the Borough of Brooklyn for his "important contribution to the world of music."

"I've been quite lucky and I still enjoy it, really." He pauses. "Oh, yeah, tomorrow's Halloween! I've gotta go up to Connecticut to play that party."

"My mother was a pianist," began third-generation Washingtonian and tenor saxophonist George Botts in an interview that stretched over two mornings at his home in Southeast Washington, D.C. "Sometimes she would sit down at the piano and play and sing. They tell me that before I was born she was a pianist and organist in church. At home we didn't listen to very much jazz but we did listen to a lot of classical music. And of course my first introduction to music was singing in the choir in church."

I had caught George Botts at several Washington-area venues in the 1980s and had written a very positive review of a performance of his combo at Mr. Y's early in that decade for the *Washington Post*. In the mid-90s—we had been out of touch for a decade—I was accompanying our dog Sparky on a backyard visit and heard my name called out. A tall and impressive figure approached me across the lawn of the house next door. It was George, and he explained that he had brought his teenage granddaughter for her weekly lesson with our neighbor, classical clarinetist Charles Stier. At Stier's house, a book that I had authored caught George's eye and Charles told him that I lived across his back fence. Incidentally, that granddaughter, Karona Poindexter, now has a master's degree in music and is artistic director for the D. C. Youth Orchestra. Her principal instrument remains the clarinet, which she teaches, and she also plays bass clarinet, saxophone, and flutes.

In an essay in his *Jazz: The American Theme Song* James Lincoln Collier makes the significant point that the so-called local jazz scene is peopled not only by dedicated amateurs but also by "musician[s] of the first quality." He adds, "It often turns out that such players were once 'on the road with Woody [Herman]'—or with Dinah Washington, as was George Botts in the early years of his now nearly six decades of professional activity as a highly regarded tenorist and bandleader.

"The whole family was musical. My mother, my father, and my cousins played. Both of my brothers—they're younger than I—played piano. My cousin Charles played the trumpet, the sousaphone, the French horn. I really enjoyed hearing him play because his family was very religious and the only time he got to play what he wanted to was when he would come up to my grandmother's and play stride piano and sing all those Fats Waller tunes. It was just a spontaneous thing. His sisters used to come by and play sometimes, too.

"My father worked as a messenger at the Treasury Department. My youngest brother never saw my father because he had cancer and died in October 1936 and my youngest brother was born in January, 1937.

"In kindergarten we had what we called an orchestra. I'll never forget, we did a song called 'Who's Afraid of the Big Bad Wolf.' There weren't any horns or anything, just cymbals and gongs. I played the cymbals. In elementary school I came up with Leo Parker, Buck Hill, and Tony Taylor," he adds, naming two musicians of future fame and the future manager of the D.C. jazz club Bohemian Caverns. "Tony's mother and my mother went to school together. Leo and Buck, they both were playing saxophone in elementary school. Buck was playing curved soprano and Leo was playing alto. Buck was a year ahead of me and Leo was two years ahead.

"The National Symphony Orchestra came to our elementary school and gave a concert. Hans Kindler was the conductor. It was amazing to me because I'd never seen that many musicians together. On the radio we had classical music and spiritual music. Sundays we used to listen to 'Wings over Jordan,' that type of thing. A lot of those tunes I have rearranged to play as jazz and bossa novas. Tchaikovsky's *Fifth Symphony*, Chopin's *Nocturne in E-Flat*, 'The Night Is Young and You're So Beautiful,' and 'Jealousy.' The guys ask me, 'Man, how do you know those old tunes?' And I say, 'Well, I used to listen to them on the radio.' I used to listen to Xavier Cugat's band when he had

Miguelito Valdes singing with him. There are songs I cannot play in public and I'll tell you real quick, 'Look, I can't play that.' Because they touch me." He names "Amazing Grace," "Poor Butterfly," and "I Remember Clifford" as examples.

"But as far as the jazz scene, I didn't really know about it. Actually, I was more of an athlete then. I was a football player and baseball player. My mother used to speak about Louis Armstrong but I wasn't getting into *listening* to jazz 'til I was in junior high school. In fact, I'll never forget the very first stage show I saw. I went to the Howard Theatre and saw Earl Hines's band with Billy Eckstine, about 1941. I was somewhere between twelve and thirteen. Brown Junior High School was kind of split shift. We were out at 12 o'clock, and on that particular Friday we went to the Howard Theatre matinee.

"When I was in high school I was working from twelve at night until eight in the morning at the Treasury Department, in the Liberty Loan Building next door to the Bureau of Engraving. Joseph Ferrall, Reeves Franklin, and I were working together sorting canceled government checks. Before the day shift came in we'd wash up and be ready to go to school in the morning.

"There were concerts at the Uline Arena at 4th Street, and the Ellington band was coming. It was near Christmas, and Joseph and Reeves and myself, we were so emphatic about seeing Duke Ellington that all three of us took off from work that night to go to the concert and we got to meet him.

"In my house I didn't have any jazz records. Reeves had a nice collection of Billie Holiday and Lester Young, who at that time had a quartet with Johnny Guarnieri. So my mom made me a present at Christmas, a hi-fi. During that period when you bought a hi-fi they would give you four or five albums. Well, of course I picked out a Duke Ellington and Stan Kenton. I still hadn't decided to play music. During that period Jay McShann came to the Howard Theatre, and he had Al Hibbler with him. This was before Hibbler became a member of the Ellington organization. And he had Charlie Parker with him then and, man, they did 'Jumpin' the Blues'!

"Joseph Ferrall was taking saxophone lessons and was playing pretty good. He was taking harmony and theory and he was trying to write like Ellington." George laughs at the memory. "One of my friends had a saxophone but he wasn't doing anything with it, named Bobby

Talbert. So Bobby said, 'Man, do you know anybody who want to buy a saxophone?' I said, 'How much you want?' He said, 'I want twenty dollars for it.' I said, 'Sold!' And I'll never forget, it was a little silver alto, vintage. I started taking lessons, fifty cents an hour, something like that, from William Miller, who is the one who got the Afro-American Musicians Union chartered here in Washington. After I got the saxophone, Reeves bought one, an alto. Joseph had a tenor and was writing these arrangements, which were kind of horrible," he chuckles, "that we played.

"During that period for the next two years I didn't do anything but went to work, came home, and practiced, did whatever chores I had to do. But as far as recreation or anything, I took away all that.

"It just started as a passing fancy, but that Christmas of 1945 my mother saw that I *really* was interested. I was sixteen, and I was complaining about the saxophone that I had because, like I said, it was vintage. So my mother, who was working at night at the Government Printing Office, she made me a present of a new saxophone, a tenor. I'm still practicing; I wasn't going to any movies, I didn't do anything but go to work, come home, and practice, then I'd go and take my lesson. I'd have to travel by streetcar to go to work at night. And then, on the weekend, I was trying to make those school dances and things.

"I had one more year in Armstrong High School. Actually, I had really wanted to be an architect but, as you know, back during that period the average black man, he did nothing but mean little jobs and I didn't want to do that. I was working at night, taking drafting in my first two periods, and I had a very good teacher, Charlie Baltimore, who used to let me sleep for one period, long as I could get my schoolwork done. And I was also playing football, so that meant that I worked at night, I went to school, and after 3 o'clock I practiced football. I'm not bragging but I was good. I made first string my first year, and that really had never been heard of before, specially at Armstrong, which was a football powerhouse. Incidentally, Charlie Rouse played there. He was a tackle.

"When it came time for a physical, I had high blood pressure. They wouldn't let me play anymore. I guess it was because I wasn't getting enough rest. What really threw me off was working at night." With one year to go, George dropped out of school.

"I said, 'Well, look, one thing, I'm a musician and if I'm a musician, I can determine my own destiny.' So that's why I practiced real hard. And it paid off because the war was winding down and I was displaced with servicemen coming home. I lost my job. By this time Leo Parker was playing with Billy Eckstine and we went backstage at the Howard Theatre and talked to him." Both the performances and the backstage visits made strong impressions on the fledgling musicians. "We admired them, we tried to emulate them as far as buying clothes and dressing like them.

"Incidentally, that last job I had I was a junior draftsman at the Commerce Department. I just took the Civil Service exam for junior draftsman and I passed it, just from what I had learned in high school. And during that period I'm a musician, I'm taking lessons, I'm about sixteen, and they asked me to contribute to the Red Cross. I told them I didn't see where the Red Cross was doing that much for colored people. So they asked me to contribute to the National Symphony Orchestra and I said, 'Well, I don't see any colored musicians in the National Symphony, so I can't give you my money.' So I got fired! That was when they said I got displaced.

"But in those two years, man, I had learned to read music so well. We had a little band—in fact, the same band that you see here in this photograph with Sarah Vaughan. We used to practice at Walter Barns's house every day. His father, Walter Barns, Sr., played a very important part as a male figure. Like I said, my father had passed. Mr. Barns taught us, every one of us, about how to carry yourself, how to dress, how to be prompt, because he was our manager. He got us a job playing at the Cotton Club, at 15th and H North East. And I'll never forget it, man, it paid us more than I was making in the government. It was paying each one of us forty-seven dollars a week, and all the food was free. And by this time my mother and uncle, they knew I was serious about this, so for the first time that I can remember, my mother and my uncle they came to see us. I was now about eighteen. The Kings of Swing, that was the name of our group. We stayed there about a month.

"From there Mr. Barns got us a job at a club out in Maryland called the Dyke's Stockade. And from there we went to the Brown Derby, up on Connecticut Avenue.

"We were hungry this particular night and the chef at the Brown Derby fixed us food." The manager told the band that they couldn't eat it in the corner of the club where they rested during the intermissions. "He took our food and set it outside on top of the trash can." The band's leader, Dempsey Combs, "cussed him out and told him that we wasn't playing there no more. We played out that night but we didn't come back. We had been there over a month, six nights a week. Then after that we started playing one nighters, Fort Meade and the Army War College. I used to go up to the Villa Bea at 19th and California Streets. It was an after-hours place. All the musicians used to go there." (In an odd coincidence, the author's extended family—parents, grandparents, two aunts, an uncle, his two brothers, and he—from the early 1920s until the early '30s rented this immense townhouse that later accommodated the Villa Bea in its garden-level basement.)

"Benny Caldwell, who owned the Club Bali, was having problems with Al Dunn's band. They were coming in late. Now we had played in special events at Club Bali and we had uniforms, we didn't drink, *and* we were always on time. At that time Local 17 had a business agent that would come by and check on your union card and stuff like that. Mr. Barns had had all of us join the union, and he was a member of the same lodge as the president of the union. The president said to him, 'You want to put your band in there?' He said that all of Al Dunn's band, their dues was behind. 'Okay, this is what we gonna do,' he said. 'You have your band settin' outside tonight. I'm gonna pull 'em off!'" George chuckles. "But Mr. Caldwell, who also owned the Crystal Caverns, was a beautiful person. He couldn't see them out of work, so what he did was, he sent Al Dunn and them down to the Caverns.

"So we started to work at the Club Bali. The first artist that we worked with there was Dinah Washington. So I'm supposed to introduce her. I'd never introduced nobody in my life, especially a star like her. So Georgia May Scott"—a writer for a weekly entertainment paper—"wrote out a little thing and said, 'You carry this home with you and you practice until you get it down.' It was very short and I still use it today sometimes: 'Well, and now, ladies and gentlemen, it is indeed a pleasure for me to introduce to you the incomparable Miss Dinah Washington.'

"John Malachi would come by just to play piano for Dinah. During that period we opened the show for Errol Garner and we had patterned our style after the way that Errol played. So he says, 'Hey, man, I can't even play my hits because you guys are playin' 'em, too!'

"What we did at the Club Bali, we opened the show and we played dance music between the sets. George Shearing came in and Cab Calloway, who had broken his band down to a small group, he came in, and of course Billie Holiday. Tell you a story about when we worked with Billie Holiday at Club Bali. We were well entrenched there; we had our own dressing room and everything. Billie Holiday's manager was John H. Levy. They were staying at the Dunbar Hotel and John Levy went into her room, took her mink coats and all her gowns and everything and cut 'em up and put 'em in the bathtub. He was there first at the Bali and he say, 'When B come in here I'm gonn' kill 'er!' We were in our dressing room. We looked at each other. Finally, Billie Holiday comes down the steps and, ma-a-an! Levy had this butcher knife"—George laughs and raises his hands about a foot apart—"that big! We said, 'Hell, man, God, man!' We just closed our dressing room door 'cause we didn't want to be no part of this. We heard 'em in there scufflin', man, they're scufflin' like mad. So everything got quiet and we said, 'So I guess he killed Lady.'" He chuckles. "We came out and there he was; he had all his clothes torn off! She had tore all his clothes off and *she* had the butcher knife in her hands! And the bun she wore on the side of her head was coming off and she had a little bruise under there. And Lady Day went in there and put that makeup on and fixed that bun and put that gardenia in her hair. When we got on the bandstand she sang 'Ain't Nobody's Business What I Do,' and when she got to the part, 'If I'm beat up by my poppa and I don't call no coppa,' the whole band broke out laughing and she had to stop singing and she was laughing. And she tell the folks, 'But it wasn't that way! I whipped his ass!'

"Leo Parker was my best friend, him and Gene Ammons. Through Leo I met Charlie Parker and all of them. In fact, the mouthpiece that I'm using right today was given to me by Wardell Gray. And those guys, man, they took me under their wing. I used to go to Leo's house every morning. I'm working at the Club Bali and he would help me with my instrument, show me how to play, like all these scales and how you transform them and use them in jazz.

"Then we went to the Crystal Caverns. They used to have floor shows there, chorus girls, Helen Penn and the Pennettes, who danced in the chorus at Atlantic City at the Club Harlem. We didn't go to work 'til 12 o'clock at night and we'd work 'til five in the morning. At the Caverns, that's when I started meeting a lot of musicians. I can remember, Woody Herman came to the Capital Theater. That was when he had Gene Ammons. Of course they didn't want Gene to play because he was black. So the whole band said, 'Well if *he* can't play, *we're* not going to play.' So they eventually let him play. The whole band used to come up to the Caverns and they'd sit in and we'd have a jam session. Every night musicians would come in, whoever was playin' at the Howard Theatre, and that would help me. I'd practice all day long, getting ready for the night. Of course, Ben Webster, he used to come by and bring his big ol' Great Dane dog.

"While I was down to the Caverns, Dinah Washington came in. She was at the Howard Theatre. And I got to meet the guys in her band. They used to come by and sit in. The whole band was from California. I was home one evening and the telephone rang and that was Dinah on the phone. She said, 'Look, I need a saxophone player, I got sixty-two one-nighters. Are you interested?' I couldn't believe it! That was in October. I told my mom, 'I'm going on the road!' And she bought me a suit and a new two-suiter suitcase and gave me a hundred dollars.

"Dinah was payin' fifty dollars a night. I'd *never* made that kind of money before. We did Ohio, we did Chicago, we did Iowa, we did Detroit, we did everything in the mid-West. Dinah rode in a Buick Roadmaster and we had a Suburban De Soto and one of those little U-haul trailers on the back. It was made like a station wagon, almost as long as a limousine, had a rack on top where the bass player put his bass. It was nine of us and the driver. We made one jump from Saginaw, Michigan, to Nashville, Tennessee, over seven hundred miles. Before the audience would get out of the dance hall, we were puttin' on our riding clothes.

"You had your riding food—baloney and your own bread and stuff—because a lot of times you would eat on the ride, make sandwiches and things like that. When you got to town it would be early in the morning and you were asleep and the guys would pick you up bodily and set you at the lunch counter to make sure that you got a good meal. Mostly they taught us that you can't go wrong with bacon and eggs and home fries, so we ate that for breakfast, lunch, and dinner. I *never* believed in saving money at the expense of my body so I would always check into a good hotel. I had the best accommodations you could get, as far as being black during that period.

"Thanksgiving night we were in Indianapolis at the Sunset Club and, man, we were in one helluva blizzard. It was so cold and snowy that when I opened my saxophone case it had a sheet of ice on it. That Friday we were in Columbus, Ohio. Okay, we played that, then the snow stopped, and that Saturday we were at the Persian Ballroom in Chicago. Dinah had the whole band at her house for Thanksgiving dinner because we hadn't had no Thanksgiving dinner. We were on our way to East St. Louis and that's when Dinah and the bandleader had a rift. We get there and Dinah didn't show. We had to have a police escort to get us out of the place. They were gonna do us in because they had paid the money to see Dinah Washington.

"We were on our way to Hopkinsville, Kentucky, and I was sitting up front and we were listenin' to Symphony Sid coming out of New York. And, man, we're up in those mountains and I looked over and Harold, our driver, had gone to sleep at the wheel. I didn't want to frighten him so I said, 'Hey, Harold, dig this tune, man.' Then I said, 'Man, pull the thing over.' He said, 'Well, man, we got to make this next date.' I said, 'Yeah, but I want to *make* the next date!' So our pianist Charlie Davis drove. Calvin, the bandleader, he called the office in New York, collect. When they didn't accept the call, we said, 'Ah, ah!' Charlie had been telling me, 'George, hold onto your money, baby, because this thing is gonna run out' and, sure enough, here we were in a deluxe hotel and Dinah was already *back* in New York. Said she couldn't work with Calvin no more and the tour was over. So the guys from California, they had no money and the hotel management had confiscated their instruments and their luggage. The car was going back to New York. So I told Harold, 'Man, you can drop me off in Philly.'" Botts laughs. "First thing that you learn while you're traveling is look out for your means.

"I came off the road then and after that I had a seven-piece group. I was courtin' real heavy then, so I finally got married. That's when we worked with Sarah Vaughan and Billie Holiday and Ella Fitzgerald, and we worked again with Dinah. In that group was Bill Hughes on trombone, Eddie Jones on bass, Reeves Franklin on baritone; Wesley Anderson played trumpet and did all the writing for the band, Bertell Knox was on drums, and Tee Carson was on piano. And of course I played tenor.

"There used to be a dance hall called Northeast Casino and we played there on Saturdays. They always got us to back up singers and horn players that was coming out of New York." He names saxophonist Lynn Hope, the Ravens, the Five Keys, Billie Holiday, Sarah Vaughan, and Ella Fitzgerald, who had Hank Jones on piano and Oscar Pettiford on bass, as some of those whom the band accompanied on those 1950s Saturday evenings. They also opened for a combo that Gene Ammons and Sonny Stitt had recently put together. "Then Bertell went out with Ella and I used George Dude Brown while he was gone.

"During that period musicians, if they got eight dollars a night, they were doing good. When we worked with Sarah at Club Bali, we were making a hundred and ten dollars a week apiece! That was a whole *lot* of money! For a one-night stand I was paying these guys fifteen and twenty dollars, sometimes twenty-five dollars, and I was making approximately a hundred dollars.

"I've read in the paper where people talk about the groups that played at the Lincoln Theater. It wasn't at the Lincoln Theater; it was the Lincoln Colonnade, which is *underneath* the Lincoln Theater! It was a beautiful dance hall under the Lincoln where all those people, Charlie Parker and all them, came, and they had dances in there every weekend. It's still there but it's bricked up. It was a beautiful place, man. When you came in, it was a door right beside the Lincoln Theater, and you came in and you went down, down, down, like you're going through a tunnel, and it was zigzag. Once you went through that tunnel, they had a cloakroom, and then you came into the dance hall. The reason it had the name Colonnade was because it had a balcony with columns all the way around it except for where the band sat.

"They had all these social clubs back then that gave dances in the Lincoln Colonnade, formal dances a lot of times, and the clubs used to see who sent out the most elaborate invitations. During the Roosevelt administration the Lincoln Colonnade used to be the place where, when the president was doing the March of Dimes thing and would have celebrations all over the city, that's where he would come, to the Lincoln Colonnade, because that's where black people had *their* March of Dimes celebration. And sometimes they would have Ellington's band or someone like that playing there then."

During the 1950s George Botts went back on the road with different bands, playing Philadelphia, New York, Newark, Miami, and other locales on the East Coast.

"After I finished one stint in Philly, I went to Troy, New York, played at the Airport Inn there, and from there I went and worked in Newark. I stayed in New York with Luther Henderson. He had a studio apartment and in the morning we'd wake up to musicians like Taft Jordan and Lips Page and all them dudes who used to hang out there.

"I'll never forget, on our way down to Miami, we stopped in Georgia and, man, it was hot as hell. We stopped in this little ol' gas station. And the thing about it was you couldn't get any water, and we were drinkin' sodas and stuff like that. It was so dry there that when you walked the dust would come up from your feet. So we stopped and we saw this faucet on the outside of the service station. We said, 'Damn, we can get some water!' And we went to turn that thing on and the white dude that owned the station said, 'Hey, boy, take your mouth off o' there,' and he wouldn't let us get any water! And to give you an idea, some of the places that you would least expect it, I'll never forget when I was on the road with Dinah, we came into Indianapolis early in the morning and the restaurant there wouldn't serve us and they wouldn't even sell our road manager, Nat Margo, who was white, anything to bring out *to* us!

"The Syndicate was just about running Miami Beach. They liked our group, and where we played, that's where they used to hang out. During that period they had a curfew at night that said that any black person working on Miami Beach, they had to be off the street or they had to have some type of pass, somethin', to say whoever they were working for and that they were working late. So we could come and go as we pleased, we could have a ball. After we got off from work at Mother Kelly's, we used to go over to another club called Snooky's Rendezvous that stayed open all night long, and we would go over there and jam, man.

"But my wife Veronica was expecting our second son and I talked to her on the telephone and she said, 'Oh, I can wait 'til you get home.'

But she didn't! She went on to the hospital. I left the band down there in Miami and got home a couple of days later. After that I didn't travel any more.

"We were staying at my mother's house at 43rd and Sheriff Road, where I was born. I couldn't find no work so Veronica had to work. Finally, they called me for a job—wasn't payin' but seven dollars a night—at a club in the Dunbar Hotel. After I left there I went to the 7th & T, playing there with singer Jimmy McPhail. A few things started opening up and I went from there out to Rocky's, a club on Benning Road and East Capitol. And then I formed a group and I was working at the Flamingo, across from the Navy Yard." Among others whose voices have been supported by George's tenor are Morgana King, Johnny Hartman, Betty Carter, and Jimmy Witherspoon.

George Botts has remained active as a working musician and bandleader throughout the years since he came off the road. He performs regularly at Borders Books, often plays the lunchtime sessions and special events of the Corcoran Gallery of Art, and makes occasional appearances at the Smithsonian Institution, the Washington Design Center, and the Friday evening sessions at Westminster Presbyterian Church. He currently works with a rhythm section of pianist Wade Beach, bassist David Jernigan, and his long-time musical associate, drummer Bertell Knox.

A veteran member of the Washington, D.C., jazz community and a musical force to be reckoned with, George's tone at seventy-six is full bodied and his phrasing full of surprises. His balladry is deeply moving, and on up-tempo romps he can swing with the best of them.

In her 1995 *Madame Jazz: Contemporary Women Instrumentalists,* Leslie Gourse included a chapter titled "Carol Sudhalter, Role Model." Were I devoting a chapter to this tenor and baritone saxophonist and flutist, I would add, "and Pioneer," for Carol has been a pathfinder as a female instrumentalist and big band and combo leader in the male-dominated jazz world.

I first observed Sudhalter in performance at Umbria Jazz 2002. She sat in on flute with violinist Johnny Frigo and pianist Joe Vita at Hotel Brufani and participated on tenor saxophone in a no-holds-barred lunch-time jam session at Ristorante La Taverna. I was much impressed with Carol's lyricism and her instant compatibility with

Frigo and Vita, two veteran musicians with whom she had never played before. At La Taverna, she more than held her own in the company of five other reed and brass players, all men. Since then, my admiration for her talents and artistry has increased, for I have observed her in a number of additional performances. In New York I attended several Sunday brunches at the Cajun Restaurant, where she leads the house quartet. I also caught her in Washington, D.C., on two occasions where she was guest featured artist, at a Westminster Presbyterian Church Friday night session and the Sunday jam session at Starland Café.

"I was born in 1943, in Newton, Massachusetts, into a very musical family," began Sudhalter in the interview we did in her Astoria apartment a couple of years ago. "My family roots reach back to Vilnius, Lithuania, Russia, and Germany. The original Sudhalters were from Russia and then one branch migrated to Germany. My grandfather Nate moved from wherever he was born, either Germany or Russia, to England and grew up on the South Side of London. His wife, Rae, I always believed, was born in Russia. Family records document that fourteen-year-old Nathan, two of his five brothers, Hyman and Geron, and their thirty-nine-year-old mother, Fanny, my great-grandmother, sailed from Southampton, England, on the liner Paris. They arrived in the U.S. on February 23, 1895, and settled in Waltham, Massachusetts.

"I always knew that there were musicians on the Sudhalter side, and every time another Sudhalter turned up around the country, even ones that we didn't know about, they always turned out to be musicians! Then came the biggest surprise. My first cousin on my mom's side, Nancy Caroline, who was a great scholar and a physician and recently died from multiple myeloma, did some research into our ancestors on my mother's side, the Stearns side. Nancy discovered that our family was teeming with musicians, cantors, opera singers, and conservatory graduates on that side too!

"My grandparents on my mother's side immigrated to the Boston area from Vilnius around 1900. Vilnius was a great center of culture and learning for the Jewish people. My brothers and I have the honor of being 'Cohan,' which is spelled in English in a variety of ways, but pronounced 'Ka-hayne.' Cohans are the high priests of Judaism. This is an honor of lineage depicting high breeding and intellect and is rewarded with great respect. In our case, it's the double lineage—from both the Stearns and Sudhalter sides—that makes it so special. If any of us were to visit a temple, even in a very remote area, and declare that we were double Cohan, we would immediately be called up to the altar, congratulated, and warmly greeted by the rabbi and staff.

"From the day I was born, I heard my father, Albert (Al) Sudhalter, playing on his Selmer alto saxophone every night for several hours. This was a wonderful experience. My father played the Ibert concerto, he played the Traxler etudes, he played along with his jazz records, and I think I got a beautiful sound into my head, a very beautiful alto saxophone sound from a player who started on violin. I believe he played violin gigs up until he was in college; he once told me that he used to bring the saxophone along and leave it in the trunk during his violin gigs. He was trying to work up the courage to take that saxophone out and play it. He eventually got very good on saxophone and got lots of offers to play in major bands around Boston. He played at the Statler with Eddie Duchin for two years; he played with the Herbie Marsh big band. He played all the Newport mansions, the society parties. He had his own radio program in the 1930s called *The Voice of the Saxophone*. We have several recordings of it. He played the basic Rudy Wiedhof material, kind of romantic but very technically rigorous, technically demanding kinds of pieces.

"When he got offers that were better and better and that required him to leave town and travel he turned them down because he was a homebody. That's the way he was when I was born. He didn't want to leave his wife, didn't want to go on the road, and went into business with his father, who had a bulk oil plant. He continued to practice doggedly every night. He was a very sweet, loving father and really enjoyed having his baby daughter after two sons. He brought me along on some gigs, where he'd plop me down in the front seat and play 'Daddy's Little Girl' to me from the bandstand. So I had a lot of nice exposure.

"My mother, Esther, didn't play anything. She loved music and tried studying violin as a kid but apparently didn't do very well with it.

"I think we all took piano first, I at seven," Carol continues, and then introduces her brothers James and Richard, both older, into the account. "I don't think Rich started trumpet or Jimmy on saxophone

before piano. But I do remember that at some point when I was playing piano, when I was maybe nine or ten, we formed a trio with Jimmy
on saxophone and Richie on trumpet, and our first piece was 'The
Tennessee Waltz.' Then my parents kind of laid down the law, 'No
practicing until you've done your homework.' So as soon as they would
go out for the evening, Richie would go barreling down to the basement and put on his records and practice trumpet.

"I have been aware of music since I was a tiny baby. I heard my
father practicing every night probably since the day I came home
from the hospital. I heard the records he was playing along with, which
were good Chicago-style jazz. We were a Bix Beiderbecke–oriented
family. I knew the Bix solos pretty much by heart quite early. It was a
music I really loved.

"I had a piano teacher, Florence Goldberg, who was a family friend.
Her husband, Louis, played violin and my father used to play classical
trios with them. I got up to the Rachmaninoff *Prelude in C# Minor*,
Debussy, and Beethoven's *Moonlight Sonata*. I must have been pretty
advanced." Carol's piano lessons continued until she was thirteen. At
some point she "took a few jazz lessons from Saul Skirsy" and still has
the notebook of the pieces he gave her. "He loved having me play
tenths. I could stretch a tenth so easily. After I dropped piano lessons
I started joining glee clubs.

"The interest in music was something I kind of took for granted
and didn't really seek out other people who had it. My passion throughout my childhood was bird watching and collecting insects. In junior
high I was into literature, reading great novels. I think the music was
already so much a part of me that I didn't really seek it out, except for
having mad crushes on all these wonderful musicians, friends of Rich
and my father, who would come around our house! Stan Monteiro, a
great tenor player; Roger Kellaway, the pianist, who was playing bass
at that time; Dick Wetmore, a cornetist who doubled on wonderful
jazz violin; Dave Wayman, who played trombone; Donny Quinn, who
played alto saxophone; and a drummer named Bud Farrington. I was
eleven and twelve and they're looking around and saying, 'When do
you think I can take your sister out?' and I'm kind of just in a whirl-
wind of fascination with these guys and their music and their personalities. My brother still sees these old colleagues. My father's best

friend, Benny Chitel, was a drummer, a fabulous guy. He would come over but I don't recall him playing.

"At thirteen and fourteen I loved Elvis and rhythm and blues and the hit parade, Fats Domino, Mickey & Silvia, Peggy Lee, and I went through a phase of country and western. I loved Hank Williams and 'Indian Love Call' by Slim Whitman. So my brother Rich gave it to me for my thirteenth birthday. I had to sign some kind of a note promising that I would never play it while he was in the house.

"This high school glee club was so beneficial. We had a wonderful conductor, Henry Lasker. He influenced so many students! He had us singing harmonies on pieces like 'Blue Room' and really fine-quality literature. I was an alto and I got to hear all those lines of harmony and what the pieces were about. It was excellent training. I continued with glee club in college and had another fabulous choir conductor, Iva Dee Hiatt. That was a very deep experience. When we sang Bach's *B Minor Mass* I remember that I was just immobilized; I couldn't do anything else the whole weekend when we performed it. It just goes so deep into your soul when you sing those parts and hear the parts moving together and the counterpoint.

"My major at college was botany because Smith didn't offer an entomology major. I was taking all my entomology at the University of Massachusetts on Smith's college exchange program. I was train-ing to be a science writer along the lines of Rachel Carson.

"I started listening to some very specific things in college—Django Reinhardt, Billie Holiday, Frank Sinatra, a little bit of Louis Arm-strong, records that I either got from Richard or purchased. I would say that was Richard's positive influence on me. He shared with me his taste and his collection. When he saw me going in a certain direc-tion he really pushed to enlighten me. He took me to my first Ingmar Bergman movie quite early. He exposed me to very good things.

"I was taken to clubs ever since I was small. I went to Eddie Condon's in New York when I was ten with my father and my brother, my mother, my uncle and aunt, and I went to some gigs at Jazz Village in Boston when my brother or father was playing there. I did follow bands around in a certain sense. I remember that when I went to college, if there were a mixer or a dance and a band was there, then my interest would be in the band and not in meeting fellows and dancing. I think there was some jazz and I was looking for that. I don't know whether it was Dixieland or what. I know that Louis Armstrong came to Smith and I went to see him and it was wonderful.

"While I was still in college, something very big happened. I was twenty, and it was the summer between my junior and senior years and I had started therapy in Boston. I was in a depression, college-age depression, whatever. After about six months of therapy, while I was hanging out near the band at one of these mixers, a little light went on in my brain that said, 'You don't need to be a groupie; you could actually play an instrument!' And this was the result of finding my inner-self in therapy. At home, where all the people who played were men, I had never thought that I could be a jazz player.

"So I went back to my dorm and asked if anyone had a flute, because I thought that would be something lightweight that a woman could play. I didn't know about women playing trumpets. And sure enough, some young lady who was studying biology said she had an old flute in the closet and wasn't using it. I just started trying to teach myself the notes, skipping dinner, putting on my records, and trying to play along with them.

"I brought it home at Thanksgiving and my father almost fell through the floor! His thought, with his musical background, was to send a daughter to Smith where she could become anything she wanted to be except a musician! Probably a scientist or a wife of a diplomat or a mathematician or a linguist would have been just fine! So it was a disappointment to him, but by my next visit home he had actually bought me a flute, a Bundy. Then I started going to local clubs and trying to sit in with the band. I don't even remember what tunes I knew well enough to sit in on. My father thought I had a lot of gall to do that, when I told him."

In 1964 Sudhalter finished college and moved to Washington, D.C., taking a position with the Agriculture Department as a science writer. After six months of feeling that she "couldn't do anything right" and "coming home from work and trying to practice and someone across the alley would complain and I'd have to shut the windows and it was so hot," she relocated to Northampton, Massachusetts, and began studying flute with Aram Bedrossian in Springfield.

"He was a beautiful player in the French school, a student of Marcel Moyse and a big influence on me. During that time, for about a year,

I worked a part-time job transcribing in a hospital and took courses in music theory at the University of Massachusetts in Amherst. I would go into some clubs in Springfield and sit in with some bands.

"Then in 1969 I moved to Israel because I wanted to go to conservatory and my parents said they had already spent enough on college, but if I was interested in Israel they would pay for that trip. I quickly got disillusioned with my flute teacher in Israel and after five months left and went to Italy. I had heard, at the Boston Public Library, a flutist that I wanted to study with: Bruno Martinotti. So I began this search through the phone books of all the towns in Italy and I found him. I stayed a month, living on just no money, just bread and coffee basically, until I got an ulcer, and then I came back home, worked for another year, partly in New York and partly in Boston, and then went back to Italy and studied with Martinotti again.

"Then I had a second teacher, Adalberto Borioli, who said that he wanted to reconstruct my embouchure. He made me come every day and just play on the head joint. He taught me stuff that no one else could have. He never charged me a penny! And he and I are still great friends, and his wife as well. So I had a very fruitful year and got a more flexible embouchure. I had some wonderful experiences in Italy and played in some clubs

"Then I came back to Boston in 1972 and stayed till '75. I was taking courses at the New England Conservatory under the tutelage of Phil Wilson and Ran Blake. Very good things happening, nice concerts, a lot of good concepts. We were exposed to Greek music, Theodorakis, Chris Connor. Ran Blake really opened our minds and Phil Wilson had a way of boosting up our morale and exposing us to a lot of great bebop tunes.

"In 1975 my father just dropped dead. He had a heart attack and he was gone in about three minutes. And the strangest thing was that from the day of his funeral, suddenly another light went on in my brain, and I decided, 'Now I can play the saxophone!' This idea had never come to me except in a dream once, when I was playing a saxophone made all out of carrots with a bobby pin mouthpiece. That was long ago. That had a very shimmering sound in the dream!

"So, since my brother Jimmy had taken my father's saxophone, I got a tenor from somewhere, started taking lessons, and joined a band, maybe a year later, called Imperio Latino, a Latin band. One night in 1978 Larry Harlow from New York was playing opposite us on a gig and came up to me and said, 'My wife is Rita Harlow; she is director of an all-female band called Latin Fever. There's an opening because Jean Fineberg is leaving the band to go with Isis. Would you like to try out?' Now, I had been looking for this Latin Fever for a long time and I didn't know where to contact them. They were the first all-female Latin band. So I was very excited. I came crashing down to New York and auditioned and got in and moved, lickety-split! And that was a great experience. I stayed with this band until they broke up. We played at Madison Square Garden, at the Salsa Festival, opposite Tito Puente. I was bowled over because I'd never seen women playing all these instruments—trumpets and trombones—and having such a dynamic sound, and the whole gestalt of it. Some women in the band wrote music for it, and lyrics as well, and it used to just make me cry. I remember there was a percussionist, Sue Hadjopoulos; Ellen Seeling and Laurie Frink played trumpets. Annette Lopez was one of the conga players. There were several singers. By the end of 1978 the band had broken up.

"So there I was in New York, not knowing what to do with myself. I was going out, I got some flute students, I was taking some lessons from Eddie Barefield on saxophone. I was doing a few club dates and I could see that club dates were something that could be a lot of fun or no fun at all." By "club dates," Carol clarifies, she means weddings and parties. "When I started doing some of the ones that were fun, like flute and guitar, some classical, some jazz, nothing too loud, then I realized that if I started my own agency, I could do more good-quality club dates. So that's what I did! I established Mix 'n' Match Music, which is now a pretty established thing and I'm in a book called *City Wedding* by Joan Hamburg. I have these marvelous clients who have weddings in special places, not just catering halls, and they want special music, not just your 'everything' club-date band. They'll actually make requests, ask for certain classical pieces, which I'll go to the trouble to prepare; and certain Latin pieces, or whatever. And I enjoy this very much. I recently did a wedding for a Persian Jewish man and a Cuban Catholic woman. We had a really great time. We played the cocktail hour. After we left, the Persian band came in. It was flown in from California. Then the Cuban band was brought in around midnight. So we got to play a lot of Latin jazz. And the food was just as varied, with tables of all kinds of different varieties."

It wasn't long after arriving in New York in 1978 that Carol put together her own quartet of pianist Bertha Hope, bassist Kim Clarke, and drummer Paula Hampton and started working with it at Sonny's Place on Long Island. Before that she had been sitting in there, sometimes called up onto the bandstand by baritone saxophonist Turk Mauro. At Sonny's she also met pianist Jack Wilson, who was instrumental in helping her record a 1985 album at that venue and was the pianist on the session, along with a drummer still in her combo, Tootsie Bean.

"Cobi Narita was organizing at that time the very first all-women jazz festivals over at Damrosch Park in Lincoln Center and then in her own place, Jazz Center of New York. She would have me bring in my group. I would basically free-lance with my own trio or quartet. I played at a lot of clubs. There was one called Peachtree's in New Rochelle. I used to play at Birdland when it was up at 105th Street, before it moved to midtown. They would call me periodically. And I was still playing with Latin bands, those ungodly hours that they keep, but I always enjoyed that very much. It just became a little too much for me, staying out till five in the morning. The parts are very challenging! I love playing flute in that Latin style; and in the meringues, the saxophone parts are very, very challenging. I went out a lot to hear music. I went to a couple of lofts."

Impressed with how tenor saxophonist Big Nick Nicholas "put all the color and the chromatics and the nuances in," Carol sought him out and studied with him. "He would have me memorize the lyrics of a tune before I'd be able to play it and repeat them to him and sing them. And then he'd say, 'Now play it, thinking about the lyrics' and, 'Now play it, not thinking about the lyrics.' Those lessons were just heavenly! They really put me on a certain path.

"Big Nick was a mentor to me because he was so encouraging and so interested in having me play right and use my energy right, not overuse it. He would have these really intense talks with me about everything and he agreed to play with my band any time I asked him, whether it was the quartet or big band. I know that was very generous of him. He didn't have to do that, having the name that he did."

Carol acquired a baritone saxophone in the early 1980s. "My feeling about the bari was that it expressed my female energy, where the tenor expressed my male energy. Now I don't know if anyone else could make sense of that but that's always the way I felt about it. And the flute was a whole 'nother thing that was like my third arm or something. My style on flute is very percussive and so that's just another energy. I recorded the tune 'Hey There' on the bari. I like to play ballads on it. Now I'm approaching it differently and trying to improve my speed on it. I took some bari lessons from Joe Temperley and he taught me a lot of things." She also plays piccolo and has her father's alto, which she doesn't play regularly because "his sound really was so perfect, sort of a Marcel Mule perfect sound, not a sound you would want to get today in a band." To play otherwise on her father's alto than he did makes her feel like she is "committing a travesty—I'm brainwashed."

In the mid-80s Sudhalter, having for years been checking out big bands, decided that Queens needed one and she would have to be the one to found it. She got charts together, called musicians, and rehearsed the band. In 1986 Carol Sudhalter's Astoria Big Band started getting work in street fairs and at other local events.

"Big Nick, who was always part of Queens jazz history, naturally gravitated toward working with our band. In 1990 we got an arranger, Charlie Camilleri, who had written for Joe Henderson and Machito. He wrote tunes especially for Big Nick and arrangements for specific people in my band. Over the years we have built up an enormous library of original arrangements. And we got a lot of press. I was profiled twice in *Newsday* with a photo of me and my baritone saxophone. We played all over Queens. We would work at the Forest Park Carousel. We always got grants for these concerts from the Queens Council on the Arts.

"There was a park up the street, Athens Square Park, that had an Italian night, a Greek night, a Bangladeshi night. I decided they needed a jazz night. So I wrote up a grant for that and, sure enough, I got it. So for the last four or five years I've been presenting Jazz Mondays in Athens Square. In Astoria alone you've got 120 different languages spoken, so you can just walk around that park and see people of all nations. And it's a very good thing, exposing these people to jazz. They react very well and it's very satisfying. Many of them can't make it to the big concerts in Astoria Park that are better sponsored. Then the Parks Department and Partnerships for Parks kind of took notice of me and decided to follow up on an idea I had of producing the first-ever Astoria-Long Island City Jazz Festival, which involved the seven waterfront parks that are so beautiful and look out on Manhattan. I was given the hegemony and the right to form a committee, choose which groups would play in which parks, and it went very, very well! Then a second year we were asked to do it again. That went even better.

"Earlier this year, La Guardia College awarded me a certificate for my active role in the development of jazz in Queens. Leonard Gaskin was a part of our band for quite some time, and at some point I developed this idea of a Jazz History of Queens Concert. Big Nick by this time had died, but Leonard knew Nick very well and had been his bass player for many years and knew Rose 'Chee Chee' Murphy, who was a marvelous singer and pianist who resided in Queens. And he had played with Louis Armstrong, who lived in Queens. So we had this whole presentation with a script narrated by Leonard with me asking him questions. We used slides and we would play these tunes with Myrna Lake singing in the style of Chee Chee and Louis. We presented it at La Guardia College and at the Queens Museum of Art. So that's what I've spent a lot of time doing. And I feel good, because it was a kind of pioneering effort and I got a lot of it started."

For a dozen or so years now Sudhalter has occupied the saxophone and flute chair at the Cajun Restaurant's noon to 4 P.M. Sunday Jazz Brunch. Since the death of Doc Pittman in 2003 she has been leader of the quartet. Singer Myrna Lake, pianist Zeke Mullens, bassist Leonard Gaskin, and drummer Tootsie Bean are her musical companions at the gig. Carol's association with the restaurant began in the late 1980s with occasional sit-ins and became permanent when the combo leader, the late Jimmy Butts, invited her to join the weekly session.

"He was a great bass player, marvelous singer, great soft shoe dancer, and a marvelous figure in jazz history. He had a column in the newspaper for many years. Very soft spoken, he had a strange sense of humor and was very sharp. In fact, to this day, certain things he said, I never knew if he was serious or joking. Sometimes he'd have me in tears, but he really was joking. Jimmy was totally a mentor for me. He taught me so much about stage presence. He wouldn't even allow me on stage if I didn't have stockings on, even in summer. He wouldn't allow me to rest my elbow on the piano; didn't like the way that looked. He was very demanding, very rigorous, about stage behavior. He really believed in me and I didn't even know how much, except that his wife, Edye Byrde, who was a famous actress who also died recently, loved me too, and when she would come in she would say, 'Butts just adores you; he thinks you are the end of the world!' and I'd say, 'Really?' He tremendously turned my life around because he believed in me, he encouraged me, and he gave me the opportunity through this constant, every-Sunday gig, to grow. It was just like I was given by the heavens exactly what I needed! So Jimmy is my number-one mentor and Edye Byrde is my number-two mentor."

In addition to these two and Big Nick, Sudhalter names as a mentor guitarist Jack Hotop, who had played in accordionist Joe Mooney's combo. "He played great Bach, played great jazz, and we began doing gigs together, more private parties than jazz, but we played jazz when we did the parties. Somehow it was just very clear to me how much he believed in my playing and in me."

Carol's working quartet "has kind of expanded into a sextet and I recorded some very, very nice things this year with it." She uses pianists Bill Gerhardt and Joe Tranchina, bassist Dave Ruffels, trombonist and conga player Jack Davis, and vocalist Myrna Lake, who, Carol says, "is my all-time favorite singer. She never sings anything the same way twice."

Carol produces her recordings on her own Carolina Records. These include two CDs of the big band, *SOON* and *Last Train to Astoria*; a quartet CD, *Carol in the Garden of Jazz;* and a sextet CD, *It's Time.*

Sudhalter has performed at a number of New York clubs, been a featured artist since 1994 at the annual Manhattan Country School Rent Party and All-Nite Soul at St. Peter's Church, and appeared in the 1998 Hartford Jazz Festival and the 1999 JVC and Buffalo jazz festivals. The many artists she has performed with include Sarah McLawler, Etta Jones, Jimmy McGriff, Eddie Fisher, Sergio Franchi, and The Spinners.

"I'm planning for Italy to be a major part of my future," Carol points out. "Since I'm fluent in Italian it's the natural place for me and I do love it there. I think I realized, probably after World Trade, that I didn't just want to be waiting for things to happen, that it wasn't really so important to just stay home and take care of business, that it was probably a good idea to travel, and that one wasn't so totally safe at home. And I began to think about Italy and write and try to establish contacts. I stayed up late night after night sending out e-mails and getting names from people and names from those people.

"I landed a couple of gigs in Italy in 2002, and that was enough for a start. One man had heard me at the Cajun, Frantoi Celletti, and he always wanted me to play at his restaurant in Milan. I knew I was going to Italy and I gave him the dates and he gave me a gig. At the same time I got a gig at Villa Celimontana in Rome, the owner of which is Giampiero Rubei. He also owns Alexanderplatz, a major club in Rome which I hope to play at some time soon. I've also performed at a festival in Bresso, near Milan, and at a small festival in Assisi as part of a Brazilian trio."

Among the musicians whom Sudhalter has found herself in the company of on bandstands from Rome to Verona to Milan during five or six visits to Italy the past several years are saxophonist Luca Velotti, pianists Giorgio Cuscito and Andrea Tarozzi, flutist Stefano Benini, bassists Pietro Ciancaglini and Enrico Terragnoli, guitarist and banjoist Lino Patruno, and drummer Massimo D'Agostino.

"I'm hearing my tenor playing flowing and I no longer feel guilty that my sound is a little bit pre-Coltrane, that my big influences are Coleman Hawkins and Ben Webster and Lucky Thompson and so forth and that I feel most comfortable with that kind of a sound. And I should add that Frank Sinatra's singing was one of the hugest influences on my playing. It was his phrasing and his delivery of the lyrics. I learned hundreds of songs from listening to him. This is something probably much different from other saxophone players.

"Things really seem to be happening for me. I'm absorbing music that I hear at a rate much faster than previously. Soaking it in, you might say. I hear the change in my playing. And I get some recognition for it."

In May of 2003 Carol Sudhalter was awarded the John Garcia Gensel Award at the annual Manhattan Country School Rent Party. In September she was invited to bring her thirteen-member big band to the next year's Mary Lou Williams Women in Jazz Festival at the Kennedy Center in Washington, D.C.

"This was overwhelming to me," she says of the Gensel award, "because I know the people who have gotten it before and they are all folks I revere, either musicians of an excellent quality or people directly involved with the jazz community who make things move. The same night, Clark Terry was given the Mentor Award and that made it a double honor. And to triple the honor, my presenter was Phil Schaap, the most knowledgeable and best-known radio personality and spokesperson for jazz in New York for the past several decades.

"As for the Mary Lou Williams festival booking, that was really the icing on the cake. It just blew me away to get that recommendation from Billy Taylor."

I had the pleasure of a half-hour conversation with Jane Monheit a couple of years ago when she was between sets at the Washington, D.C., Blues Alley. On being introduced to Jane by her manager, Mary Ann Topper, I remarked that the final number, "Over the Rainbow," had left not a dry eye in the house. I then observed that along with the largely favorable press she had been receiving, there had been some sour notes—for example, the recent observation in the monthly column of a veteran jazz critic that she did not measure up to Ella Fitzgerald and Billie Holiday.

"I'm only twenty-three!" she exclaimed, laughing.

Two years before our meeting she had placed second in the prestigious Thelonious Monk competition. One prominent jazz magazine editor had noted, not long after my conversation with the singer, that Jane Monheit "can turn an audience into putty." This, in fact, was the impression I got during that Blues Alley set, at a performance in Oratorio Santa Cecilia at Umbria Jazz 2002, and at New York's Carlyle the night before I interviewed her in the spring of 2003 at Cafe Orleans on St. Mark's Place, New York.

"I started singing at the same time I started talking," Monheit began as we sipped our cappuccinos, "which for me was kind of early. I was sort of an early talker and from that time I've constantly been singing and performing for anybody who would watch and listen. The earliest recordings my family has of me singing date from when I was eighteen months and two years old and it was 'Over the Rainbow.'

"My mother tells a story, she brought me to a family wedding when I was just a tiny, tiny baby, and there was a singer during the ceremony, and I started singing along. I couldn't use words yet or anything but I just started to, 'La, la, la,' really loud. My mother had to bring me out of the wedding. I remember in kindergarten I got in trouble. I got a note sent home from school because there was a bathroom in the classroom for the kids to use, all cinderblocks, so it was echo-ey in there. I would go in there and I would shut the door and sing at the top of my lungs, just in the middle of class and I would get in trouble for it. So, yeah, it's been since the beginning.

"I grew up in a very, very musical family, which was such an incredibly essential part of my development. My mother, Marjorie Monheit, is an amazing singer, an incredible singer and a wonderful actress. She studied theater and dance and was definitely a triple threat. My father, David Monheit, is also a wonderful singer and bluegrass banjo player. He still plays, brilliantly. His teacher is Tony Trischka, who you know is one of the greatest banjo players out there. So there was bluegrass from that side of the family and also classical music, because his mother and sister were opera singers. On my mother's side there was all the jazz and musical theater. With all of that and my younger brother David and me listening to pop and rock 'n' roll from the time I was a baby, I was surrounded by every kind of music. This was really wonderful because, for all of those formative years, I was learning so much about everything, even though I was always focusing on jazz.

"In elementary school, I was always the kind of kid that was putting on shows at home for my family. I've got this younger brother, David, and I was always dressing him up and forcing him to sing songs and dance with me and act the other part in the plays that I would write when I was little, and that was a lot of fun. I was kind of a ham, for lack of a better term.

"I remember when my elementary school chorus teacher gave me my first solo and I was very nervous. It was at Christmas time. My town, Oakdale, a little town on Long Island, had their big town Christmas tree at the railroad station. We had a tree-lighting ceremony and I got to sing 'It Came Upon a Midnight Clear' for everybody in the town. I was eight! And that was it!" she says, laughing as she recalls the first occasion, apart from school performances, that she sang to a big public group. "My parents have a videotape of it. Very cute."

I suggested that, although she obviously wanted to be a performer from a very early age, that experience constituted a sort of epiphany for her.

"Well, I think I knew way before that. I don't think there was ever a time in my life when I didn't think this is what I was gonna do. In fact, I can recall lots of other things I wanted to do when I grew up, but it was always like, 'Well, I'll be a doctor during the day, and then at night I can play shows. I'll be a doctor and a Broadway star. Or I'll be a marine biologist and a jazz singer.' It was always like that because there are a lot of teachers in my family and there was a lot of stress on academics and getting a good education, so that was really very important to me. But through all of it, I always knew I would do this and my family always knew I would do it and they were completely supportive. Every teacher I ever had, whether it was a music teacher or for some other course, was supportive—every friend I ever had, everybody I ever knew was always just completely behind me, as far as, 'You're gonna do this someday.'

"Luckily, I attended a public school system, the Connetquot school district on Long Island, that had an incredible music program, starting in the elementary schools. I had this teacher, John Leddy, who just happened to be a jazz drummer on the side besides being a band teacher in my school district. He was starting us on jazz. I had had a lot of it at home and he and I talked a lot about it. He knew I was interested and he started giving us lessons in addition to our regular band lessons. We'd come out of class once a week and I'd play our scales and things on the clarinet and he started giving us jazz lessons where we would learn different things like the blues scale and how to improvise over twelve-bar blues and things like that.

"We loved it so much because for us kids, eight, nine, ten, eleven years old, we were improvising, we were expressing ourselves on our instruments, and that wasn't something we thought we could do. Being in band, where we had to follow all the rules and play all the notes exactly the right way, it turned out that all the cool kids ended up being in jazz band. It became this thing that all the kids really loved.

"We didn't listen to too much radio. I listened to a lot of radio later on when I was listening to more pop music and rock 'n' roll and stuff like that. It was mostly records being played around the house, old movie musicals. In fact most of these standards that I love, in many cases, the first versions that I learned were Fred Astaire and Ginger Rogers, or Judy Garland, or the original Broadway cast recordings in the case of Richard Rodgers tunes or something like that. So at a very early age I developed a really strong respect for the composers' original intentions for these tunes.

"When I was a kid, the live music in my life was mostly Broadway shows. I grew up an hour from here, so I saw lots and lots of musicals. And I went to the ballet and the opera. I went to a lot of bluegrass shows. I can remember when I was a little girl going to a Mel Tormé concert, a big outdoor summer thing on Long Island. I remember being amazed because he did something where he was scatting with a Bach invention and then improvising over it, and I was just completely blown away, because at that point I hadn't even thought about mixing genres of music like that. I was just thinking about standards and that sort of thing, and so I was very impressed. I didn't go to a lot of jazz shows when I was little. Of course, when I moved to the city I was unstoppable; I was out at the clubs every night.

"All of this continued to develop through junior high. I joined the school show choir, I started doing musical theater, I started acting and dancing and loving that as much as I loved the singing. And through all of that experience, which continued through high school and into early college, I was still doing some community theater at home on Long Island. That's where I really learned everything I know about performing and being on stage. I think now I'm probably more comfortable on stage than I am off, I feel so at home, and I think it's really because I've been doing it since I was such a little kid.

"The summers I was in junior high I went to an amazing music and art day camp for kids called Usdan on Long Island, which was really important for me. I learned so much there. So basically, for all those years, from the time I was eight years old to the time I was seventeen, I was just completely immersed in jazz and musical theater and studying them as hard as I could with all of these wonderful people, and surrounded by kids my age who were studying the same things, my best friends. It was wonderful.

"And just having that access to the theater has always been such a huge inspiration for me. The first Broadway show I ever saw I will never forget. It was December 7, and it must have been 1988, because I was in sixth grade, and it was *Into the Woods*. I love Sondheim, I loved that show. I was so excited. I borrowed my mother's dress. I could wear her clothes because I was as tall as she was. I'll never forget that day. I've seen so many amazing people in the theater. One person I've never had a chance to see live who's one of my absolute idols is Barbara Cook. I've never heard Barbara sing live and I just adore her. But I've seen Rebecca Luker sing live many, many times and she's one of my great idols, too. Even though she's not a jazz singer, by listening to her I've learned so much about beautiful production and how to make beautiful tones and it's so easy to apply that to what I do."

I asked Jane to tell me something about her high school years, with respect to her development, pointing out that it was not so long ago.

"Yes, it was about eight years ago when I graduated. Connetquot High School was wonderful because I really came into my own then. I had an incredible group of friends who shared similar interests with me. I was completely focused on theater because my school happened to have a wonderful theater department. We also had a great jazz choir and in my senior year I actually coached the jazz choir during our meetings. My teacher would just go in his office and hang out and I would basically take control of the group. That was a wonderful learning experience for me and something I really enjoyed, something I kind of hope to do again some day, work with a jazz choir.

"I had choral teachers, wonderful choral teachers. But I never had a voice teacher until college. I never took any private voice lessons until I met Peter Eldridge. I always wanted to take voice lessons, but my family—and I'm very grateful for this now—actually didn't want me to take lessons when I was young because if you study with the wrong person, you can learn some very bad habits that can cause some damage and be very hard to reverse later on. So they made sure I was listening to the right singers and learning good technique from them. My mother would put on Ella Fitzgerald and Barbara Cook and people like that and say, 'Copy this, make these sounds.' And that's where I learned good technique. Once I started voice lessons, Peter basically said, 'Well okay, technique's covered, let's move on to other things.' That kind of stuff. It wasn't until later that I was hearing the classic vocal versions of things, like Frank Sinatra and Billie Holiday and Sarah Vaughan and Carmen MacRae and all of the great singers.

"I always heard a lot of traditional instrumental jazz at home, people like Benny Goodman, Duke Ellington, and the great jazz orchestras and swing bands and stuff like that. It was later on that I started listening to more modern instrumental jazz, like Bill Evans and John Coltrane and Miles Davis. By the time I got to that point, I already knew the original versions of the standards, the original changes, all that sort of thing. So when I heard these very modern jazz versions, it was so incredible for me, because for someone who has always studied music and someone who really loves interesting, beautiful harmony, seeing the possibilities now for all of these pieces of music was really wonderful. I think that's what really made me decide to pursue being this sort of vocalist rather than going into musical theater or something like that.

"Then I decided to go to the Manhattan School of Music, solely because Peter Eldridge taught there and I knew I wanted to study voice with him. It was where I got my degree and met my husband, Rick Montalbano, and all of that good stuff. It was wonderful going to school there; from the second I walked in the door, I was surrounded by great New York musicians and that's the best education you can get—going to the clubs and playing and listening and talking to people. So the experience of going to college here in Manhattan was really, really important. I think I could have gotten a fine education in music at some university in the middle of nowhere, but I wouldn't have gotten the experiences and the exposure that I did and that was just priceless.

"The first time I ever went to a jazz club in New York was the Vanguard. It was the Monday Night Band and I was just completely blown away. You know what I mean? 'Oh my gosh, I'm in the Village Vanguard, I can't believe it!' Just looking at the pictures on the walls! The ghosts in that room! It was unbelievable. I think one of my favorite live music experiences was seeing Take Six for the first time because they were a huge influence on me growing up. I loved them, and to hear them and to find out that they sounded that perfect live as well as on the albums was just amazing. Both times I saw them was at the Blue Note."

I asked Jane to talk about the past four years—what kind of a life it is on the road and where she has been.

"These four years have gone by faster than any other four years in my whole life. I think it's just because I've been so incredibly busy since I started. I've been lucky enough to be able to work quite a bit and tour quite a bit and I'm very grateful for that, and so are the members of my band. I love touring with these musicians that I've known and worked with for years here in New York. We're all best friends. My husband is in the band and we have a very, very strong, very important musical bond, he and I. I've learned an awful lot from him. And so it's a really positive experience for us. We're really a family, which means that we may argue a little bit because we can, because we love each other.

"Basically, the touring experience has been wonderful. We've traveled all over! Japan, Brazil, Europe, United States. We do several big European tours a year; we get to Japan at least once a year, and our second trip to Brazil is coming up in the fall. It's been really incredible.

"We tour a lot in the UK, a lot in Germany, Austria, Switzerland; we're in France and Spain and Italy and Portugal all the time, and we've been to Turkey. We've been to a few of the Scandinavian countries, but generally we do the bulk of our touring in the UK, Germany, France, Spain, and Italy. I hope to travel to Eastern Europe because I do have roots in those countries. That's one thing I love about traveling in Europe. I'm a bit of a mutt, you know. If I had four hands, I could list all the different nationalities I am. My family's history is very varied.

"We've been tracing the family genealogy and discovering a lot of things we never knew. On my mother's side I've got roots in almost every country in Western Europe, except for Italy, and I just married an Italian man, so my kids will be Italian. So there we go. And on my father's side it's Austria and Eastern Europe—Russian and Polish—and that's the Jewish side of the family. So almost everywhere I go, I get that feeling, 'Wow! I've got some history here!' And that's really exciting. So touring in Europe is always interesting for me.

"We've been to Brazil, which is my favorite place on earth next to New York. We traveled to Taiwan for the first time in January, just had one concert there but it was a big one; it was very exciting. It's always an incredible thrill to travel to some place you never dreamed you'd go, and when you get there you find out that all of these people already know who you are. It's amazing. We did the Montreal Jazz Festival several times.

"We've covered the states! Basically, any time we're not doing a European tour or a Far East tour or something like that, we're filling in with dates all around the States, traveling whenever we can. I work a lot out in California; I play Seattle's Jazz Alley a lot—one of my favorite clubs; I love that place. I play the Plush Room in San Francisco, several places in Florida. I play Atlanta very frequently, New Orleans, Chicago, Boston a lot, Cleveland, Detroit, and those kinds of places. We get out to Colorado a lot; we play Denver and Aspen and Beaver Creek. We do Texas, Vermont, Maine. We do some concerts at colleges—not as frequently as we play other sorts of places, but we have played quite a few colleges in Connecticut and California and in the mid-West, Long Island. Generally we're doing one-nighters in concert halls. It's been that way for a while now. It's hard to remember all of it.

"Right now we're at the Carlyle. Cabaret rooms are the greatest places to play. It's so wonderful playing some place like the Carlyle or the Algonquin or the Plush Room. I did the DVD at the Rainbow Room—a dream come true. I think right now those are my favorite sorts of playing situations, a small cabaret room where people really come to listen. There's this intense respect for the music. It's really wonderful. Those rooms are meant for singers. I can remember one of the very first nights I ever played at the Algonquin, when I was first starting out, and certainly the first time I'd ever done cabaret, so I was a bit nervous. Wynton Marsalis was sitting directly in front of me and I had never met him at that point, so I was just like, 'Oh my gosh, oh my gosh!' I remember being incredibly flattered that he came to the show. Since then there have been a lot of experiences like that. I think probably the biggest one was doing Concert for America.

"The other night at the Carlyle we had some technical difficulty, some troubles with the mike. The cord was loose and the monitor was making these awful crackly noises, and then the cord fell out of the mike and it was this whole ridiculous thing. Of course I'm cracking up laughing, which is my first instinct when this sort of thing happens, and making everybody else laugh too, and it ends up bringing the whole room together. In a concert hall, if something like that happens, you get ten guys running onto the stage to help you out and it's harder to turn it into the kind of situation where you can bring everyone together. For me, I kinda love when things go wrong because it's a great opportunity to make everybody laugh.

"The DVD just came out and I'm not sure when I'll be in the studio again to record another album, so right now we're really focusing on touring. It's gonna be a really full year. I've got three big European tours before the year is up—May, July, and November. We're going to Japan again in October, Brazil in November, and tons of dates all over the United States in between, just basically constant touring. I think I'm off in August. So it's gonna be an exciting year. I feel very grateful to have the opportunity to work this much in these sorts of times. It's difficult for everybody in the entertainment industry and to have this much work is very, very reassuring."

When asked what singers have been the strongest influence on her, Jane says without hesitation, "Ella. Definitely Ella Fitzgerald and Sarah Vaughan, a little bit of Frank Sinatra, and some Carmen McRae, those are the strongest of the jazz singers for me. But, you know, Barbara Cook was a huge influence on me, and Bonnie Raitt, Joni Mitchell, some wonderful folk singers and pop singers as well. Actually there's this incredible Irish folk singer, Maura O'Connell. I wish she were better known because she's an unbelievable vocalist and she had a real influence on me and it was bluegrass. Her first albums, the ones I was focusing on when I was a kid, were produced by Bela Fleck— he's playing on them—and Jerry Douglas, those kinds of musicians. Beautiful music. I learned so much from her about having just a very pure, relaxed sound, which I think is really important.

"There are a lot of younger artists that I really like, for all different reasons. I really appreciate Sarah McLachlan's music because she sings in a very simple, touching way and she writes really beautiful songs. She's a great performer, she's a great musician, she plays instruments. And the new breed of super pop singers with all of the chops, someone like Christina Aguilera. I listen to her and I say, 'Wow, that's an incredible instrument!' I can really appreciate what she's doing. I listen to a lot of singers. Of course I love what Norah Jones is doing. I think her album's beautiful and I'm so excited to see her success. I love Diana Krall. Her sound is so specially hers; it's so beautiful and natural and real. And I love Brazilian vocalists. I listen to a lot of Ivan Lins—especially right now, since we're going to Brazil again in the fall. His singing is just so natural. I love people who have their own really special sound, whether it's virtuosic and perfect or whether it's a flawed, natural, really human sound.

"I've also had the chance to work on many other artists' albums. This is one of my favorite things about this line of work, collaborating with other artists that I really respect—people like Terence Blanchard and Ivan Lins and Freddie Cole and Mark O'Connor. I'm about to go into the studio to work on Frank Vignola's record; he's an amazing guitar player. I've recorded with Steve Tyrell and Les Brown, Jr., his dad's band. It's been very exciting.

"In terms of listening to live music, I'll go hear all kinds of things, especially since my closest friends are jazz instrumentalists. There's something to be learned from everything and there's inspiration to be found in everything; I think it's all really valuable. I just enjoy hearing people express themselves in a sincere musical way, regardless of what kind of music it is. I've always tended to fixate on music. I'll find one thing that I'm really into and I'll just listen to it constantly and take everything I can from it; then I'll move on to something else. For those early years, it was the great singers. And then in college it was more instrumentalists, and now I've been concentrating on Brazilian music, which is really wonderful for me."

Aware that many readers want to know about the technical aspects of a singer's instrument, I asked Jane about this.

"When I was younger, I was a true, true soprano. I had a G above high C. It's just a freakish note, you can almost never use it. I mean, I'm not exactly going around singing Mozart arias, so what the hell do I need a G above high C for? But I don't have it anymore. My voice deepened a bit as I got older. If I were doing musical theater or something like that I would consider myself a mezzo, because I feel very comfortable in the upper part of my range. I notice as the night goes on and my voice gets warmer and warmer, my range consistently moves up; it gets higher and higher and higher. I used to have a D below middle C all the time, and with all the touring and all the singing, as my voice gets stronger and healthier, I'm losing a little off the bottom and gaining a little on the top. My range is not as wide as it used to be. It's hard to say how many octaves it is, but I guess it's maybe less than three now. When I was a kid, my range was just enormous, and even though I've continued to work with it and stretch it over the years and do all the exercises and things, it has decreased a bit. But it's nice to finally hear my sound maturing. It takes a very long time for a vocalist's voice to mature and it's nice to feel my voice settling into its own sound."

I asked Monheit how she thinks of herself as a singer in relation to the materials that she performs. Does she get involved in the lyrics, is she an actress acting them, is she interpreting the lyrics from the perspective of her life experience?

"Oh absolutely! For me something that's really, really important is choosing songs that have lyrics that reflect my own life, my own experiences. I'm not exactly going to start singing 'Lush Life' right now because it just wouldn't be plausible, that sort of thing. So I try to choose songs that mean something to me, even if it is a youthful experience. For instance, I could be eleven years old and singing 'The Man That Got Away' and taking myself perfectly seriously, because that seventh grade crush, you know, that was the biggest thing I had ever felt at that point.

"The training in acting and all the experience with that makes it much easier to get in touch with those feelings. For instance, every time I sing 'Over the Rainbow' I'm practically overblown with emotion because of everything that song means to me and my family. The other night I was singing it at the Carlyle with my mother sitting directly in front of me, and I didn't even know if I was gonna be able to get through it. When you study acting, you learn how to get in touch with your emotions and how not to be afraid of being vulnerable in front of people and letting those things show. So the theatrical experience was essential in my learning how to be free with my emotions. And now maybe I'm a little *too* free!" she says, laughing. "But I think it's a good thing. I want people to know how much these songs mean to me, and when people see emotion in me, they're seeing the real thing, for better or for worse."

One afternoon at Umbria Jazz 2000 I hung out for a set at Perugia's Piazza Della Repubblica and was gratified that the Johnny Nocturne Band was offering, gratis, their splendid musical fare to a delighted, even mesmerized, thousand or so instant fans of all ages. There was no language barrier as singer Kim Nalley communicated her mischievous come-ons and no-nonsense rejections with palpable body

English and unequivocal inflections on "I'm Stickin' with You Baby," "I'm Checkin' Out Go'om Bye," "Minnie the Moocher," and other classics of the genre.

Nalley was out in front shimmying to the beat and belting the blues, the tassels of her dress swinging to one side as her posterior bumped to the other; leader John Firmin's hard-swinging tenor saxophone was egging her on, the three other horns riffing beneath her seductive vocalizations. With a four-piece rhythm section stoking the furnace, the Johnny Nocturne Band all but moved back the walls of the adjacent medieval structures. If given the proper exposure, I mused, this outfit could well introduce the young generation—then so taken with *faux* Retro Swing bands—to the real thing, for the Johnny Nocturne Band is authentic to its core.

I enjoyed the band during my subsequent visits to Perugia's annual July jazz event, and on one of these ten-day stays I sat with John Firmin and talked with him about his life and career.

"My father, Lewis Firmin, was born in 1914 in Hugoton, Kansas, where he was raised on a large wheat farm," Firmin began. "He heard the territory bands of Jap Allen and Gene Coy when they came through during harvest time to play country dances. It was in one of these two bands that he heard Ben Webster for the first time. He also heard King Oliver when Oliver traveled through Kansas in the early 1930s. My dad took up the tenor sax in the late 1920s and almost immediately started playing in bands that roamed around playing dances. In the mid-30s he ended up in Kansas City with one of Al Stoval's bands that traveled throughout the Southwest. It was during this time that he heard all the great musicians playing around Kansas City at the time. He told me he used to see Lester Young on the trolley car late at night or early in the morning. He and his buddies made a special trip to hear Charlie Parker at a small joint when their gig was over at some uptown hotel. He said Parker was pretty much a "wunderkind" from the start. All the musicians knew about him.

"World War II and the U.S. Army took my father to Alaska, which he liked so much he returned there after his discharge in 1945. He spent the rest of his musical career playing in the many strip joints and bars in Anchorage, which was really a frontier town. He used to rehearse in front of the quonset hut where we lived. He also taught all his children to play various instruments, but I was the only one to follow in his footsteps as a professional musician. He was the biggest influence on me personally and musically. He died after suffering a stroke in 1971 at the relatively young age of 57.

"I was born in Anchorage on April 20, 1947. I have four brothers and a sister, all of whom played musical instruments at one time or another in a rather patriotic family band that used to play at all the Sons of America get-togethers. My family can trace its roots in this country back to the American Revolution.

"My father actually made a living for many years just playing music and working for the railroad as a machinist. The music scene in Alaska thrived because of a lot of construction after World War II, various military projects, the defense against the mighty Russian bear, and the threat of communism. So there were a lot of single men up there; there was a lot of night life. The bars were open twenty-four hours a day. And so he was able to work as a musician and as as a machinist and raise his family.

"My first musical experience was basically listening to him rehearse in the front room. He actually rehearsed a lot of the music that I to this day aspire to play in some way, music that was similar to the Johnny Nocturne Band in that front line of four horns. This wasn't a band that my father gigged with; it was a band he rehearsed with for fun. It was kind of a jump band, a Count Basie–inspired band. He also played a lot of bebop arrangements of the time, which now, fifty years later, I realize were an attempt by the beboppers to play a kind of popular music. The musicians at that time picked it up and were trying to play it on gigs. I remember he played 'Buy Us a Drink' by Don Byas. I still have all my dad's music. It was handed down to me. So I can look through it now and realize what I was actually listening to.

"We didn't have television. We listened to the radio a lot. The radio up there was basically the same old Hank Williams tunes everybody in the United States heard. My dad was a fan of traditional New Orleans jazz. His group would rehearse that a lot of the time. There weren't a lot of bass players in Alaska at the time so he bought a bass saxophone to kind of fill out the little Dixieland band he had.

"We moved from that quonset hut in 1953, so this would have been, like, the first six years of my life. I literally remember when my dad bought the Gerry Mulligan Quartet records. They were 45s and I remember him taking my brothers' and my record player away and listening to these, which he really enjoyed. I remember hearing 'Bernie's Tune' and all that stuff. My dad also played in polka bands, all kinds of stuff, so I heard all this. These things you don't forget.

"The musicians' union would have picnics and we'd go and hear all these various groups that were playing in Anchorage at the time. They would show their stuff on these affairs. Anchorage didn't have that many people; it was mainly a support town for the two military bases, and there were a lot of musicians in the military who would cross over and play with these local bands.

"I took up the clarinet in fourth grade. The instruction was pretty poor and I wasn't really interested, but by the time I got to the seventh grade I was playing it and we started a little band. My father would write these little arrangements out for trumpet, clarinet, and alto sax and we'd play little versions of rock tunes at school assemblies.

"The band that really grabbed me first was Cannonball Adderley's. That's when I decided I wanted to be a saxophone player. I didn't put the clarinet aside, I still played it, but I got my dad's alto and started trying to play that. I remember all this in chronological order. The Stan Kenton stage band thing was goin' at the time—this would be the late '50s, early '60s—and I got into the high school stage band, even though I was in junior high, because I had a tenor. There were a lot of alto players but not a lot of tenor players. I started playing in this high school swing band, or stage band they called it, with these people who were a couple of years older than me.

"And then I got into a surf band. This predates r and b. There were a lot of guitar bands around and then these guys grabbed me to play in their rock 'n' roll surf bands and Duane Eddy cover bands. And those bands, even though I was only fourteen or fifteen, actually got gigs playing in bars. I mean, it seems odd but I put my repertoire together at that age. I started playing 'Night Train' and 'Honky Tonk' and 'Harlem Nocturne' and 'Stella by Starlight' for dancers. We'd play on the military bases, do a lot of work playing for the lonely G.I.s. And this is all before the British Invasion so it was a lot of rhythm and blues and instrumentals.

"Surf music predates the Beach boys. It was very simple blues-based guitar-oriented garage-band music and usually they would have a saxophone. It's all instrumental, so you get a bunch of fourteen-, fifteen-year-old boys together, kids that were probably too shy to sing, and you could build these bands up; you could play dances, and then you would kind of branch off into rhythm and blues. The whole singing thing started with the Beatles, and the Beach Boys were popular sort of simultaneously with that. But the surf music thing in the '60s was a garage-band movement that was all over the United States. You could sit in your basement or your garage, learn the stuff, and go out and play a teen dance. It was some of the first music ever to be played really loud.

"We would actually play Cannonball Adderley tunes with the surf band. 'Sack o' Woe,' 'Work Song.' We didn't have a keyboard; it was saxophone, two guitars, bass, and drums. The big deal was if you got a Hammond B3 organ in your band. That was a huge, *quantum* leap, if you could find some kid to play organ.

"By the time I got to high school my father would send us down to the record store every so often to get these records that he'd read about in *down beat*. I became an avid record collector as a result of that and I've still got thousands and thousands of albums. He sent me down to get my first Cannonball Adderley record, my first Ornette Coleman record, and of course he had all kinds of Gene Ammons and Freddy Martin records. So I've listened to almost everything, every saxophone player there is. Biased that way.

"I can't say that I played in bebop bands or anything like that. Once I got involved with the r and b circuit we were playing Jimmy Smith tunes, a few Gene Ammons tunes, and what they called soul music at the time. If we'd play a Horace Silver tune, that was a big deal. Remember, we're playing nightclubs, we're playing for dancers. At that time I would go to jam sessions but I was kind of persona non grata, I couldn't play well enough to really get up. 'Cause there's all the military guys that were *really* good players. A lot of them were veterans of big bands and guys that came out of New York and L.A.

"Also, when I was in high school, the Dave Brubeck Quartet was very popular so we learned to play 'Take Five.' I played with Lowell Fulson, the blues guitarist, for a weekend. That was the first important musician I played with. I played with a lot of famous strippers, like Miss Stella by Starlight, Miss Wiggles. They were well known on the dancing circuit. Miss Wiggles had worked with Louis Jordan. She was a contortionist; she didn't totally strip. She's probably the most famous one I worked with. Marylyn Moore and Her Twin Forty Fours was the stage name of one of them. I'll never forget *her!*" John chuckles.

"I went to Alaska Methodist University and the University of Alaska. I majored in history, which was just a ruse to read about anything I wanted to. I liked American history. I like to read about the social development in the United States, a lot of cultural stuff. I've read every jazz book there is, including those of Royal Stokes. I'm reading *Distant Mirror: The Calamitous Fourteenth Century* by Barbara Tuchman for about the third time. I wouldn't say I'm an intellectual; I just enjoy that stuff.

"All during this time I played in r and b. This is during the time of Otis Redding, Sam and Dave, early Aretha Franklin, Bobby Blue Bland, B. B. King, and all these bands. These were racially mixed bands and we would cover this stuff. Sometimes we'd play nightclubs; sometimes we'd just play dances. And then, Etta James came to Fairbanks when I was going to the University of Alaska and we backed her up for a weekend. Boy, I haven't thought of a lot of this stuff for a long time. Played with Good Rock 'n' Roll Brown. He was doing a residency in Alaska that lasted about eight years.

"And then, about 1969, I moved to the San Francisco Bay area. I was going to college around there, just taking extension courses, trying to stay out of the Vietnam War, and I started going to sessions with more serious, jazz-oriented musicians. I hate to say they're more serious because some of the best musicians I ever played with were in lounge bands. I mean, those guys have incredible ears; they can sing, they play multiple instruments, and they understand how to entertain— and that in itself is a neglected art. I mean, people just forget that this is not something you can do easily. It's something that you have to learn to do and it's a craft.

"When I moved to Berkeley I was hanging out with Bert Wilson, who was a saxophonist extraordinaire. He was in a wheelchair and had a lot of students. He's originally from L.A. and he lives in Tacoma, Washington, now. He's a pretty outrageous saxophone player. I would hang out at his house. A whole infrastructure of musicians would come around and jam constantly because it was hard for him to get out of the house—guys from Charles Lloyd's band. Rahsaan Roland Kirk came by once, believe it or not. His house was always full of people and you had to wait in line to get to play. A lot of guys were based in bebop technology. It was kind of freebop, sort of avant-garde at the time. I was there in Berkeley about a year. It was a good experience for me because I saw a lot of my heroes for the first time. Duke Ellington, Charles Mingus, Pharoah Sanders, Miles Davis. I saw Sonny Rollins at the Jazz Workshop. I was twenty-one, twenty-two.

"Then I moved back to Alaska and began my career in the engineering business. I'd done this off and on for years. I'd work in the summer, usually in construction, and in the winter as a musician. I worked on the trans-Alaska pipeline and the highway to Fairbanks. I would fly out in a helicopter and survey vast tracts of Alaskan wilderness. I spent most of my time running a chainsaw, cutting brush so I could see with the surveyor's transit.

"I did that until I was about twenty-seven and then I moved to Woodstock, New York, and went Creative Music Studio. I just felt that I was getting to a point in my life when I needed to make a decision about whether I wanted to pursue music full time or get more involved in this engineering business. Then a call came in from David Bromberg's roadie. Bromberg was looking for a saxophone player who could play flute and clarinet. At the time David had a highly visible band that played folk-oriented, rock-sort of New Orleans traditional music. He had a great trumpet player in the band, Peter Ecklund. I got the gig and I never went back to Creative Music Studio.

"So I'm in that band and it was a godsend because here's this pantheon of American music, so to speak—everything from New Orleans to gospel, rhythm and blues, a little swing stuff. It was perfect for me because I could play clarinet and saxophone, and I learned enough to play the Irish tin whistle. I still play with them. We go out on tour about once a year. I said good-bye to Anthony Braxton and Karl Berger and free jazz, and joined a folk-rock band. They've never forgiven me!" He chuckles.

"I spent the next five years touring all over the world with David. That band broke up in 1980 and then I moved to San Francisco. It didn't *totally* break up; it did a couple of tours a year, but it wasn't touring full time. I just played with everybody I could in San Francisco, until about 1988, and then I started the Johnny Nocturne Band. Over the years, I backed up a lot of people. I'd get these jobs where you're part of a backup band for different blues people, rhythm-and-blues artists. And then when I first started the Johnny Nocturne Band we didn't have a vocalist, so we would get these tours backing up Johnny Copeland, Laverne Baker, Otis Clay, Charles Brown, lots of them! And saxophone players too. Sil Austin, Big Jay McNeely, Lee Allen, all these r and b sax guys who are kind of neglected but are heroes of mine.

"I was always interested in that kind of gray area where swing and r and b all came together in the late 1940s, when the bands had these four-horn front lines with a couple of saxes and a trombone and a trumpet. And I was always interested in that because I liked the idea of its being organized enough to have all these people playing on the same page but loose enough that you can have a lot of soloing, and behind the soloists you can have interesting background parts. So it's loose but organized.

"I would go back to Alaska and put little bands together and play this one nightclub up there about once a year, Mr. Whitekey's Fly by Night Club. And this is not just jazz, what *you* would call jazz. I was incorporating a lot of surf music and r and b instrumentals. I've always done a lot of Gene Ammons type stuff, and King Curtis. I always felt that you could take the saxophone, and without a vocalist, you could put together a nice show that would keep the average person interested.

"I've been very fortunate; I've had very little personnel change in my band. You want to work with people who are fun to play with. As David Bromberg pointed out to me, you can always find better musicians but it's harder to find better people sometimes. So you look for people who are sensitive to what you're trying to do, who don't try to hassle you and are fun to be around. The biggest change in my band has been the vocalists; that's because we do an album and they get popular and they leave. We've done five albums now and the trumpet player I have has been with me since the beginning and it's the second trombone player I've had. I've had problems with baritone saxophone players. Nobody wants to play the instrument anymore. We've had a lot of baritone players.

"So the band really is a reflection of my general interest in a lot of different types of horn-oriented music, whether it's from Memphis Stax or Cannonball Adderley or Count Basie. I indulged myself and the band kind of accidentally took off. When I started in the late '80s nobody knew about this swing revival, which has come and gone already, but it was kind of starting to happen. I got a lot of jobs in San Francisco backing up other artists that weren't touring with their own bands. They'd come through and we'd play at Slim's, which was the preeminent roots-music hall in San Francisco. It isn't anymore; the scene's changed a lot since the '80s.

"When we started out, we played all the time and that led to the Monterey Jazz Festival, San Francisco Blues Festival, Mississippi Valley Blues Festival, Vancouver Jazz Festival, and eventually we, fortunately, ended up here at the Umbria Jazz Festival in 1997. Carlo Pagnotta heard us at Monterey and hired us and we've been coming back ever since. The trick in any music business is you gotta be out there banging on doors all the time.

"I'm at the point in my life where I have a wife, Linda, and an eleven-year-old son, Jake, who has his own band already, and I don't really like to be on the road in a van—a 'penalty box', as we call 'em. Most music is youth-oriented. When I started the band there was more of a market than there is, to some extent, now, 'cause people that follow the kind of music my band plays only go out on weekends. They come to jazz festivals; they don't go out to nightclubs. They sit at home during the week, watch the NFL. So we supplement what we do—the festivals and the traveling—with playing a lot of corporate parties. That's always been a big source of income for bands like mine. Even Ray Gelato just played Paul McCartney's wedding. San Francisco is a big corporate party town, so you can play a lot of parties just staying in the Bay Area. I try not to travel unless it's a career move, like going to the Vancouver Jazz Festival, which is great and which we've done a number of times. We go up to Portland once in a while. But to go out and just play strings of one-nighters, which don't really further the career of the band or make you any money, it's not what this particular group of men and women is into. We've all done it; we're older now, we're not a bunch of surfers anymore," Firmin concludes the interview, chuckling.

America's loss is Europe's gain, what with singer and Oklahoma native Shaunette Hildabrand settling in the Netherlands as a member of Swing Cats, a quintet led by multireed player Frank Roberscheuten.

At Switzerland's Jazz Ascona festival several years ago I noted how Hildabrand applied a convincing irony to "I Cried for You" and was delighted as she brought down the house with a gorgeous, old-worldly "Bei Mir Bist du Schön," which stilled the crowd with its evocative overtones of passion.

At the next year's Jazz Ascona, in a late-afternoon set for ristorante patrons seated at tables in Piazzetta Ambrosoli, Roberscheuten's versatility was nicely on display in the three opening instrumentals, one of which, "12th Street Rag," he took at a fast walk, leaving space for thoughtful solos by pianist Dirk van der Linden and bassist Karel Algoed.

Singer Shaunette Hildabrand then opened with a medium-paced take on Gershwin's "Someone to Watch over Me," soft traces of her southwestern accent effectively surfacing. She slowed the proceedings down with the verse of "Tea for Two," strolling through it dreamily, and then, over the sizzling drums of Onno de Bruyn, kicked the tune into overdrive, delighting her audience with her polished vocal skills, stage presence, swing, and sheer charm. The set-closing "Just One of Those Things" became an untrammeled jam, Hildabrand's pipes and Roberscheuten's tenor taking turns leading the uproar.

The next morning Shaunette and I sat on a balcony three floors above a flower-bedecked courtyard as she talked about her life in the United States and abroad.

"Both of my parents, Herbert Hildabrand and Betty Bair Hildabrand, grew up in the same town, in Enid, Oklahoma, roughly one hundred miles west of Tulsa. I would say they were of middle-class background, maybe in the lower section of the middle class. They divorced and both remarried, and my father has divorced again.

"I was the fifth child, in 1962, and I was supposed to be the last one. My younger sister ended up being a surprise. There are five girls in the family, Sabrina, Sonrisa, Starlene, myself, and Sharilyn, and there's my brother, Shayne, who was third in line. He passed away eight years ago, in 1993. My father has a thing for S's. I was supposed to be a boy, too, and therefore my name is Shaun-ette. They wanted to name me after the Irish name, Shaun, a different spelling from Sean, but as I turned out to be another sex they just improvised and added the 'ette' to the end. It was a lovely experience being in such a big family.

"My background in music started because my mother insisted that all of her six children take piano lessons. She never had the opportunity and always felt like she had missed something. She'd really wanted to study piano. I actually wanted to take up the violin but she said she wouldn't listen to the practicing. I think in the beginning stages when you study violin it must be very painful for the people at home—or maybe even the neighbors. So all of us had the chance to study on the little Wurlitzer that we had at home.

"My mother's parents went through the Depression, and my grandmother was divorced. Her husband, my grandfather—O'Daley was his name—was of Irish descent and he was a bit of a drinker, a carouser. But he did sing for radio; he sang commercials. He left my grandmother when my mother was about two, so my mother was raised for a couple of years by a single parent, and then my grandmother remarried. Circumstances were just difficult back then.

"One of my earliest recollections is that after I could play well enough, my mother *loved* to sit next to me and have me play old songs. And I didn't even realize these were jazz standards. I would just play them and she would sing them. It's very nice that I got to learn things that way—really unconsciously. She had me singing 'Bye Bye Blackbird,' 'As Time Goes By,' 'The Nearness of You'—from all those *Reader's Digest* collections. From the time I was about ten or eleven, I was playing those types of verses. I was not the most serious piano student but I was all right. I think I studied about twelve years.

"In Oklahoma you didn't have a big offering of cultural events. You did have different types of music, but not much classical or jazz. There was a lot of country and western and a lot of territory bands back in the earlier years.

"Both my mother and father loved music. My father had a *big* collection of records and even today I don't know how much material he has. I do know I went to visit him and he has a store—he used to design kitchens for people—and half of his store is dedicated to what looks like a record section. I remember all different types of artists. He had Sinatra; he would listen to Al Hirt or Herb Alpert or Harry Belafonte or just *anybody*. He actually even listened to the Beatles. He didn't listen to much classical music or hard-core jazz instrumentalists. I was influenced by what he liked because he'd play the records at night after we'd gone to bed.

"Of course there was the influence of my brothers and sisters, too. The older ones, who would have a bit of pocket money, could go out and buy the latest thing that they were listening to on the radio. My second oldest sister listened to more folk and country things. But that was later, when my sisters were in their teens. I think I had a very nice, well-rounded background.

"We did the gamut in my piano training, starting out with the easier ones, the pieces written for children. So you had people like Tchaikovsky and Schumann. Then, as I developed and increased my skills, I went on to Schubert and Beethoven and even pop tunes. I wasn't a very diligent piano student, not at all. I maybe practiced a half an hour or twenty minutes a day. The piano became much more interesting when one of my brothers or sisters sat down to play. It's that possession thing; as soon as somebody else would start to practice, then I wanted to. We were required to practice a certain time of week. My mother was pretty adamant about that, of course, because she was spending money for lessons and she wanted her children to do something with it. I was one of the only ones who kept on with piano. A lot of my brothers and sisters quit because it was a struggle to get them to practice, and if they didn't, they'd go to the lesson unprepared. The sister that's fourth in line took up the flute and did very well with that instrument. The one that was interested in country and western music took up the guitar. So we all found our niche.

"At the university I met a teacher, Ivy Boland, and I studied with her for a year before she retired. She was very, very strict and that's where I really developed my piano skills to a very high degree. You just did not go to your lesson unprepared, oh, no! She was a frightening figure! But that way you were very sure to practice and with the practice you improved. When she retired I left piano studies. The singing was always more interesting to me.

"I started singing when I was in kindergarten and was asked to solo at Christmas programs. I didn't have any formal training until very late, but I've always sung. For me, it was fun and there was no pressure. There was pressure with piano. Something made me quite nervous about being behind a piano, but singing was just a normal thing. In elementary school we had music lessons and learned the folk songs of the states; I hope they still teach these in the American school system. We learned things like 'Erie Canal' or English songs that have stayed in our cultural tradition. And in Christmas programs I would sing, solo, 'Silver Bells' or something like that.

"My mother and father were staunch Baptists, so we went to church about three times a week." Shaunette laughs. "And one of those times was a choir rehearsal. As soon as you got to a certain age, you were allowed to sing in the choir, and then you picked up all the church songs and different hymns; I enjoyed that a lot. Sometimes I was asked to sing a solo for the morning or evening service. And I got a lot of experience singing that way—hymns like 'Have Thine Own Way' and 'Just As I Am.' I still do 'His Eye Is on the Sparrow,' but in church we did it much more in a steady tempo and we weren't allowed to improvise off the melody. Most people just sang their parts. Everything was printed out in four-part harmony. By then, you could hear that I had a nice voice so they allowed me to do solos for the choir and that was fun; I loved that very much.

"I went to university in Texas in a little town called Wichita Falls and the university was Midwestern State University. I was offered a scholarship there and from various other colleges, and I chose this one because of the voice teacher there. He seemed to know what he was talking about, and also, honestly," she concedes, laughing, "it was the farthest away from home! They had a very good music department and you were also required to take general academics the first two years. Then the last two years you spent only on music—things like theory and music history courses, voice lessons, piano lessons, repertoire class, opera class, recital class every Wednesday, where you have a chance to actually perform these pieces. We did all different things. I remember singing the role of Blanche in *Dialogues des Carmélites*, an opera by Francis Poulenc. We did this in English, of course, because in Texas I don't think many people would sit through two hours of French.

"I went on with my training after university because my voice instructor knew of a teacher in New York, Cornelius Reid, who's fairly well known in classical circles. He was involved with the Ford Foundation, writing a dictionary of vocal terminology. I think he probably was the biggest influence on my life as far as vocal technique and building voice in the classical direction is concerned. I still see him when I go back to New York and he also does master classes in Europe. So that was another four-and-a-half years of study that I did, 1986 to '91. During that time I lived on the Upper West Side on 83rd between Amsterdam and Columbus and I worked for Morgan Stanley as an executive secretary and just took my lessons. I went back to do a few concerts in Texas when I was invited to do things like the soprano solo for the *Messiah*. And when I eventually moved to Europe I did a few classical performances here before I started moving into the jazz direction.

"No, and that's really a shame," said Hildabrand in response to my asking whether she went to jazz clubs in New York. "I even remember that, at university back in Texas, the choir did some exchange programs and we were in New Orleans and I saw the French Quarter and I thought, 'Oh, what is that?' I couldn't really profit from anything like that at the time, not even in New York. It was quite a shame."

In 1992 a romantic involvement persuaded Hildabrand to relocate to Germany and settle in Bonn.

"It was there, in 1994, that I was asked by a friend to do a program for her fiftieth birthday and I asked a pianist friend to accompany me. We did things from *Carmen* and some George Gershwin in a musical theater style. The people were *so thrilled* and *so enthusiastic* and I said, 'Oh, I think that's fun.'

"I then looked for a pianist who could do all these types of things, classical and cabaret and this and that, and I met Norbert Kemper, who was an amateur pianist and a pharmacist during the day. He was absolutely obsessed with jazz music. He had had a few years of lessons and he said, 'Why don't you try singing in a jazz direction? Listen to Billie Holiday, listen to Dinah Washington,' and that's how it all started. And right from the start, everything seemed to go so well that I never ever thought to turn around and ask, 'What happened to the classical upbringing?' I never thought about that anymore. Everything just kind of clicked. I still occasionally do classical things or musical theater or film music.

"I didn't want to go to a jazz school or study again, for sure. So I just did a lot of listening and working on things and finding out things myself. I think a lot of things come through intuition; you *feel* whether something is in good taste or not. Especially, if you listen to artists who have *really* good taste, you're bound not to go wrong when you start to work on a thing by yourself.

"Everybody had their own little circle, especially in a small town like Bonn and it was hard to get things going. People would already ask for certain names for certain concerts. It was very difficult, especially because I didn't have very many German language skills. The first couple of years there I had to learn the language and try to get about and notice the differences in the society and the culture. I taught voice lessons and I enjoyed that a lot. You learn a lot yourself that way." Hildabrand became an autodidact in a relentless pursuit of jazz knowledge.

In 1995 Shaunette was invited to be the singer in Norbert Kemper's Bonn-based Chicago Footwarmers, a group of amateur German musicians with day jobs. She was sometimes asked to perform with other European bands. In 1997 the Footwarmers were booked at Switzerland's Jazz Ascona. The serendipitous substitution of Dutch clarinetist and saxophonist Frank Roberscheuten for the band's reed player Matthias Seuffert, who had a conflicting gig in Paris, was the initial step of her association with the Swing Cats, who were led by Roberscheuten and based in Valkenswaard, Holland. The artistry and established professionalism of the Swing Cats greatly appealed to Hildabrand. She was soon joining the band at gigs throughout Europe. Two years later she relocated to the Netherlands, where she still lives.

"I'm very grateful to Norbert Kemper for steering me in a good direction, but when I met him I had already worked very hard on my musical skills. My biggest help in this music was, and is, listening to the jazz greats. I was very lucky to meet up with the Swing Cats because they are a fine group of musicians. I've been given a lot of freedom to try out different things, explore how far I can go, select my own repertoire, and really develop myself. And that's been a lot of fun and a big challenge the last few years. A lot of people, especially singers, don't have that chance. It's hard for singers. They have it a little bit more difficult than an instrumentalist. So I consider myself fortunate that I met the boys from the band.

"*East of the Sun* was our first recording together. Two years later we did the *Night and Day* album, then we did a live recording with multi-instrumentalist Tom Baker in Hamburg in 2001. That was only a few months before his death. Our last CD is actually a compilation of ten or eleven years of Tom playing with Swing Cats, and there are a couple of my vocals on it.

"Frank [Roberscheuten] is the Swing Cats' organizer and he's really incredible. He does the calling and arranging, although I also set up some dates. We're mainly busy during the times of year that jazz musicians are busy, March until the mid-summer, then a few weeks off, and then you start again in August or September up until Christmas. January and February tend to be a little bit slower, which is fine, because you need that time to work on yourself. Of course, you can work when you play or sing on a job, but not really in terms of studying some new numbers or doing something different. At least half the work is at festivals, and then a lot of it is club dates. You have also private party things. We're in Italy in the fall, which means we'll stop back in Ascona, and we do things in Holland and Belgium. We're *all* over Germany. The Germans take very good care of the jazz culture and are good listeners. And the boys have traveled as far as Waihiki, New Zealand. I hadn't met them yet so they already had the contract set for that and I didn't go. Frank Nagel-Heyer—we have recorded for his label—is very interested in putting together a vocal album of me because, apparently, in Asia they're crazy about singers. So he wants to compile something and send it out that way. And I would love to go and perform with the band in Asia. I think that'd be a gas, yeah.

"The Swiss make up a large portion of the people listening here at Ascona and they have been just a *fabulous* audience. It's really something to have a room that's *absolutely* quiet and you feel like you can deliver a song and you get something back. There's a certain level of respect that they give to the music and to the musicians themselves.

"It's a little bit different in Holland. Sometimes we play certain clubs or festivals there and the Dutch are very much what they call *gezellig*," she says, chuckling. "They like to enjoy themselves and then you get a little bit more of a bother in the room when you're performing, and sometimes it's a little annoying. But you know it, you expect it, you have no big expectation. If you get the room silent once a night, then you think, 'Yes! I have achieved something!'"

The setting was Perugia's Piazza IV Novembre, with the Cattedrale San Lorenzo looming behind the temporary stage set up as a principal non-ticket venue at Umbria Jazz 2002. Standing there, I was astonished at the energy, flair, and musicianship of the septet holding forth. It was the London-based Ray Gelato Giants, and I was riveted to my square foot of pavement for the entire set, so carried away by the Swing Era–style impact of the music that I forgot to take notes.

I got together with Ray Gelato the next day in the lobby of Perugia's Albergo Rosetta, where he and his band were quartered, and he talked about his life and career. He began by briefing me on the tunes of the set that I had caught.

"We did 'Air Mail Special' last night and I featured Richard Busiakiewicz, my piano player, Enrico Tomasso on trumpet, Alex Garnett on tenor sax, and Andy Rogers on trombone, and I played on it too. We did 'That's Amore,' 'Sophisticated Lady,' and an Italian song called 'Americano.' We did 'Sing Sing Sing,' which featured my drummer Steve Rushton. We did 'Memories Are Made of This,' 'My Kind of Girl,' 'Solitude,' featuring Enrico, and 'After You've Gone,' again featuring Enrico. Yeah, we mix it up."

I told him that Steve Rushton's feature on the great Benny Goodman and Gene Krupa number blew me away and that moving him and his drum set to stage-front captivated the thousands in the piazza.

"On the big stage I like to do that. See, we have *two* features there: 'Sing Sing Sing' and one that I wrote, 'The Man from Uncle,' which is a kind of minor drum feature. Steve is a fantastic drummer, the most musical drummer I've ever worked with. He's a cultured musician and a dedicated professional. In fact, that goes for everyone in the band. You know, we're playing fun music but we're damn serious about what we do. Everybody in the band can get up and play jazz; everybody in that band knows hundreds of songs. They're great players.

"I grew up in London," Ray continued. "My father was a G.I., a 1950s American conscript from New Jersey. He came over to England and met my mother. My earliest memories of music are from his record collection. He had all the rock 'n' roll records of the day— Little Richard, Bill Haley and His Comets, Fats Domino, all that kind of thing. He also was mad about Sammy Davis, Jr. I was a tiny kid and always loved that kind of stuff. I was never really interested in what was on the radio in England 'cause when I was growing up it was Beatles and Rolling Stones, and that kind of stuff never really moved me. I was a kid three years old when the Beatles came on.

"So it was the records that were around the house, Dad's kind of thing. I remember 'Strangers in the Night' by Sinatra. Later I remember 'Hello Dolly' by Louis Armstrong, and his 'Wonderful World.' I liked Louis as a kid and it took me years to realize that he was a jazz musician and not just a singer. And I liked Barbra Streisand. Then I remember a big, very big influence on me musically was the film *Jungle Book* with Louis Prima singing the song 'King of the Swingers.' I remember as a kid I loved that song.

"That was what was happening until I got in my teens in the late 1970s and there were things like punk rock and all the kids in school were listening to that and a lot of the heavy metal things. I never really went toward that kind of stuff. I got more into the rock 'n' roll records my dad had. We used to go to clubs in London that played a lot of rock 'n' roll but some of the deejays, they were into different things, more black r and b. I don't know what you call 'em in the States—cult clubs, I guess. In England at that time there was a whole different scene going on. There were Mods, Punks, Teddy Boys, and rockers. They all had their own kind of music. It's homogenized now, but it was very different at that time.

"When I was at school in the 1970s there was the usual crap on the radio and I was not really interested in that, except maybe a couple of songs. But when I left school, because of these clubs where they didn't play just rock 'n' roll but used to play people like Louis Jordan, I got interested. In fact, I became fascinated with Louis Jordan, with the saxophone solos and the trumpet solos. That was more interesting than my dad's collection. I bought a tenor saxophone, left school, and started practicing along with records. I liked the sound of the tenor, and the saxophone breaks on the records were tenor. I picked up the saxophone pretty quickly. I kind of learned note for note without really knowing what I was doing. I knew nothing about music. I never went to music college; I couldn't read a note. I had played violin and recorder in school, but gave it up, not really interested in it.

"I was seventeen years old and working in a regular job and really became fascinated with the saxophone. I got in a band that was playing 1950s stuff, mostly bop and blues. We toured up and down the country doing one-nighters. When this band rehearsed, I could pick things up quick—I don't know why, but quick. I was becoming discouraged with the attitude of the guys in the band. I didn't feel they were particularly interested in what they were doing. It was like more of a laugh to them. I wanted to try and understand the music. I had a fascination with it, and through listening to Louis Jordan and a lot of the rock 'n' roll people, I started to go back to wanting to understand what was before that.

"So I found a guy in the paper one day and started studying with him and understanding what I was doing. Through him and a few other people I got a wealth of knowledge about these people that I really came to love very much. Illinois Jacquet was a first influence. He played in a similar style to players on my dad's records, 'cause those guys on the early rock 'n' roll sessions, as you know, were jazz players, most of them; they were hired in to do the job. They were great players. I mean, those guys on Fats Domino records, they had great sounds, like Sam Butera with Louis Prima. They could play. I discovered Sonny Rollins, all the usual guys. Some of them were guys that nobody talks about anymore, but they're still big heroes of mine: Arnett Cobb, Eddie Lockjaw Davis. At that time people like that were still around and coming over to England. They played at Ronnie Scott's club. We used to go check these guys out. I went to the Nice Jazz Festival every year and made an effort to see these people.

"In the meantime, I was going to jazz courses, these two-week club courses you could go to, and I was practicing pretty hard and gradually getting my sound together. I'd left the band and formed another band called the Chevalier Brothers. The guitar player was Patrice Serapiglia, but he was calling himself Maurice Chevalier. He played a mixture of Django Reinhardt and Charlie Christian. He didn't read or know about music, but he had incredible natural ability. We did a lot of Louis Jordan material and some Benny Goodman. Patrice taught me a lot about how to play, especially about the kinds of harmonies and the times that he used.

"The Chevalier Brothers was a hit with the college kids. At this time—1981, '82—you had the pop scene and the punk scene, and we were really pioneers in the resurgence of swing. We weren't the best musicians, but we weren't the worst. We were studying; everybody was studying up, trying to play. And while I was playing with that band I'd always do other gigs, too, little combos, quartets, quintets, trying to get a repertoire of songs together."

The Chevalier Brothers played a big role in reviving interest in the jump music and early r and b that predated rock 'n' roll. Serapiglia encouraged Ray to sing. By early 1983 what began as a duo had expanded into a five-piece combo and was gigging in the London clubs. The added members were Roger Beaujolais on vibraphone, Clark Kent on bass, and John Piper on drums. The stage garb was zoot suits,

which for the time was a different look, compared to the rest of the
pop scene. The band played such London clubs as Dingwalls, the
Dublin Castle, the Fridge, and the Half Moon; they toured the college circuit, appeared on television, were booked for the Montreux
and North Sea jazz festivals, and performed in Japan. The band broke
up in 1988.

"I met a lot of my heroes during that time—for example, Jacquet
and Arnett—and I used to watch what equipment they used, that kind
of thing. Seeing those people live really influenced what I do. I saw
Lionel Hampton a lot of times and I was knocked out at the way he put
the band across to people. I realized how he communicated to the people,
which is something that I've always wanted to do. That's why I enjoy
singing. I've never been into the sort of jazz that doesn't really communicate. It's not me, it's not my personality. And seeing guys like Hamp
and the guys I mentioned made me realize that's what I wanted to do,
communicate with people. Even Dizzy Gillespie does that. He took
the music across in a nice way, a way that people would appreciate,
even if the band played something technical or complicated.

"Louis Prima never came to England," Gelato points out, adding
that the Chevalier Brothers had not included Prima's materials in its
book. "He never traveled overseas. He just used to work in the States.
I never got to see him. But they used to play his records in these clubs
in London, 'Buona Sera' and 'Just a Gigolo,' so I discovered Louis. I
loved his trumpet playing. I listened to his early stuff and the 1950s
stuff on Capitol. Again, it appealed to my sense of how to communicate with people. And I loved Louis's way of singing. It's loose; it's
like the way the saxophone sings, that loose phrasing. It's not conventional singing; it's not studied singing. It's got so much heart in it,
and that's the way I approached him. I spent many years, in a way,
copying Louis Prima. I've gotten away from that a little now. Louis
had a great band, too.

"I've been fortunate enough to see and meet Sam Butera"—who
spent two decades with Louis Prima as saxophonist, arranger, and
comic foil to the leader—"a couple of times and talk to him. I was
always a big fan of Sam's playing. I always felt Louis played good
music; he never compromised the music but always, again, communicated with the people. He was a popular entertainer. To me, there's
nothing wrong with that at all.

"When the Chevalier Brothers broke up in 1988, I wasn't the leader of that band. I formed my own band, Ray Gelato and the Giants of Jive. I always liked the big band; I was getting very much into the big band sound. I loved Count Basie and Duke Ellington. But I can't afford a big band. Who could take a big band out now?"

Gelato took Kent and Piper from the Chevalier Brothers and put together a seven-piece unit—trumpet, trombone, alto and tenor saxophones, piano, bass, and drums—that played scaled-down big band arrangements of 1940s-era jump and swing tunes. It went onto the club and college circuit and toured frequently, especially in Italy. Highlights included appearances at the Nice Jazz Festival, the Lugano Jazz Festival, and a New York concert. The band recorded three albums.

"In 1992 we played in Carnegie Hall with Renzo Arbore, who's here at this festival this year. He got us over there to do a thing called Napoli Del Mondo. That was a great experience. Since then I've lived in the States. Last year I lived in Florida for nine months, had a band there, and I go back pretty frequently. I go to Philadelphia, D.C., New York City, that kind of thing. Hire guys there. I've got some good friends in New York who can put a band together. I was in the States as a kid once to see my grandparents, in New Jersey."

In 1994 Gelato started his present band, the Ray Gelato Giants. His emphasis now was on American popular music and jazz in a much broader sense than before, drawing from Nat King Cole, Frank Sinatra, Duke Ellington, and others and retaining his Louis Prima–influenced vocals.

"This specific band that I have today has been together since 1995. I changed the concept, and, basically, we play anything in this band that I like. I don't limit it to just the 1940s or '50s, I play anything. I write songs; we play a mixture of some Louis Prima stuff, a little bit of Dean Martin, some jazz. We got 'Whirly Bird' and 'Apple Honey' in the book. I've got a jazz repertoire if we need it; we do ballads; I feature some great guys. We got a wonderful trumpet player, Enrico Tomasso. Enrico's father was a famous British jazz musician, clarinetist Ernie Tomasso, who knew Louis Armstrong from the 1930s and played with him. When Enrico was eight his dad arranged for him to meet and greet Louis when he arrived in Britain by plane. Enrico played for Louis, and hung out with him at several gigs!"

The Giants are well traveled, having made the festival and concert scene through the British Isles and Western and Eastern Europe.

"This band is my main project but I do a lot of other things. I've got a bebop band with my tenor player Alex where we do a lot of that Eddie Lockjaw Davis/Johnny Griffin/Gene Ammons/Sonny Stitt kind of stuff. I'm heavily into that style.

"The myth that's happened in jazz that you can't enjoy yourself and communicate with people playing music, I think that's bullshit, excuse my language, because you can and that's what we try to do. I look at it this way. There's a lot of unhappiness in the world. If I can contribute a little bit of happiness to people, that's great. We're still presenting good music without playing garbage. But to me, I'm doing something I was born to do. There's enough people coming out of college playing the more modern thing and there's nothing wrong with that. I play tenor like my heroes; I play Texas tenor, that kind of style of saxophone, 'cause that's exactly how I fit. I like Ben Webster, all the guys like that. That's the way I want to play, and the same with the singing. I like to mix it up, little bit of Louis Prima, maybe a bit of Sinatra, I try to get my own thing in. So we're doing pretty good.

"Do you knew how many times people come up to me and say, 'My husband's sick and off in the hospital' or 'My boy friend's left me' and 'You've helped me forget that it happened.' That, to me, is *the* most important thing that you can do. The world now is so uncertain after 9/11 and this terrible thing in Israel and Palestine. You think people aren't learning. That's two latent world wars and it concerns me very much. Really, I say, leave 'em happy; that's so important. I mean it!"

2

Modernists

"Jazz is American, it's all of us, and I just want to get that over. It's *got* to get over. It isn't black, it isn't white, it's *American*! Music has no color lines." Art Blakey

"We have given nowhere near the kind of attention that we should have to make sure that women got an opportunity to be heard. Many women who could have made *enormous* contributions were not given the opportunity to do that, and we're trying to correct that." Billy Taylor

"Somebody says jazz is dead. I don't think so. Jazz is not for a thousand thousand people. I've never seen for classical music a thousand thousand people. Should we say that opera is dead?" Carlo Pagnotta

The last of the many times I caught Art Blakey's Jazz Messengers in action was at the 1987 Jazzfest Berlin, a four-day event that annually began at the end of October. The then sixty-eight-year-old drummer and bandleader would die three years later in that very month.

At that booking, the Jazz Messengers' other members were each about one-third the age of their leader. Blakey estimated toward the end of his life that about two hundred young musicians had passed through his band during the three decades of its existence. Most had gone on to lead their own groups. On that Berlin evening Philip Harper was on trumpet, Javon Jackson was on tenor saxophone, and Benny Green was at the piano.

The Messengers mounted the stage of the Philharmonie, the city's symphony hall, at about midnight as the program's final group—and they roared, Blakey giving as good as he got. I could not recall ever seeing the Messengers cook with as much energy as they displayed for that hour-and-a-half set.

A half-hour or so after the evening's conclusion, photographer W. Patrick Hinely and I saw Blakey being dropped off at his hotel. We followed him into the lobby and greeted him. I handed him a copy of the current *JazzTimes;* the cover story was a profile of Pat Metheny, which I had written. I remember that Patrick addressed Art as "Dean Blakey," in honor of the virtual school of music that his combo had long represented.

"*JazzTimes,*" Blakey said, taking the magazine from me.

We addressed some remarks to him as he turned the pages of the publication.

"He can't hear a word you're saying," a member of his road team called to us from across the lobby. "He's stone deaf."

"I'm on my knees!" the weary drummer announced to us in his gravely voice and turned toward the elevator.

Oddly, the very same roadie who had told us Blakey couldn't hear then approached him and informed him of a jam session that was soon kicking off in a nearby club and asked if he wanted to go. Blakey did not reply, looking at him blankly, and stepped into the elevator, staring at us all until the door closed.

"He arrived in Berlin yesterday," explained our informant, "got his band settled in the hotel, and took the Concorde back to the States. He got back here this evening."

A decade before our encounter in Berlin I had conducted an on-air interview with Art Blakey on my radio program *Since Minton's* on public radio station WGTB-FM, Washington, D.C. What follows is the transcript of that show. Interspersed in the half-hour conversation were selections from albums by the Jazz Messengers. Before we went on the air, Art pointed to a yellow legal pad I had before me and remarked, "You got a whole book of questions there! I don't need no questions, once I start talking!"

This indeed proved to be true.

* * *

"That was a cut called 'I'm Not So Sure' from an album released a couple of years ago by Art Blakey and the Jazz Messengers," I back-announced, "who are currently appearing at the Childe Harold and will be there through Sunday night. We have Art Blakey here in the studio with us. First, I'd like to make a couple of comments, actually, read a couple of quotations, some things that have been said about him; this first one is by a German jazz critic, Joachim Berendt, who refers to him as 'the wildest and most vital of all the jazz drummers to emerge from bop.' And Nat Hentoff commented that 'he is perhaps the most emotionally unbridled drummer in jazz' and 'there are times when his backgrounds resemble a brush fire.' I'd like to start off asking you what you're doing now in terms of your music and where you're appearing and who is in the group you have together now."

"Well, we're doing everything we possibly can. What we're trying to do, we try to promote America's art form, which has sort of fallen by the wayside for some reason. I don't know why, because there's plenty of room for everything, but we Americans, we're so one-track minded. [Jazz musicians] spend most of our time in foreign countries to make a living. It *shouldn't* be, but it just happens to be that way. I don't understand it, I guess they don't propagate it here and yet we have the best media to propagate it. We find in foreign countries that we go to that we're best known, *more* known, than most of our jazz stars are over here."

"It's always been like that since the very beginning."

"Yeah, absolutely. It's just ridiculous. It is our art form and we seem to ignore it and it seems to have gone underground. Until, oh, a couple of years ago we were strictly buried; we never got to appear here in this country. We're always gone, 'cause there was no work for us here. And now in this new generation that's coming up they have just discovered it and they're beginning to like it. This music is so technical, kids can't just go into it. You can't start at the top; you have to work from the bottom. It takes years to build up the technical ability.

There's a lot more to being a musician than just playing music. [Musicians] have to learn how to get along with people, and first you have to learn how to be a man. There are other things going on and you have to build up to that. You have to learn the chord progressions and why Louis Armstrong did this, why Art Tatum did that, why Bix Beiderbecke played this way. These men have put down something, just like Beethoven and Bach, and it shall never perish. I don't see why they choose to ignore it, but I think they should give it to the kids. Anyway, the kids have found it and we're back once again."

"What sort of a reception are you getting from young audiences here?"

"*Fan-tas-tic*, fantastic, I tell you; they feel that it's a new thing, and they say, 'Well, wow!' Jazz is an unspoken language and people understand it everywhere. They just won't propagate it here, and when they do, you have to waste a lot of energy jumpin' around on the stage and dancing. People say, 'Well, entertain us!' We're there to play music and all the energy you spend jumpin' around on the stage we got to put in our horns or in the other instruments with the technical ability it takes to play."

"Do you play a lot on the club scene in this country—for instance, the type of club that you're doing right now, the Childe Harold? And what is the audience like in terms of age in the clubs?"

"Well, this type of gig at this club is very rare. We have very few of them throughout the country like this club that caters to young people. It's a good club."

"Let's switch to that overseas situation. Where have you been traveling? You've been all over the world?"

"Yes, you name it. Everywhere. We go to the Soviet Union, where nobody else goes."

"And what sort of a scene was it there in terms of where you play?"
"Beautiful, beautiful."
"Where do you play, in concerts?"
"Play concerts, yeah, mostly in all countries we play concerts."
"Big audiences?"
"Aw, yeah! Fantastic! And they know more about jazz than anybody. We have a young *and* old audience over there, young and old."

"Let's take a pause now to hear a standard that you did some time ago, 'Along Came Betty,' from the album *And Then Again*.

"Yeah, 'Along Came Betty'; it's a tune by Benny Golson, our ex-saxophonist and arranger. He was with us when we did the movie *Les Liaisons Dangereuses*, which we did in Paris. Years ago we were doin' music for movin' pictures.

* * *

"That was a standard called 'Along Came Betty' by Art Blakey and the Jazz Messengers. We're talking with Art Blakey here in the studio. He's appearing down at the Childe Harold through Sunday night. I want to get into something about your drumming, Art, perhaps not getting too technical. Tell us something about your style of drumming or your approach to drumming, in that what you did, really, was to help bring about an entirely new approach to jazz drumming, introducing polyrhythms and the use of melody in drums."

"I started in junior high school in Pittsburgh, Pennsylvania. I was a pianist. I played by ear; I couldn't read music, and I worked in a club. I was very young at that time, about fourteen, and I had an eighteen-piece band. A big show came in from New York, Tondelayo and Lopez, and I couldn't read the music, 'Powerhouse,' composed by Raymond Scott. We rehearsed it all day and I said, acting like a big shot, 'Run this down.' So they ran it down and got to the piano part and I couldn't read it. Raymond Scott, he jumped all over the paper. So this little guy sitting in the corner said, 'Can I try it?' I said, 'Sure, go on and try it,' and he listened to the record, went to the piano, and went straight through it. Well, in the meantime, I had been runnin' back and forth showin' the drummer how to play it. I played drums in the school band, messin' around with the drums, 'cause I always loved 'em. And the little guy played it on the piano, ran through it like a dose of Epsom salts; he just played it so beautiful. And it was Errol Garner! So they told me, 'You want to work here, you play the drums. That's where I came into playin' drums, and I liked it, and I been playin' the drums since.

"How I started to develop this instrument, I listened to Kenny Clarke. His was a different style from before, when Jo Jones and Ray Bauduc and these guys come out of the West. They played western drums, played from the hi-hat. The eastern drum style that Chick Webb and Klook—Klook we called Kenny affectionately—played was from the top cymbal.

"Kenny said, 'Well, one thing we got to do, we got to identify ourselves.' Now you're not playin' a melody instrument but you got to identify yourself on a record, because drums have a tendency, one sounds just like another. So I identified *myself* by making a press roll."

"When did this happen—about what year?"

"When I first started recording, with Billy Eckstine."

"About the mid-'40s. You were also playing with Fletcher Henderson and Mary Lou Williams."

"Yeah, I was developing then. I was with Fletcher Henderson and Mary Lou Williams and I went to Boston, I had my *own* band then at the Tic-Toc Club. I had the house band and I left and joined Billy Eckstine. I joined B. with Charlie Parker and that's when the whole thing started."

"That was the first real bop orchestra."

"Yeah, and I was listenin' to Kenny Clarke droppin' the bombs and Max Roach and I had to come in with the press roll. And this is the way I've identified myself. Like the young musicians today, see, the problem is, they're so busy keepin' time they can't identify themselves. One drummer sounds just like another; it doesn't make any difference who you got. But immediately, if you put on a record, 'Oh, that's Max,' 'Oh, that's Elvin Jones,' 'Oh, Philly Joe Jones,' 'That's Kenny Clarke,' 'It's Art Blakey.' You can identify *us* because we identify *ourselves*."

"I was down to hear you last night and I noticed that you have a very definite identity there on the bandstand, but you also leave a lot of room for the other musicians. That's one thing that really impressed me."

"What I'm tryin' to do on the bandstand is get musicians to play. I try to get the best out of 'em. Nat Hentoff says it's a 'fire.' Well, the drummer is the stoker of the group. He's the fireman."

"That's true."

"Then you got personalities to fool with. That's the reason I like combos instead of big bands. You got four or five personalities to fool with. This guy may get in an argument with his wife before he comes to work. When you come on that bandstand you may not get another chance to get back up here to express yourself. So you have to play like there's no tomorrow; you have to pull these guys out of their doldrums or whatever they're in and make them play. It's up to *you*.

So with our type of music, if you sit up there and the drummer has got that fire up under you, you try to play. If you don't, we just roll over you like a steamroller. I try to get the young musicians because they got it; they got a lot of ideas, they got a lot of wild ideas, they got a lot of energy. What you have to do is trade off with *your* experience and *their* energies, and fair exchange is no robbery. You show 'em which way to channel their energies and how to present themselves. I've heard many, many great musicians who don't come across the floodlights. Whatever you got to do, you must *sell* it; it's got to be sold. And that's what happened to us in the modern jazz era; that's what helped us to die, because the cats could play but they didn't sell it—they began to play for themselves. After all, you're up there to entertain the people."

"Why don't you tell us something about the group that you have down at the Childe Harold."

"*Fan-tas-tic.* I just don't know, I'm just so lucky in musicians. Most of the time, my apartment in New York, it's like an employment agency. The guys call from all over the country, all over the world, in fact. There's some that come in from Russia, they come from Japan, they come from every part of the world to join the Jazz Messengers. The *majority* of them have gone out on their own and they have all become stars, because we teach them. I'm not a leader at the top there just to sell myself; I'm up there to sell the artists that's with me, because we need *more* leaders and more modern jazz groups. That's what keeps the clubs open. So we try to build them up and when it's the right timing, then we put 'em out on their own."

"Well, who are the musicians with you now, the present Jazz Messengers?"

"David Schnitter is a fan-tas-tic tenor player and he comes out of Newark, New Jersey."

"I heard him do 'I Can't Get Started' last night and that was really quite beautiful."

"Yeah. And then we have Bill Hardman on bass. He has been with me throughout the years; he comes and he goes—twenty years he's been off and on since he was about, oh, twenty. Bill is steady; he sets a good example for the younger musicians; he makes time, he's always doin' his job. On the piano we have John Hicks. John has been with me off and on. We use several pianists—Walter Davis, Ronnie Matthews, Al Dailey. And our bassist is Chin Suzuki. He's Japanese. It's a very wonderful bunch of cats and they can really play and they work together good. I don't get a group together just because they're great musicians; *spirituality* has got a lot to do with it, how they work together, how much they like each other."

"Let's hear another piece now, a ballad called 'Love for the One You Can't Have.'"

* * *

"That was 'Love for the One You Can't Have' by Art Blakey and the Jazz Messengers."

"What we're tryin' to do is put this American art form out there. It's American, it's all of us, you know, and I just want to get this over, it's *got* to get over. It isn't black, it isn't white, it's *American*. You see some musician, he says, 'Well, this is *black* music.' God knows, if it wasn't for America, it would *never* have happened. African music has nothin' to do with us. We have descended from Africa, but this society brought forth jazz. No America, no jazz, and that's the way it happened, and all of us helped to make it. It was white musicians, it was black musicians, it didn't make no difference. Music has no color lines.

"I stretch myself, from back in Dixieland all the way through swing, modern jazz, the bop era, and up to now. I just happened to live through all of it because I'm so mean and evil and I'm just *gonna* live through it, because I'm gonna prove my point; I *got* to prove my point. I'm not out here to make money; I'm out here for the art form, and I think these men who have gone before us should be given the credit. Duke Ellington has passed through our ranks, Louis Armstrong— these men did not get the credit that is due them. Awright, take the money but for God's sake give 'em the credit! They didn't even give 'em the credit."

"I'm going to just return for a moment to the European scene, the overseas scene, because you've been all over the world. How often do you travel—how much time do you actually spend traveling abroad?"

"As much as we possibly can, because guys got families and they like to exist. We have to work as much as possible, and we *have* to play. You got to play all the time. It's important that you play every day. It's like anything else, you can't be dormant."

"You find that you have to go to Europe to survive."

"Yeah, but I'm very thankful for one thing. I see all these men and the presidents and they're stealing and going on just to go down in history. Well, I'm already there. All I have to do is just play and be myself, and I'm very thankful for it. And the only way I could've done that is be here, born in America. I'm very happy about that. So I've made it and they got to get it. Where I've gone, they've got to come. So they're spendin' money, goin' through all the politics, and deceiving people. All I had to do is just be Art Blakey and play my drums. So I think I'm very lucky."

"So you'll be down at the Childe Harold through Sunday night. Where do you go on from there?"

"We go to a place called Orange, New Jersey. It's just a small club like the Childe Harold, Club Orange. We play there for two weeks and then we go into the Village Gate in New York. And then we go on tour with the Newport Jazz Festival and we'll be quite busy doin' that. We go to Cannes and North Africa and we leave that and play Ronnie Scott's in London; then we go to Japan. It's fan-tas-tic."

"When do you think you'll be back in Washington?"

"I hope very soon because I really love this club. What I want to tell you is that last night, a teacher come in and she told me she said to the kids in her class, 'Well, Art Blakey's comin' to town,' and the kids said, 'Who is Art Blakey?' So there's a little kid there who just came in from Vietnam; he jumped up and said, 'I know who Art Blakey is' and he told 'em. He explained every detail, all the men in the group! He knew all our histories, where we were born and everything!"

"If you want to experience the music of one of the truly great jazz drummers, a musician who was one of the founding fathers of modern jazz, you can catch Art Blakey and the Jazz Messengers down at the Childe Harold through Sunday night. Well, I want to thank you for being with us this evening, Art, and I'm looking forward to coming down to hear you again tonight."

"Okay, and thank *you* very much, Royal."

In the sense of being a pioneer, pianist and composer Patrizia Scascitelli is the Mary Lou Williams of Italian jazz, as the following account of her life and career will amply verify. I had become familiar with her playing via several CDs she sent me, and I caught her with her trio a couple of years ago in New York at Shutters Bar and Café. David Croce was on bass and Carlos Cervantes was at the drums. I interviewed her the next day at her apartment on the Upper West Side.

"I was born in Rome, October 15, 1949," Scascitelli began. "My mother, Maria Tiglio, was the big influence for me because she used to sing. Not professionally. She used to sing at the college, special college for girls, and with the sisters in church. She had a beautiful, unbelievably beautiful, voice, and great passion for music. Her father, my grandfather Vincenzo Tiglio, was an eccentric man, and I think also he was the big influence in my family, even if I never met him. He died when my mother was young, only eight years old. He was a poet and loved music, opera.

"So this passion for music came from my grandfather to my mother, even if she really never studied music. 'Til today I go to her with my latest CD and I ask, 'What do you think about this?' She always has the right answer. It's unbelievable. She has this talent for music. But then, at a certain point, she had an accident, and her singing voice disappeared. It was like a trauma and she was not able to sing anymore. This was before I was born. She was very young, maybe eighteen. This was during the war and they were having incredible stress. My mother was from a very, very poor family. It was really a struggle, a difficult life. She was born near Naples in the country of the bel canto and the music of the people. She went to Rome when she was only eight with sisters and her mother. My father was from the countryside near Rome. His family had nothing to do with music.

"So all of this music came from my mother. When I was two or three years old I was listening to the radio for hours. And so, little by little, she saw that I had a passion for music. She told me that I was a very independent person, that I was kind of strange, for a child. I used to just go and do my own business, playing music. She told me that one day she punished me and said, 'Okay, I don't want to talk to you,' and I started to sing a song! I was only three years old. She was really amazed because that was kind of weird. I really loved music.

"So my mother started to investigate how I can get into music. But not singing, she said. 'No, you have to play an instrument.' When I was eight, I had piano lessons, and that was very intense. I used to seriously practice three and four hours a day. I could not really wait to play, to do something with the piano, with music. I started writing my own first compositions.

"My father was working for the government, at the mint. I remember we didn't have much money. It was really hard. My mother had a really hard time to put a meal on the table. But we always had a nice home and she took care of us. I grew up in Monte Sacro, a middle-income section of Rome, with some housing projects not far from us. My mother managed to put some money together and introduce me to a few music teachers. I still remember there was, like, an odyssey, going to five or six different teachers. I would go once and my mother would say, 'This is not good for you.' So she decided to get me the best teacher. She went to the Conservatorio di Musica Santa Cecilia, even though she didn't have the money to pay for lessons, and she got the names of the big teachers there. One of these was Tito Aprea."

At the audition with Aprea, the nine-year-old prodigy displayed polished technique and performed difficult pieces with ease, but it was evident that she could not read music and had learned the music by ear. Her mother made an arrangement with the professor to bring her daughter back for another audition in six months. During that half-year period of practice and study, Patrizia learned to read music and mastered some Bach and several of Muzio Clementi's sonatinas. She passed the audition with flying colors and was awarded a scholarship at the conservatory.

"I always remember, they had this huge stairway you have to climb, and everybody was saying, 'What's this little girl doing here?' Everybody else was much older. Still today, when I have a hard time with some music, I always remember when I climbed those stairs and I say, 'Wow! I climbed when I was ten! I can climb today!'

"Once I was in the conservatory, I was with the best teachers, very famous teachers." Scascitelli's teachers included, in addition to Aprea, Armando Renzi, Pietro Scarpini, and Giorgio Gaslini. "And always I have very high marks in music, even my diploma was a ninety-five out of one hundred. I was a very artistic type, really crazy; I always wanted to do what I decided to do. So maybe that's why they never wanted to give me one hundred, a little bit to punish me because I was not really, how I can say, too academic oriented. I wanted to always take risks. So that's my story with classical music.

"Nobody was playing jazz in my family. I don't know how I heard this word *jazz*, but I was going around asking people in the conservatory, 'Do you know jazz?' and 'What is jazz?' Nobody was able to answer me. And then somebody gave to me a 45-rpm record. It was Louis Armstrong and I was playing it over and over and over. This was my first jazz record.

"Then, in 1965, when I was fifteen, I went to this vacation place and I met this guy who was older than me and he started taking me out. It was really crazy. I was going in these night clubs when I was a teenager and listening to Ray Charles. I was very wild, crazy, really experimenting, drinking cognac. My mother definitely didn't know I was doing this. It was in northern Italy, Ventimiglia, on the border of France.

"I had friends, a group of teenagers, different from other friends that I have in the conservatory, who really stuck with a classical environment. I hung out with this group of people my age when I was seventeen, eighteen, and had some experiences different from my friends from the conservatory. Also, my neighbors in the housing projects liked rock music and popular artists. We listened to a lot of Led Zeppelin, Cream, all the rock of the time. For maybe three years, I was very deep into this culture. In 1968, when I was eighteen, I saw Jimi Hendrix live in this small theater, Teatro Brancaccio, his first concert in Italy. I saw the Rolling Stones live. I was going to all the concerts, which was really unusual for somebody going to the conservatory. My teachers were kind of sad to see me always going with these guys, but they could not really say too much because I was very good with classical, too. Some time I went to the piano lesson and I was a little high on marijuana, or maybe I was drinking a little bit, but I was able to play—not a problem with my music.

"Then something incredible happened. A couple of my friends stopped listening to all the rock 'n' roll music one day and said to me, 'Watch, we have something new now,' and we started listening to Ornette Coleman! That was 1968. Ornette and also Charlie Mingus.

"Of course, there were musicians in Italy who knew about this music, but it was like a small group of appassionati, the people that were really into jazz, and mostly in northern Italy. It was not really popular like today, when the young generation can go and see a jazz concert. At that time it was more like a few clubs. So for us it was a discovery, these albums by Mingus and Ornette. We really started listening to jazz after that, by the time I was eighteen, nineteen.

"I didn't know really what direction I would go in. But always I have this idea of a different type of music. And then I saw in the conservatory of Rome, for the first time, and this was a historical event, Giorgio Gaslini, who was, and is, a very well-known musician, a pianist and composer. He was giving this jazz course, something special, something extra, in the conservatory. They called it *Straordinario Corso di Jazz*. That was the first time there was jazz in a conservatory in Rome. And I read about this and I was, like, 'Oh, wow! Jazz! Finally, I can see what jazz is about!' So I put my name down and I went to this *Straordinario Corso di Jazz*.

"Of course, Giorgio was like a hurricane inside the school. It was unbelievable! Gaslini's personality was really unbelievable. The special course, the special workshop, was three years. A lot was going on during this course. I was able to meet other musicians, and not just from the conservatory, because it was a mix of classical musicians and street musicians. Gaslini opened the door to everyone, and I remember they gave us this big basement where we could play music.

"So in 1971 I get my degree, both in classical and jazz, and with a one hundred this time, summa cum laude. I wrote my thesis on the influence of classical music on Chick Corea and they loved it, because Chick Corea also knows classical music." A year later she performed, in trio format, two numbers—Milt Jackson's "Bluesology" and her own "Living in Blues"—in a program produced by Gaslini, the Conservatory's, and her, first jazz concert.

After this, Rome's Conservatorio di Musica Santa Cecilia chose not to offer any more jazz instruction. "That was really enough for them, it was so wild," Patrizia explains. A new conservatory was founded near Rome, the Conservatorio di Frosinone. "It is like the Manhattan School of Music. They have great jazz programs, contemporary music, electronic music. It is a very lively conservatory.

"Then I started playing with other musicians. Bruno Tomasso, bassist, was one of the first musicians I used in my combo, and alto saxophonist Massimo Urbani. Roberto della Grotta was another of my bass players. He was my boyfriend and he was going to school studying to become an engineer, but when he met me he changed and became a musician. It was very hard to find drummers, so I used to use one guy, a big name, Franco Tonani, who was the drummer with Giorgio Gaslini. For me it was very important to play and sometimes I was playing for nothing, no money. I'm short but I'm very strong, and I used to move my electric piano by myself on the train. Some of those guys, they didn't really want to be bothered traveling from Rome to Milano. So I would say, 'Please, come on, we gonna have fun.'

"Then I start getting into a big crisis at a certain point, because I was getting really far away from my classical music. And I thought, 'My goodness, I really like classical music; what am I gonna do?' I could not have time to practice classical music and was really starting to feel very bad. This crisis has been going on with me for a long, long time, because I love classical music. But it is impossible for me to do both.

"I became famous in jazz, but I didn't know much about jazz. I could not possibly know jazz, because I had been listening to it for only three years. Giorgio Gaslini started with the blues and Billie Holiday and Armstrong, all the beginnings of jazz, but I didn't know much. And for me to go around and play at these big festivals with such incredibly big names, I felt embarrassed, to tell you the truth. It was kinda weird. Also, it was kinda hard for me because I was a woman. It was very hard for me to be a leader, but at the same time because my personality is, I could say, wild, I always tried different things. I could not really stop; I was really a girl who liked to dip into everything."

I suggest that, because she started so early, she was artistically and intellectually precocious.

"Yes, exactly!" she concedes, laughing. "*Precocious, yes!*"

In 1973 Scascitelli was booked to play in trio format at the first Umbria Jazz, for which she put together a selection of her own compositions and some arrangements of Italian folk themes. The program at the festival that year included the Thad Jones–Mel Lewis Big Band, Dee Dee Bridgewater, Georgio Gaslini, and Weather Report.

"The next day I was like the new personaggio, the new personality, in Italian jazz. I had pictures all over the place. Another festival that I did, a very, very important festival, was Bologna in 1974, again with my trio and again I did all original compositions. This festival was unbelievable. First of all was Gato Barbieri. I played that night, thanks to him, in front of 100,000 people. There was also McCoy Tyner, there was Dizzy Gillespie, Stan Getz." She holds up a faded newspaper and reads aloud a phrase, "'Il grosso e favoloso successo della pianista Patrizia Scascitelli,'" and then translates another, "'who was able to reanimate the show.' I was, like, 'Wow! I was playing all my music,' and I had had an accident!"

The accident had occurred three months before the festival.

"I had this injury because, first of all, I was in this stupid relationship with this guy who was driving me nuts. So I left his house on my motor scooter and I got cut off and the brake didn't work and I fell off and broke my right hand. I was lucky I didn't die because something happened to my leg, as well. I went in the hospital, not a very good hospital, and for one week nobody looked at my hand. And I'm a *pianist!* Nobody really listened to me. Crazy, really crazy situation. So anyway, I called a friend; somebody came to the hospital, and they fixed my hand, finally."

In the 1970s Scascitelli began a series of visits to New York, first in 1973 with a jazz workshop group organized by Gaslini. Attending the Newport Jazz Festival in New York on her initial visit, she saw "all of these incredible artists—Cecil Taylor, Rahsaan Roland Kirk, Thelonious Monk. I went completely crazy. It was an incredible experience for me.

"Then, in 1975 I came back to New York. There was a lot of free jazz here then. I went to the the Five Spot in the Village. I was living on St. Marks Place, very close to this club. I saw a lot of musicians there. I met Don Cherry and I was able to tour with him when he came to Italy. I went to see Ornette Coleman. He was watching all these videos he made and I was able to see how he works. I became friends with Sam Rivers. The loft scene was unbelievable. After two months in New York I didn't have any more money and I decided to go back to Italy.

"When I went back to Italy, festivals like Umbria Jazz didn't interest me anymore; I was more into the alternative scene. I was playing free jazz. I liked Cecil Taylor at the time. I was not playing much like Cecil, not so percussive. I was playing melodies in my music, but pretty much free. I can't believe that I was playing two hours in concerts, no stop, with Italian jazz musicians. I was looking for a drummer, and a bass player introduced me to this guy, this man who became my husband, Marvin Boogaloo Smith. He was an African-American musician from New Jersey and was there in Italy playing rhythm-and-blues music. He's from a very famous jazz family. His brother, bassist Buster Smith, has played with everybody."

Life Force, the group that Scascitelli put together, consisted of percussionist Karl Potter, saxophonist Larry Dinwiddle, drummer Smith, and Scascitelli. "At this point, they started talking about 'Patrizia Scascitelli and Life Force.' This completely changed everything, because I was not just the first jazz woman in Italy but I was going around with three black men. It was kind of crazy! Going to Sicily on a train at night, me with three black guys. It was insane. We would need four or five more tapes for me to really tell you what I went through to go around like this. When we were traveling, it was really hard. But for me, everything was a challenge. I am the type of personality, I really didn't care. In a hotel, some time I was sharing a room with Marvin, and I didn't care. There was a lot of embarrassment—for *other* people, not me. I didn't care. I was, like, 'Hey, this is my personality.' But for the people who were organizing things, oh, it was *shocking*! My family didn't really want me to do this. My father didn't talk to me for a long time. We started in 1975 and Marvin and I married in 1977. I stayed married for eight years. I traveled with this group from 1975 to 1978. We broke up the group then because I got really tired of the sound.

"I came to New York with Marvin in 1981 and I was, like, 'Wow! I can get different experiences.' I was so excited because he knew all the big musicians. Donald Byrd came by one day, and Buster Smith, Marvin's brother, knew everybody, all the cats! The first thing Buster told me when I was playing the piano for him, he made me really angry; he said, 'Wow, you have lots of technique, but you don't have a story!'" Patrizia laughs heartily. "And he was right! Because I was playing a lotta notes. I got the story after I lived here a couple of years, because I started playing with big musicians.

"When we moved to New York in 1981, I didn't think I'd stay for twenty years. I thought, 'Okay, I go there with my husband, we stay a little bit, maybe four years, I get my experience, then we go back to Italy, play there, go back and forth.' My husband was traveling all over with Archie Shepp. Thank God I was able to get to Barry Harris's workshop for a couple of dollars. I stayed there all day and learned and met a lot of different musicians. Finally, I start playing with story in my music, because I start to understand jazz a little better. Barry really helped me a lot. At that time I started meeting some musicians in New York. I had a trio with bassist Jimmy Garrett and drummer Stanley Bailey. We were able to play with Clifford Jordan, Maxine Sullivan, David Fathead Newman, a lot of people.

"I went to live in Harlem," continues Scascitelli, having mentioned that she separated from Smith in 1983. "Four-room apartment—beautiful, but winter time and no heat, no food; it was a struggle. I was really crazy, but I was playing with a lot of different musicians. In 1987 I met my companion, Steffan Finkle, and moved to this beautiful apartment. All my struggles, I can pretty much say, were over.

"From 1990 'til '97 I really stopped performing in Italy. I could not play in my country because I was here in New York doing all these gigs, making money. Like I said, after all my struggles, I didn't have nothing! Then, in '97, I was having a big crisis and I decided I have to go back and play in Italy. I said, 'Gee, after ten years they completely forget about me.' I went to Italy and I went to see Gaslini. I had spoken to him maybe two times in ten years. I thought he was gonna say, 'I don't know you'; but when he saw me, he was, oh, so happy! He said, 'You must make a recording here!' So I started to play again in Italy and I made a recording there in 1998." The recording was the well-received *Homecoming* with Paolino Dalla Porta, bass, and Giampiero Prina, drums. Two years later she returned to Italy and recorded the stunning *Live in Rome*, a solo effort that has her paired with Gaslini on one selection— a medley of "Lover Man" and "Night in Tunisia."

"And by then all the magazines in Italy started to write about me again. The last time I went there, in March, I did three days of lectures in the Conservatory of Frosinone. I'm going back in November for a big concert of my compositions in Rome. I was also at a festival in Verbagna, in northern Italy, last year, accompanying a lot of musicians.

"I have my own jazz group, five pieces, sometimes three pieces, and I also play with a lot of different people, too. I'm very versatile. Sometimes I play Latin jazz with different groups. I play cabaret music. I work with different groups because I play different styles. Mostly, I don't play with big names, because I'm always oriented to my own compositions. I work as a leader. I play with Carol Sudhalter when she calls me. I accompany singers. Oh, yeah, I have to mention this singer, Tessa Sauter, because we have worked together for a year. She's from England and she is a great singer. She's not well known but she's gonna be now. Our group is called Three Flags Jazz Trio. David Croce is on bass."

In a three-decade-long career Patrizia Scascitelli has toured Europe and Japan, performed and lectured throughout Italy, and played in many New York clubs and numerous other venues in the city, including Madison Square Garden, Columbia University, Hunter College, and St. Peter's Church. She has released recordings under her own name and appeared on CDs of prominent jazz artists.

"I have experienced a lot in my life. Now I just do my music and I feel tremendously free at this age. I'm really happy that I can play here in New York and that I can play in Italy. There is this group, the International Women in Jazz, that really helps to add, how you call it, a niche, right? Something that you know you can be recognized for. I'm one of the female jazz players in New York, and I'm the only one from Italy, so I'm very well recognized."

Howard Johnson has turned up over the decades in so many different contexts and formats that it's difficult to pinpoint just where and when I saw him in performance. One memorable occasion was at Umbria Jazz 2000. The Monk Tentet All Stars mounted the stage of Teatro Morlacchi at midnight, and in my review of the evening for *JazzHouse.org* I cited as one of the highlights of the two-hour set, "baritone saxophonist Howard Johnson's and trumpeter Don Sickler's interplay on 'I Mean You.'"

During one of three visits I made to New York to interview musicians for this book, I got together with Johnson at his Manhattan loft and taped the conversation from which the following account is drawn.

"I was born on August 7, 1941, in Montgomery, Alabama. My father, Hamilton (Hammie) Johnson II, was a kind of itinerant domestic at first—chauffeur, gardener, things like that—for various well-off white families. And he actually did pretty well at that because he was very good at it. In fact, *his* father would have been known as a landscape artist these days, because he did that sort of thing, for really no money, for the white families around there. It was just garden work as far as they were concerned. My father was good at the so-called gardening-landscaping thing, too.

"When I was two-and-a-half my father went to check out where there were steel mills during the war. They needed workers 'cause so many had gone into the services. So there was a big exodus from the South to those places where they were producing steel—Gary, Youngstown, Cleveland, Pittsburgh. Our family settled in Massillon, Ohio. Even though I was raised mostly in the North, I was in a black community that mostly came from three counties of Alabama. It was almost like an Alabama colony in that town. The churches were southern, the food was southern, and the way your mama raised you was surely southern," Johnson says with a laugh.

"As far as music was concerned, the radio was always on! In those days we didn't have any jazz stations or r and b stations or gospel stations, but if you knew the radio you could dart around and get black music. You could get an hour of gospel here and a half-hour of something else there and there were always dances being advertised, mostly in Canton and Akron. There were even bands coming through. They didn't come through my town and I wasn't old enough to go to where they were, but my bobbysoxer older sister saw that I was into it and had a lot of the records. So my earliest musical memories are of Lionel Hampton and a little bit of Duke Ellington and people like Tiny Bradshaw, Lucky Millinder, and most powerfully of all, Louis Jordan. I'm one of that legion of people that can blame Louis Jordan for them being a musician, because he really laid out a way that showed you could be so much. I mean, he was a great instrumentalist; he would sing really syrupy ballads and low-down dirty blues, do a lot of comedy material, and even do what you could really call rap—in the 1940s.

"My mother's name is Peggy, and she was the one in the family who always wanted to make things better. My father was pretty easily pleased. If everybody was eating he was okay. But she really wanted to give us a much better life and fought for things like a real refrigerator instead of the icebox. We were a poor family; we were in basic abject poverty, even with the stable job in the steel mills. My father wasn't a guy who drank up all his money; he was just real tight with it. I have three sisters: Thressa, who is ten years older than I am; Mary, four years older; and Connie, four years younger.

"I was never thinking about being any kind of musician, except for one thing. There was a friend of our family's named Ruppert Chapman, who had a set of drums in his house, and he practiced. And I thought that was amazing, to be able to do that. I thought I might like to do that. He gave me a set of sticks and showed me a couple of things and said, 'Check out what you can get from school.' I'm in about fifth or sixth grade and I had enough skill with those sticks and with the way music was read that I was able to get in the junior high school band—as a very poor drummer! I loved clanging around on the cymbals and beatin' the bass drum and just having a good old time!

"I never did have music teachers; I never had music lessons. I always liked the tuba section. I liked the tubas' role in the music. I was already into the bass line anyway. I was just oriented toward that. I could hum along with the bass before I learned the melody, in most cases. And I particularly liked staying over at my uncle's house, 'cause he lived over a jukebox joint and he'd make me a pallet on the floor. In a lot of cases the songs I heard coming from that joint were ones that I knew, and the bass line was highlighted through the floor. So I would put my ear to the pallet and that's how I could hear the best. My uncle's name was Charlie Lewis and he was also sometimes called Charlie Bell.

"I was in the late part of the eighth grade and the band director was Max Reed, who was an outstanding clarinetist. When they finally formed the Canton Symphony he was the first principal player in that. He was serious about music; the whole town was serious about music. Mrs. Dorothy Farrell, who was my highly influential first grade teacher, had to be able to play the piano. There was a piano in every classroom. So music wasn't so far away; it seemed accessible. Seemed like it was close at hand at all times.

"There wasn't any official segregation in that part of Ohio but at that time there were no black people in the school system teaching. There didn't get to be until I was in about the seventh grade. And I think there were probably only two by the time I graduated from high school. The football teams were integrated in the 1890s. Massillon was one of those underground railroad station towns on the way to Canada. There's still a tradition of sanctuary there. They have a church, the same church as back then, which is now a much bigger church, and they have people from El Salvador and people who can't get documentation and are in sanctuary at that church.

"One day I was in the room where the instruments were stored, with a girl who wasn't in the band. I was kind of interested in her, and she was looking at all these things and said, 'Goodness, what's in all these cases?' I was showing her that you could tell what was in them by the shape of the case when I ran across this humpbacked case and I had no idea what it was. I tried to bluff it until I opened it. And when I opened it I still didn't know what it was because we didn't have anybody playing one in the band. So later I asked Mr. Reed, 'What is this instrument?' He said, 'It's a baritone sax. You wanna play it?' Mr. Reed knew that he could do without me in the percussion section and he also had some down time that he was trying to fill, so he said, 'What are you doing such-and-such period?' I said I had a study hall that I'd love to get out of and he said, 'Well, come down to the band room and I'll teach you how to play this.' And I did that. He taught me about scales and how to deal with a reed and gave me some way of relating to the paper.

"But then his schedule changed and he said he was sorry about that but he wouldn't be able to teach me anymore. He said, 'Well, nobody's playing it in the band so why don't you just take it home and see what you can do until the end of the year.' So I did that and I could make a sound on it and get around it a little bit. And then I started hearing what a baritone sax does! I'd never really noticed before. But I picked out Harry Carney in the Ellington band, and a lot of the r and b bands at that time always had that bop, bop bop"—he sings on beats 1, 4, and 7 out of 8—"that kind of thing. It was, like, 'Oh, yeah! That's pretty cool!'

"I was twelve then. I didn't use a neck strap for the whole first year; I just put the sax on the floor and reached up to it. I found out that the baritone sax parts were much like the tuba parts! I didn't know why, 'cause baritone sax didn't have the punch that the tuba did. If your band didn't have a tuba player, you could get those notes by making your worst saxophone player play it on the baritone sax. You didn't use anybody that you needed as a saxophone player. It was one of those instruments that people got relegated to. Even in big bands, the guy who wasn't valued as an alto or tenor player often was the baritone player. And it's kind of like that in schools now. They often make the girl play baritone. 'You can be in the band, but you have to play baritone.'

"It was fun being in the band. The parts were not very challenging and I was in there, I was doin' it. So I played sax that summer and in the junior high school band the next year. One day I was playing a part when I noticed that what I had to do with my right hand on this chromatic figure was the same thing that the tuba players did with their valves. I thought that was kind of fascinating. So I started learning the fingering consciously and seeing how it compared to whatever I was doing. And after a while I thought, 'Hmm, I think I know the fingering for a whole chromatic scale.' And so I wanted to see if I really did. But the problem was that we were not allowed to play other people's school-owned instruments. So I waited till Mr. Reed was out of the room and I picked up a tuba and played the chromatic scale down, the chromatic scale back up: I had the sequence both ways. I thought that was kind of interesting and when I started to play it again, I looked up and Mr. Reed had come back into the room and was looking at me.

"Now, this was grounds for a lot of detention, having to stay after school, and so I just kind of skulked back over to my own chair and he came over to me and he said, 'How long have you been playing the tuba?' I thought, 'Oh God, he's got me dead to rights now; he's trying to get me on some stuff I didn't even do.' So I said, 'Mr. Reed, I know I wasn't supposed to do that and I'm very sorry but I never did it before and I promise I'll never do it again!'" Howard laughs at the memory. "Seems kind of ironic now! But he said, 'No, no, what I mean is, how are you able to make a sound? How did you learn the embouchure? When did you start playing?' And I still didn't understand. So I said, 'No, I didn't play anything before just now.' And he said, 'Well, you know, people who want to learn this instrument or who are being taught this instrument go for months without being able to get any kind of decent sound at all, so what did you do?' I said, 'Well, I thought I was just doin' what the other guys were doin'.' And then he said, 'Well you're going to the high school next year and they don't march a baritone sax. They're going on this trip to Pasadena for the Tournament of Roses parade and they need tuba players. They're graduating five and they don't have any coming in. So you'd stand a better chance of making it that way. I mean, there's a lot of competition on the drums and you were never that good in the first place, so you might think about playing the tuba.' So I said, 'Yeah, okay.' But the only thing I registered was that I wasn't in trouble, I had got out of that, I didn't have to go to detention. I wasn't thinking about what it would mean to take up the tuba or anything like that.

"So from then for about nine weeks I had what seems now remarkably fast development as a player. I extended my range and my technical capability and, probably because I didn't have any teachers, I tried everything. I really blossomed; I became a pretty good tuba player in that nine-week period.

"In 1958 I went into the service to kind of get that out of the way—August 1958 to August '62—because I thought there would be some kind of war in the sixties, for which I'd be prime beef, so I tried to get in and get out and maybe do a little music while I was at it in the navy's music program. But I got thrown out of that for a variety of silly reasons and spent the next three years on an aircraft carrier not being a musician. I was based in Boston for three years. I met Tony Williams and was a boarder at his house for the last two years that I was there and played with the Boston people. Alan Dawson, Herb Pomeroy, and some of the Berklee guys who were emerging, including Chick Corea and Gary Burton—mostly in school situations with those guys and at the Stable with Herb Pomeroy. I'd do gigs around Boston with Tony and a pianist named Phil Moore III, son of the pianist and vocal coach who helped a lot of singers in the '50s. I was playing baritone. I didn't own a tuba yet."

After a brief period in early 1963 in Chicago, where he met Eric Dolphy and had his first exposure to John Coltrane in performance ("I couldn't believe it!" Howard exclaims), Johnson moved to New York, where he has remained except for a four-year residency abroad in the early 1990s.

"I was at Manny's on 48th Street looking for tubas and ran into Eric Dolphy. I said, 'Eric, I took your advice, I'm here!' I bought the tuba that I still play. It's forty years old. And that Sunday I went to a jam session at a place called the Phase II. Now this was back in the days when people who could play would show up at jam sessions. In fact, nobody else would be there. That's when I got introduced to a lot of people, like Paul and Carla Bley and Roland Kirk. I hadn't played tuba in five years, but I really couldn't stop. I just played until

I couldn't make the embouchure any more. It felt so good to play. And even when my capacity was diminished it was still beyond most people's expectations. So I was still having fun and still making an impression. And I knew my stuff. I knew the tunes; I was ready to play any jam session. I just needed a few weeks to build up my chops, and I was right back in it. I had a muscle memory. I used to go out to play some nights, not knowing where I'd be, with both instruments. It was like, 'Let me get out there and do somethin'.' I was just excited in that way. There was a place called the Speakeasy that I'd already been playing in a lot before I had my tuba—with Pharoah Sanders, C. Sharp, Henry Jenkins, Larry Willis, Jimmy Owens, and Joe Henderson.

"I was workin' at the NYU bookstore during the day and I was the cook at a place called the Limelight, just off Sheridan Square. It was a kind of hangout for the theater crowd; there were always actors and other kinds of performers there. I don't know if I was fired or left or what, but I was gettin' more gigs at that point, so I probably just left.

"It was good to be a baritone player. People using slightly larger formations, they would call me for things, and also I was a guy who was sober and on time and pretty reliable and worked hard to make the music happen. That's how I got to know Slide Hampton. He had written some stuff and needed a baritone player and somebody recommended me. And that's how you get around; you get recommended. People would say, 'Well look, there's a guy who can do it.'"

In the fall of 1964 an opportunity fell into Johnson's lap. In a scenario that he describes as "one of those B-movie stories," Howard happened to be in the Five Spot checking out Charles Mingus's quintet when the legendary bassist and leader got the news that Red Callender, who was to play tuba on Mingus's upcoming Birdland gig, couldn't make it. Pianist Jackie Byard said to Mingus, "There's your tuba player over there."

Mingus was ready to start the set when Byard pointed Johnson out.

"So Mingus pulls up the mike and he says, 'That kid back there?' And Jackie says, 'Yeah.' And Mingus says, 'He's got a tuba but can he play it?' Jackie says, 'Why don't you ask him?'

"By this time the audience is looking at me and looking at Mingus and turning back and forth. I'm in the back of the Five Spot trying to be obscure and trying to be small. And all of a sudden all this attention was on me. So Mingus was saying, 'Does he play behind the beat?' and Jackie says, 'I think he's pretty good.' Suddenly Mingus says, 'What tunes do you know?' I said, 'What tunes do you want to hear?' And the audience went, '*Whoooooooaa* !' And Mingus says, 'Oh, you bad, huh? Well come on up here and we're going to see about this.'

"So I got auditioned right there on the spot. The audience was on my side; I was the underdog. He had me play a blues, and right in the middle of it he says, 'Oh yeah yeah, okay!' And then he says, 'You couldn't handle, like, a real up-tempo tune, could you? I mean you couldn't play "Cherokee"?' I said, 'Oh, sure.' 'Well let's hear "Cherokee,"' and he counts 'Cherokee' off pretty up tempo. I play a chorus or so and he stops me and says, 'Yeah, right, okay, the rehearsal will start here tomorrow at two.'"

In 1966 Howard began a musical association with Gil Evans that lasted until the great arranger's death in 1988. As Mingus had done before, Evans "stretched me beyond my own concept" and from him Howard "got some things that I didn't even know were doable on the tuba."

Johnson's musical life was from this point on characterized by variety. He went on the chittlin' circuit with Hank Crawford; he did studio work, some of it for pop records; he recorded the album *The Real Thing* with bluesman Taj Mahal, subbed for Harry Carney in the Ellington band, led the Saturday Night Live band from 1975 to '80, made many European tours, including one with Paul Simon, formed his own multi-tuba combo Gravity, and spent four years in Hamburg, German, playing in the North German Radio Big Band.

"I just kinda keep things going," says Howard Johnson. "At sixty-one, I'm looking forward to having a bunch of fun."

Four summers ago in Perugia, Italy, during a well-attended end-of-festival press conference, I rose to my feet in the back row, and with an Italian- and English-speaking interpreter at my side, brazenly delivered a five-minute rebuke to Carlo Pagnotta, Umbria Jazz Artistic Director and co-founder of the now three-decades-old festival, for the absence of women's groups and the pitifully meager representation of women instrumentalists at his festival that year. I pointed out that the only women instrumentalists present were a couple of horn players in U.S. college bands and a baritone saxophonist, Gabriella

Grossi, with Marco Zurzolo's Naples-based Banda MVM. In my remarks I put great emphasis on the salutary effect that the presence of women instrumentalists, especially when performing on the outdoor free-admittance stages, would have on young Italian and European women, encouraging them to believe that there are other avenues into a career in jazz for them besides being a vocalist or pianist. It was at this juncture in my reflections that I was gratified to see a number of women turn their heads and greet my observations with smiles and affirmative nods. This was in startling contrast to the largely negative reception I was greeted with that evening on taking my seat for dinner at a table occupied by a half-dozen male journalists from different nations, one of whom led off by scolding me for having "hurt Carlo's feelings."

Basically a shy person, I cannot imagine what possessed me, although I do enjoy the memory of having had my public say on an issue of discrimination that has long and deeply troubled me, an issue that the jazz community worldwide should also be disturbed about and should make a vigorous effort to rectify. Regrettably, women horn, string, and percussion players almost never perform with men except in combos and big bands that they themselves lead.

Carlo booked the groups of two female singers, Dee Dee Bridgewater and Dianne Reeves, at the next year's festival, and the year after that the Umbria Jazz 2002 program included pianist Carla Bley's virtually all-male big band (her daughter Karen Mantler was at the organ). It was at that festival, two years after my 2000 confrontation with him at the press conference, that I saw Pagnotta looking on at a noontime jam session in Perugia's Ristorante La Taverna. As we watched and listened, tenor saxophonist Carol Sudhalter blew the walls back on number after number, holding her own and then some in the company of five men on horns on the bandstand. They included tenor stalwarts and bandleaders John Firmin from California and Britisher Ray Gelato. Carol, incidentally, was not on the festival program but had only dropped by as a paying customer for three days on her way to gigs in Rome, Verona, and Milan.

The crowded eatery's patrons—and not just the women in the audience—cheered every time Carol took a solo. Five senior male journalists from Bologna, old friends of Carlo Pagnotta, left their table in the back of the room and stood at the side of the bandstand, again and again calling out, "Brava!" as Carol soloed. I glanced over in their direction and saw that Carlo had joined them. He was smiling—and he was definitely digging what Carol was laying down.

To give credit where credit is due, the very next year after that La Taverna jam session, Pagnotta booked the all-female sextet Sisters in Jazz, led by alto saxophonist Christine Jensen and presented at Umbria Jazz 2003 by the International Association for Jazz Education (IAJE).

I interviewed Carlo Pagnotta at Umbria Jazz 2002 in his office across the street from the eight-hundred-year-old palazzo that houses the Galleria Nazionale dell'Umbria. I mention this medieval structure to alert the reader to the glorious architecture as well as the many historical monuments that Perugia boasts.

"My family had nothing to do with music," he began, "except my cousin was a good musician and moved to Rome to join the Italian Radio and Television Orchestra. In 1949 I was in college, Convitto Nazionale Cicognini, in Prato, near Florence. I didn't like the music that was done in Italy. I'm not a fan of Italian songs or Neapolitan songs. At the time I was listening to French radio, and one night the music I heard was new to me. It was the 1949 Festival International de Jazz in Paris. I started buying records. My first jazz record was a Dizzy Gillespie big band LP."

For the sixteen-year-old university student that broadcast was an epiphany. However, although Pagnotta remains a self-confessed bebopper, he has learned to face up to the economic realities. To verbalize the obvious, when you book big jazz names you have to pay them big bucks. To cover those costs you need big crowds. Carlo Pagnotta has programmed his festival to attract tens of thousands of fans not only of jazz but of pop, blues, gospel, zydeco, and other genres. Umbria Jazz provides ticketed concerts of, for example, Wayne Shorter, Chick Corea, and Patricia Barber for the purist, while for the crowds who throughout the afternoons and evenings throng the Centro Istorico's outdoor free venues on Corso Vannucci, there are the bluesy Johnny Nocturne Band; the crowd-pleasing Swing Era–style Ray Gelato Giants; the high-decibel electronic Gotan Project from Argentina, replete with hi-tech sampling, beat programming, and a deejay at turntables; and Sean Ardoin & Zydekool, a high-energy sextet from New Orleans that turned cheering audiences on with its funky beat.

"My first vacation abroad was in Cannes in 1949, where I heard bebop live for the first time. From the mid-1950s onward every year I went to the jazz festival in San Remo, the first jazz festival in Italy. There I heard Art Blakey and the Modern Jazz Quartet for the first time. In 1958, with a group of friends from Bologna, I went to Cannes again for the International Jazz Festival, where I heard Ella Fitzgerald for the first time. In Bologna I had met the people who would invent the Bologna Jazz Festival, the most important festival in Italy in the 1960s and the beginning of the '70s, Alberto Alberti and Cicci Foresti.

"In 1955, together with Adriano Mazzoletti, I founded the Hot Club Perugia. The first concert we organized was with Louis Armstrong, followed by Chet Baker, Johnny Griffin, and Dexter Gordon. In 1960 the Hot Club changed its name to Jazz Club Perugia, of which I was president, and we proposed a festival to the Regione Umbria, the Umbria regional government.

"So in 1973 we had the first Umbria Jazz festival and it was completely free, changing almost every day. But we had many, many problems those early years—too many young guys who were political—and we gave up for one year, 1977. 'Okay, let's wait,' we said and we started again in 1978. We had the same problems and started again in '82. By then the political faction was out of the music and we discovered that people were willing to pay for concerts.

"Of course, we were maintaining the outdoor free concerts, but they have to be easy listening music, as you can see in the street and on the two free stages. So we have a free concert like the other night, the Gotan Project"—the Argentine group attracted thousands of revelers for a late-evening show—"that has nothing to do with jazz. And then we have what we can call 'real jazz' inside the theaters.

"Since 1973 many things have changed. At that time we could have Stan Getz, Miles Davis, and Art Blakey. Now, we lost Ray Brown last week. I mean, it was much, much easier to organize a big festival in the '70s and '80s. There are a lot of good musicians now. But just to make an example, I love Eric Alexander, but how can we talk about Eric Alexander when I just mentioned Stan Getz?

"Somebody says jazz is dead. I don't think so. Should we say that opera is dead or classical music is dead? Of course, because of my age I prefer acoustic piano. I enjoy much better at night listening inside to Pat Martino, Larry Willis, Peter Washington, and Louis Nash than staying in the street. So we can have the Gotan Project. Last year we had Paulo Conte or we had James Taylor three years ago. We have 85, 90 percent jazz. Montreux Jazz Festival has only 10 percent. So I think that, for this place, for Perugia, we have done a good work, thanks to some volunteers and professional people.

"Also we have Umbria Jazz Winter in Orvieto from December 27 until January 1, 2003. It is ready. The winter festival is going up much, much faster than Umbria Jazz in the summer. We don't have the outdoor concerts there because it's too cold.

"We think every year, what are we going to do next year? Of course, we don't want a supermarket festival. It's like this: there are two different kinds of people. The Gotan Project at night was an exception because this is the group that everybody wants to listen to. They sold in one month 50,000 CDs. It's unbelievable. So, okay, for Heineken Night, the Gotan Project. Yesterday we had a free concert by the British Ray Gelato Giants, but at the same time we had the George Russell Orchestra in Teatro Morlacchi. Even if it is an expensive special project, we like to bring the George Russell Orchestra. We try to maintain this balance.

"Last year we had again the Gil Evans Orchestra, almost 90 percent the same band that played here in 1987, except George Adams, of course, who died, and George Lewis, who couldn't come. In 1987 we had the Gil Evans Orchestra with Sting, and Sting said, 'The boss is Evans, not Sting.' When I made the contract with the Gil Evans Orchestra to be here for ten days, meeting in New York with Evans, we agreed, one concert with a special pop star, in order to sell more tickets. At the time I was thinking of Sade, because the movie *Absolute Beginners*, with Gil Evans's music and Sade, was just out. But Sade wouldn't sell so many tickets. And I heard that Sting was at Ronnie Scott's in London listening to the Gil Evans Orchestra.

"This has to be a jazz festival for the jazz followers first; then if there is something special, why not? I'm a jazz follower and I know that I prefer the night concerts in a small venue, a club. This year for the first time we had the Jazz Apertivo in the Sala del Cambio of Hotel Brufani. Yesterday, I was very, very surprised to see, for an Italian jazz trio—even if it was Renato Sellani, one of the oldest Italian jazz pianists—that at seven o'clock they had sold so many tickets people were standing.

Every year we try to do something different, and sometimes it is working, sometimes not." I point out that the duo of violinist Johnny Frigo, now in his mid-eighties, and pianist Joe Vito had also had people standing in the aisles nightly in the same room.

"Umbria Jazz is the top jazz festival in Italy. Umbria Jazz Winter festival comes in second. I do think that we are at the top. We had to work very hard to stay at this level. We can do more, of course. You know better than me that jazz is not for a thousand thousand people. You can have 30,000 people in the street and maybe you have 1,000 paying tickets. If jazz is the classical music of the twentieth century, I've never seen for classical music a thousand thousand people. Jazz is not rock; jazz is not pop.

"I read in the newspaper that they say they don't like what we do in the street. Okay, don't stay in the street; go to Assisi, go to Gubbio, go to Todi. It's not necessary to stay all day if you're coming to be a tourist; it's not necessary to stay in Perugia. You visit Umbria, the green heart of Italy, and you come back in the evening; you forget what is going to happen in the street, and you go instead to jazz in the clubs or in the opera houses.

"Let's count how many tickets we sell for Gary Burton and Makoto Ozone. And then watch how many people will be in the street. It's a completely different audience. Most of the people, they don't pay, they don't pay for one ticket, because they want Ray Gelato. Ray Gelato is coming back, yes. Keith Jarrett is coming back. This is the two different audiences.

"Our problem is the venues. I would like to have a venue like Vienne, France. They have a Roman amphitheater that can seat 8,000 people. I don't understand why Julius Caesar built a Roman amphitheater in Vienne, France." He laughs. "He could have come to Perugia and now we could sell many more tickets for Keith Jarrett or others!"

I remarked that two days earlier I had sat in the Galleria listening to a solo recital by pianist Uri Caine. There were three hundred people in the room and there was total silence and attentiveness. I had explained this to myself in terms of the European cultural tradition and a decided respect for the arts here, the same respect that is shown for opera. I asked Carlo to comment on this phenomenon.

"Compared to some of the American jazz festivals, the Italian audience—we can say European audience—is much better. I remem-

ber at the Hollywood Bowl I was listening to the Carnegie Hall Orchestra and in the next box was a family doing a picnic. If you try to
do this in Italy somebody will kill you. About twelve years ago I made
a mistake; I invited Chuck Mangione, not for the street, but in the
Giardino del Frontone" —a ticketed outdoor venue for big-name jazz
artists like Keith Jarrett, Enrico Rava, Pat Metheny and Michael
Brecker, Dianne Reeves, Buena Vista Social Club, and a double booking of Ahmad Jamal and Brad Mehldau. "You cannot present Chuck
Mangione to an Italian jazz audience. Chuck Mangione is music for
family. Don't tell them it is jazz because they don't want it. It was
'Boo! Boo! Boo!' In Italy, if I put Kenny G in the Giardino, the main
stage, where you have to have a ticket, they're going to kill me. This
is the difference. There is not a big audience for jazz, not in America
and not in Europe. But of course the jazz audience is a real jazz audience. Normally, in Italy, we don't drink so much like in Northern
Europe. We sell beer because Heineken is our main sponsor. But we
don't let drunk people listen to real jazz. You can meet some drunk
people in the street, but you never meet drunk people at night in the
venues at Umbria Jazz where you buy a ticket.

"Also, let's not forget that for eighteen years the Berklee College
of Music of Boston has been coming to Perugia for two weeks during
the festival for the Berklee Summer School at Umbria Jazz Clinics.
Every year for this occasion about two hundred fifty students come to
Perugia, 25 percent of whom come from outside Italy.

"My first New York experience was in 1971 and I can still remember with what emotion I went into Carnegie Hall for the first time to
listen to Duke Ellington. After twenty years this is the first year I
don't go to New York, not since last November. Not because of September 11 but because I decided to see if I needed a break. I said,
'Okay, let's do by it mail, by telephone.' But you need to go around
and listen. This is why I go to the other festivals, because there's
something to learn every time.

"Normally, I've been to New York eight times in one year. I go to a
club every night for two weeks. For seventeen years I'm doing this,
except one year I'm going to New Orleans. I was the first festival artistic director who booked a brass band, Ambrosia Brass Band. Now other
festivals copy. Next week it will be the Monterey Jazz Festival and there
will be a Jazz Festival Organization meeting. And the European Jazz

Festival Organization will come in September, after the Montreal Jazz Festival.

"It was these New York experiences that gave me ideas about Umbria Jazz. Usually, a jazz festival consisted of a single evening concert with two or three groups. In New York I went to midday concerts at the Carnegie Room, free afternoon concerts, evening concerts at Carnegie Hall and Avery Fisher Hall, and afterward to the jazz clubs. In New Orleans I was able to appreciate the climate created by a marching band in the streets and this is how Umbria Jazz's winning formula was born. I haven't invented anything new, but from all these experiences the formula of Umbria Jazz is now street parades with marching band, midday concerts, afternoon concerts, free outside concerts, main evening concerts, and midnight concerts in theaters and clubs. Each festival can teach a lot to the other festivals. I must confess that I'm learning a lot from the other festivals, especially the festivals that don't do straight jazz. We have some meetings with the other festivals."

I asked Carlo to reflect on some of the great musical highlights during his thirty years as artistic director of Umbria Jazz.

"Well, of course, it may be because it was much more emotional that I have to go back to the 1970s when we had Charlie Mingus and we had Bill Evans with Philly Joe Jones. Miles Davis came in 1984. That was the first time I was able to bring Ahmad Jamal, the first time we had Brad Mehldau in a small venue playing for twenty people. I don't pretend to be a talent scout, but I was very impressed when ten years ago I saw Brad play with Joshua Redman. In 1996, a completely unknown Diana Krall performed for a week in one of the festival's midnight clubs. One evening I took Tony Bennett to listen to her.

"We have to stop and think what we will do for the thirtieth anniversary in 2003. There's a good staff working, just a few people working during the year.

"The problem is I try to watch around to see who's going to replace me. In Italy we say, 'Morto un Papa se ne fa un altro.'" My Italian is strong enough to understand the proverb, but Carlo translates it for me anyway: "One pope dies, we have another pope."

It can't have been easy for a female teenager in the late 1960s to take up jazz guitar, much less contemplate becoming a professional musician in an art form then—and still—dominated by men. Of course, the casual indifference that today too often prevails vis-à-vis women jazz instrumentalists is a far cry from the outright hostility that a female horn, string, or percussion player confronted back then. But Monnette Sudler persevered, and today, after three-and-a-half decades on the scene here and abroad, she is considered by many to be one of the most creative guitarists in jazz.

I was much impressed with her virtuosity and artistry when I saw her in performance several times in the 1980s, and that assessment was renewed a couple of years ago here in my home territory of Washington, D.C. Of course, I had been keeping up with her recorded output over the period in between. Sudler had come here to provide the music for an early evening reception for the Pennsylvania contingent of the Congressional Black Caucus. It took place at the 701 Restaurant only a few blocks down the street from the Capitol. Monnette was in a quartet at this crowded affair and I seemed to be the lone individual giving the music my undivided attention, although most of those passing by the area occupied by the foursome sent fleeting smiles their way as they continued on through the throng.

Monnette and I met up later that evening at HR 57, the Center for the Preservation of Jazz and Blues, where she sat in for a cooking "Softly as in a Morning Sunrise."

Although Sudler did not begin to study the guitar seriously until she was in her teens, guitar music was in her orbit early and she seems as a youngster to have already begun to think of herself as a guitarist.

"I was born in Philadelphia and I grew up there in a section called Nicetown-Tioga," Sudler began our conversation about her life and career. "The singing cowboy type thing was pretty popular then, which I know sounds pretty corny. In fact, I have a photograph of myself with the guitar when I'm about five years old. Going upstairs in our house there was a landing and I'm standing there with my little toy guitar and pretending I was playing something.

"I spent a lot of time with my grandmother, Bertha Goldman. She really enjoyed guitar music and would go to parades to hear the string bands. I guess the Mummers were pretty popular in Philadelphia. She would listen to recordings of show tunes and the Nat King Cole Trio and Johnny Mathis and Dinah Washington and Ramsey Lewis, and she enjoyed classical music too.

"My mother, Lea Sudler, sang quite a bit—church music and classical styles. Juilliard heard a demo record that she made and offered her a scholarship.

"I have three younger brothers, Truman, Warren, and Duane. My brother Truman is the closest thing to being musical. He became a deejay. But as far as playing an instrument or singing or anything, it didn't happen for any of them. I spent a lot of time in the church growing up. I used to sing in the youth choir in the Tioga Methodist Church, 19th and Venago Streets. The choir director there was named Sue Smith McDonald. I started piano lessons when I was eight and studied off and on, from three different teachers, over a period of four years or so. I would kind of practice right before my lesson, but I always could do the lesson.

"My uncle Nathan was a brilliant inspiration. He would come over and play the piano, jazz and show tunes, and he used to work in the clubs. I would just sit on the floor and listen to him when I was about seven. I loved the music and I wanted to play the piano so badly, but I really didn't want to practice. I just wanted to sit down and play like he did right away. I fought against the piano. A couple of years later I was given this guitar and couldn't play it and my mother used to hide it from me because she wanted me to play piano and do more classical things. She'd put it in the closet and every now and then I'd go pull it out and she'd hide it again.

"This guy used to come over to visit my stepfather and he kind of played guitar by ear. I would sit and watch him. He played blues and flamenco style. I don't remember him singing anything. He would show me little things, but he couldn't really tell me a lot. I didn't start studying guitar until I was fifteen.

"What happened was the church had a youth camp in the Poconos and my mother sent me there. They had a talent show. There were a lot of people there who were playing guitars and it really just reminded me that that was something I wanted to do and that I had the guitar at home and I should be playing it. I was old enough to make my own decisions. I'd had the guitar for at least three or four years."

This being the mid- to late 1960s, I asked what impact the Beatles and the British Invasion had had on her.

"Surprisingly, not that much. I didn't even like Jimi Hendrix that much at that time. I liked Jobim and the bossa nova type music, and my mother had lots of Nat King Cole and stuff like that. I was listening to Wes Montgomery and Fats Domino and the Motown sound—the Supremes, the Marvelettes, the Miracles, Martha and the Vandellas, and all those groups.

"I do want to name my aunt, Marlene Robertson. She was working at the Warton Center, 22nd and what was then called Columbia Avenue, in North Philadelphia. I was living in Germantown at that time. There was a woman named Carol Friedman who taught guitar there and my aunt introduced me to her and kind of set up the guitar lessons. She bought me a music stand and my grandmother bought me a guitar case, or it might have been the other way around but, anyway, they both helped me and got me started. I just never stopped after that.

"Carol Friedman was basically coming from a folk style—that was her thing, Joni Mitchell and Joan Baez, that type of stuff. After a little while I said, 'You know, I would like to learn some jazz things.' I was going around asking my neighbors, 'How can I find jazz on the radio?' and 'Where are the jazz stations?' It wasn't 'til I got to my late teens that I really started listening to Jimmy Smith and Hugh Masekela and Herbie Mann and John Coltrane, Yusef Lateef, those people.

"Carol Friedman introduced me to a man named Bob Zatzman, who taught me more chords, like major seventh chords and minor sevenths, and different songs, like 'My Favorite Things' and 'Malaguena.' My next teacher was Harold Golden and we did more ear training, sight reading, and chord-melody type things. And then from there I went to Joe Sgro, who was a good friend of Dennis Sandolis, a guitarist and music instructor that many musicians studied with. Joe Sgro was more like a bebop-type guitar player and we did a lot of bebop tunes, a lot of writing solos, different picking techniques, chord scales, inversions. I really enjoyed that.

"One of my first performances with the guitar was at Tioga Methodist Church in duo with Freddie Smith, who played snare drum. 'Autumn Leaves' was the song. The pastor there was Dr. Thomas Snowden, who was a jazz pianist. His trio also played that day, in the style of Les McCann and Ramsey Lewis. I used to listen a lot to his Nina Simone and Aretha Franklin tapes.

"In the early 1970s I met Khan Jamal, the vibraphonist. I was working at a Y, teaching guitar and art, and this guy was working there and he said, 'Oh, my friend plays vibes and you guys should meet.' So he introduced us. And then Khan came over to my house and brought his vibes and we just played all day. We met a couple other people and for the next month we just played music all day long."

Other than occasional duo sessions with another guitarist, this was Sudler's first real involvement with other jazz musicians, the first time that she "really had a chance to play in a band situation." They formed a group called the Sounds of Liberation. Its instrumentation was congas, bass, vibes, and guitar.

"We worked at some bars, some community centers, and outdoor festivals. I'll never forget the first time we worked and we actually got paid some money and I said, 'Wow! I can really do this! I like this!'" She laughs, recalling this revelation at the age of about twenty.

"Later on, saxophonist and flutist Byard Lancaster joined the group and we recorded an album with him. We started doing some jobs in Boston and some of the festivals in New York. At that time the Wild-flower Festival"—the 1976 avant-garde event out of which came five albums on the Douglas label—"was going on and saxophonist and pianist Sam Rivers started his loft scene, Studio Rivbea. I recorded with the Sam Rivers Big Band, but I don't know whether he has ever released that session. I got my first record deal from someone who had heard me playing with his band. I worked with drummer Sunny Murray's Untouchable Factor and I recorded with him on the Apple Cores label. I worked with pianist Uri Caine, who is from Philadelphia; tenor saxophonist Odean Pope; bassist Tyrone Brown; and the Change of the Century Orchestra.

"During the loft period in the '70s, saxophonist David Murray and drummer Stanley Crouch had just come to New York and I would go up and we would all hang out. Dave also played with Sunny Murray's Untouchable Factor and he and Stanley shared a loft together, so we would all stay at the loft and practice and rehearse. Byard introduced me to trombonist Janice Robinson and I did some things with her. In the early '80s I kinda moved to New York for a little bit and started to work with trumpeter Hugh Masekela. I lived in New York about two years. I worked pretty much at the Tin Palace and a couple of the lofts. I would just go and hang out with trombonist Steve Turre and pianist John Hicks and bassist Reggie Workman and all those guys that were working around the area. It was stiff.

"During that time I started traveling to Europe and just kind of moving around a little bit more. I did festivals in Switzerland and Norway and Germany. I had a quartet. Oliver Collins was on piano, Newman T. Baker was on drums, and Kenny Kilham was on bass."

Aware that Monnette Sudler has devoted much effort for many years to community causes, I asked her to provide some details of that aspect of her musical life.

"I enjoy working with youth and with children and have done quite a bit of work in that area. In fact, we just finished a play this weekend. It was great. It was at the Art Sanctuary at the Church of the Advocate here in Philadelphia and based on two artists here, Walter Edmonds and Richard Watson. It told the story that the murals in the church are based on and I wrote the music to poetry that Trapeta Mayson wrote. The children also contributed their own work. Ms. Mayson worked with them with poetry and I worked with them with music. We did a three-day performance called *North and Beyond*. It's the second year that they've done performances with the children. This is my first year involved with them. It was great, a great turnout.

"I also do work in youth centers and correctional facilities for young people. There's a place called the Youth Study Center here where juvenile offenders stay. I go there on Saturdays and do music and poetry workshops, along with Ms. Mayson. I've also been involved in arts in education in Buffalo, New York, doing the same thing, music and poetry. I go to the prisons periodically to do performances and also have been an artist in residence at the State Correctional facility in Chester, along with the drummer Leon Jordan. We do workshops. I work for an hour with the guitar and bass players and Leon will work for an hour with the drummers and then we will combine and do an ensemble on the music that we taught for that day. I've been doing that for the past couple of years.

"Of the last few tours I have been on, one was to Japan. I went as a duo with pianist Barry Sames to play with the Japanese Soul Chorus, which was led by Nathan Ingram, a Philadelphian who has been living in Japan for quite a few years now. We toured all over Japan for a couple of weeks performing in jazz clubs and concert halls. I also did the Jamaica Festival with Byard Lancaster and vocalist Barbara Walker. The last thing I did was in December when I went to South Africa and did the festival in Durban as a solo guitarist and worked with some South African musicians there. That was a great experience. I haven't been to Europe in the past few years."

I mentioned the Congressional Black Caucus reception at which she performed.

"I am definitely involved in the political side of it, so you're liable to see me playing at functions like that. Senator Vincent Hughes"— of the Pennsylvania State Legislature—"is very active in the community and I try to take part in some of the things that he does. There are a lot of different functions based out of his office that I really feel I should contribute to in one way or another."

I first met baritone saxophonist Claire Daly at the Kennedy Center's second annual Mary Lou Williams Women in Jazz Festival in 1997. She was there with Diva, the all-female big band. Several years later I saw her at the International Association for Jazz Education (IAJE) meeting in New York. I also had a chance to chat with her backstage at the Kennedy Center after her guest appearance with the Billy Taylor Trio in 2001. A couple of years later I got together with Daly in her Manhattan loft for a long conversation about her life and career. I had caught her a few nights before at Nolita Tavern in Soho with People like Us, a working quartet that for fifteen years has been featuring the compositions of its pianist and leader Joel Forrester, tunes with intriguing titles like "Zen Soviet Blues" and "The Baker Bounce."

"I was born in Bronxville New York and grew up in Yonkers," Daly began. "I remember as a really little kid having some 45-rpm records—'Flowers on the Wall' and 'Don't Sleep in the Subway.' I was maybe four or five. I had older siblings and they listened to music. They were four and five years older than I was and I have a brother who's almost twenty years older who would watch *American Bandstand*. I was sort of always tagging along seeing what they were doing. I don't know that they had favorite groups but I remember when the Beatles came on Ed Sullivan. I was very little and we all got very excited about that. My sister and I used to listen to a transistor radio, looking for Beatles songs on different stations. As a kid, I would say I listened to the Beatles, AM radio, pop songs from the '60s and '70s, whatever was on the radio. I wouldn't say my parents listened to music, except on the car radio.

"I went to a small Catholic grammar school. They were gonna start a band and I came home and said, 'I want to play in the band.' At this time my father, Patrick Joseph Daly, sat down with me and explained different instruments, what they sounded like, and sort of presented some options. I randomly picked the saxophone. Then, to support my looking into this, he started coming home with tickets to concerts, to show me what saxophone players were doing. I think he liked the music, too. He had played cornet and sousaphone when he was in high school. I think he had fun exploring the jazz world with me.

"I got my first horn, a rented Conn alto saxophone, when I was twelve. My father said, 'Look, let's rent one to start with. We'll see if you stick with it and then we'll get a really good horn.' A year later I bought the alto that I actually still own.

"At the same time I was going to see rock concerts with my friends. I saw people like the Grateful Dead, Yes, Poco, the Allman Brothers, The Band, Sly and the Family Stone. And funk music, also; I really loved funk music—Parliament Funkadelic and Tower of Power. When Bob Dylan came back I tried to get tickets to his return concert and couldn't. We were still pretty young, my friends and I, but when you have older siblings you tend to get turned on to more music because you think what they're doing is cool. It just seems to me like music at that time was not as compartmentalized as it seems to be now. You could turn on the radio and hear a variety of styles, even on the same station.

"My first experience with jazz was at twelve when my father got tickets for a big band concert at the Westchester County Center. Vaughn Monroe, Bob Crosby and the Bobcats, the Tommy Dorsey band, and Gene Krupa and somebody else were sort of reuniting there—just a whole bunch of jazz artists. The last one on the bill was the Buddy Rich band, who did 'Norwegian Wood,' a Beatles song, and I could identify with it. I mean, I was just completely blown away at this concert; the top of my head just blew off, and I was completely out of my mind in the best way. I stood on my chair, I was screaming! Very exciting. I remember Al Klink was there and there were other tenor players. When the Buddy Rich horn section stood up it was just unbelievable, playing those fast-burning soli. Flipped me out. For me it was an epiphany. I still have some of the autographs from that night.

"I can remember seeing this Timex All-Star show at Avery Fisher Hall, which I also have autographs from on the wall. I loved getting autographs. Duke Ellington and Count Basie sitting at concert grand pianos opposite each other and playing back and forth. I mean, unbelievable! They were both there with their bands. I saw Ella Fitzgerald many times. What can I say? I saw a lot of the greats! Freddie Hubbard, Return to Forever, Blood Sweat and Tears.

"We went to another concert where Gene Krupa was playing and we asked him—'cause he lived in Yonkers—if he knew any saxophone players who gave lessons. He suggested Carl Jenelli, who was my first teacher outside of school, when I was thirteen or fourteen. My very first teacher was a guy at my grammar school, Tony Trotta. I'd go to Carl's and take a lesson every Saturday morning. My high school didn't have a band, so I played for the Elmsford Marching Band. I did shows and musicals at another high school in the pit band. So I found extracurricular ways of playing music. I just took lessons and played as I could. I did my first gig ever with the Associates Jazz Rock Experience at the White Plains Bowling Alley. We did a lot of Chicago, a lot of instrumental jazz-rock. And, yeah, that was really fun. My first gig ever, while I was in high school."

During high school, Daly continued to listen to rock records with her friends; she recalls that her earliest purchases were albums by Janis Joplin, the Who's *Tommy*, and *Jesus Christ Superstar*. She had also bought some Stan Kenton and other big band albums, and her father had given her some of Louis Armstrong's Hot Five and Hot Seven albums. Then, fortuitously, a friend of the family had forsaken jazz for classical music and was giving away his jazz records. He presented her with a stack of LPs that included Miles Davis's *Kind of Blue* and Gerry Mulligan playing the soundtrack of *I Want to Live*. These recordings inspired her to acquire John Coltrane's *Transition*.

"I put it on and I totally didn't get it," Daly confesses. "It was completely over my head at that point.

"Various people told me about Berklee College of Music. 'Cause I would get autographs and just ask questions, talk to people. I was just a kid but I was curious; I wanted to know what people thought I should do. My family was in a suburban New York situation and it wasn't like there was a lot of exposure to the jazz world there. I wanted to go to Berklee and I applied, got in, and went.

"I studied with Joe Viola, who was a great master of playing saxophone and of teaching it. There were a lot of good teachers there. Andy McGhee was there, Bill Pierce, George Garzone, lots of great players. I always talk about the Fringe when I talk about my Boston years, George Garzone's avant-garde trio. When I first got to Berklee I befriended a trumpet player who is still one of my dear beloved friends, Willie Olenick, and he said to me, 'You have gotta hear this band, you've gotta hear them, it's unbelievable. They play Monday nights over at Michael's Pub,' this little dive nearby. And so I went with him. It was Garzone on tenor, Bob Gullatti on drums, and Rich Appleman on bass. I didn't know quite what to make of what I heard, but it opened up this whole other world to me and I knew that I had to keep going back. I went every Monday for about a year. Michael said to me, 'You're here every week; why don't you just be the bartender?' So then I was the bartender for the next two years.

"I think that was one of the deepest musical experiences of my life. The Fringe is just a tremendous unit. John Lockwood now plays bass. They're just phenomenal. They've been together something like thirty years now. Anyway, that opened up the door to more avant-garde music for me, which I just jumped on. All of a sudden I found the Art Ensemble of Chicago and the World Saxophone Quartet, a much freer crowd. In 1977 I discovered Rahsaan Roland Kirk. And he is another one who I believe changed my molecules somehow. I saw him once. He was gonna play at the Jazz Workshop shortly after school ended, so I stayed there just to hear him. I was gonna go hear him every night. The first night I went he was three hours late and angry and dropped his horn. He was struggling and it kinda broke my heart. He died three months later.

"I left Berklee in 1980. It's funny, I feel like I was part of a whole bunch of different scenes there. I loved the Fringe and I loved the outside world. Pat Metheny used to play at a little joint in Cambridge once a week and I'd go hear him. It was all music to me; I didn't have a lot of compartments for things. I just heard a lot of different stuff. The fusion scene was more at a place called Pooh's Pub in Back Bay and I'd go there. There was a jam session at Wally's, also in Back Bay, every Sunday. There was a place on Mass Avenue right before the bridge to Cambridge that I used to go to with John Neves the bass player. He was an older guy and I loved going to hear music with him because he would point out subtle things in the music for me to listen to and really teach me how to listen.

"I had bought a tenor while I was at Berklee and I did some gigs at Michael's Pub and restaurants around town. I'd get a rhythm section and usually one other horn player because at that time I didn't want to be the only one in front of the band. It was always fun; I liked playing, I just wanted to play.

"There was a rock band that was auditioning saxophone players and I went and got in this sort of Top 40-ish rock band. I went to my graduation and that same day I left and drove down to Cape Cod where I started a six-night-a-week gig with that band, the Ina Ray Band, an all-female rock band. I worked with them for a couple years. That began about five years for me of being on the road almost all the time. That band lasted about two years, then four of us mutinied from it and started a band that was a sort of Bowie-esque funky rock band. It was a very good band and we traveled a lot. You'd get a gig for three to five nights somewhere, then get in a van and go off and gig somewhere else. We did one-nighters too. We did a lot of the New England East Coast area, just driving around playing. Then we'd go back to Boston for a day or two, where occasionally I would have jazz gigs on Sunday or Monday nights. I was based in Boston, living largely on the road—schlepping equipment, drag all that stuff inside, set up, play, drag it all out, and drive to either a motel or the next place we were going. The band folded and I moved to New York in 1985. And that started the whole free-lance New York experience, which covers everything from the ridiculous to the sublime. Everything!

"I didn't own a baritone yet. At that time I played alto, tenor, and soprano. Leni Stern is an old friend of mine from Berklee and she and I got a little trio gig down here in Chelsea once a week. And I just started pounding the pavement. You just find the places where there is music and you try to get gigs. You meet musicians and make yourself available and to whatever degree it can, the work will start coming. I began getting a couple of little steady nights a week in town, trios and stuff, and pursuing club dates and any other kind of work that I could think of to do. Latin bands, the whole free-lance scene here, I did a lot of that. It's kind of a scuffle, the free-lance shuffle thing, just trying to keep working.

"Shortly after I moved here, I heard about a baritone for sale. I went and tried it. I had a little money in the bank so I thought I should look into the baritone! And I had probably my second musical epiphany, playing this horn and just instantly recognizing that I loved it. Bought it on the spot.

"As time went on, I realized I really love the baritone; that's the one I want to be playing, regardless of what it's like to carry it around. I always say about the horn, I think the baritone picks you. I think people that play the baritone are playing it because they have to, because it's such a cumbersome, fragile, big thing to do. To carry it around and play it is very physical. You have to really want to do it. I recognized that pretty much immediately. I'll still play tenor, alto, and soprano once in a while if I get a call for something, tweak 'em up, get them in practice.

"One of my first real gigs on baritone was with Kit McClure's Big Band on the Robert Palmer tour in 1986. I worked with her and with many big bands. I feel like I subbed in all of them. It just seems like I've always worked a lot. That's probably because I've had to. But I also like that; I like to be playing a lot, so I find myself doing quite a variety of gigs—anything from parades to concerts, just anything. That seemed to happen for a long time. I had made my goal to make a living playing, and I was making a pretty meager living. At various points I would decide that I wanted to up the level, make the stakes a little higher. Every once in a while I do what I call trimming the fat: I just look at all the gigs that I'm doing and sort of weed out the ones that I'm not crazy about. Usually you make room and some other stuff comes in.

"For example, one day I was doing my laundry and across the street there was this big restaurant, in London Terrace, and I walked over there while the dryer was goin' and I said, 'You know, I think live music would really sound great in here! Hire us on a Wednesday night; I'll give you a trio and you'll make your money back, we'll bring people in.' You know, you make stuff up, 'cause you have to! 'And I think when you hear what it sounds like in here, you're gonna love it.' And they did. So then they said, 'Why don't you do Sunday brunch?' So we had this steady gig for a couple of years, playing tunes on Sunday mornings, making a little food money, and getting a free meal.

"Then I heard about this place in the Village that wanted to have a brunch. When you're working these clubs, the same people are all moving around; they pop up, and if they need music, if they know you from some other place, they'll call you and say, 'You wanna do a thing here?' It starts to happen like that. So this guy called me and I got a Saturday and Sunday brunch that lasted for four years! And I used different people all the time. I could call anybody and ask them if they wanted to come play a brunch. It was a nice little gig.

"Word went out at some point that there was an audition for female players. Every so often somebody gets the idea to put an all-female band together, as if they've discovered something new. I'm always of two minds with these situations. But work is work. So I thought, 'Well, I'll go to the audition, yeah, great.' And really, I thought, the best women players in town were all there and the audition was fun. Not a lot of baritone players showed up, so I got to keep playing the baritone book. And that was the beginning of Diva and I got in the band then. And I have to say, my experience in Diva was largely a positive one. Stanley Kay and Sherrie Maricle really started that band with all the right intentions and did an amazing job of getting a big band up and running and continuing to work in this day and age. Diva continues to employ a lot of women players in a situation where it's hard to get employment these days: a big band that's playing concerts and festivals. I went all over the world with Diva. We backed up amazing people—Joe Williams, Rosemary Clooney, James Brown, all kinds of show biz names. We did the Songwriters' Hall of Fame one year. They are still swingin'. I was in the band for seven years; it was 1997 when I left.

"The same time I started in Diva was when I met Joel Forrester. And I was always working with him parallel at that time. The band was Dave Hofstra on bass; Denis Charles, drums; Joel, piano; and me. In '95 we made our first CD and we got a few festivals and were able to get some nice work. I feel like it's in my design to play Joel's music. I absolutely love doing it. It gives me deep, immense joy, playing his tunes."

Joel Forrester, it should be noted, was in the early 1980s under the wing of the Baroness Pannonica de Koenigswarter, the patron of Thelonious Monk and Charlie Parker. Joel established a rapport with Monk, who was then nearing the end of his life. In a very real sense, pianist and composer Forrester is a musical descendent of Monk, deeply influenced by his music.

As for those whom Daly counts as influences, they are numerous and disparate.

"I would cite Sonny Rollins as a role model, because I feel he is one of the most generous players I've heard. George Garzone, because he's so completely unique and is such an honest player; he really lets it all show. As far as bari players, I love different qualities of all of them—Harry Carney had wonderful phrasing; Joe Temperley is such a great soloist; Ronnie Cuber can *kill* in any style; Serge Chaloff was so sweet and Gerry Mulligan so melodic. I loved Leo Parker's big sound, Gary Smulyan is burning, Howard Johnson is so soulful, and on and on. I never met a bari player I haven't liked for some reason or another." Claire adds Pepper Adams, Sahib Shihab, Charlie Fowlkes, Nick Brignola, John Surman, Hamiet Bluiett, and Leroy Cooper as others she has listened to and admires

In addition to her long-standing association with Forrester, Daly frequently works with singer Nora York.

"I first started doing gigs with Nora in the mid-'90s," says Daly, "and that's another close-to-my-heart important thing that I do, working with her. The artistry of Joel and the artistry of Nora are thrilling aspects of my life. Nora has such brilliant ideas. It's just so much fun and it means a lot to me to work with her. I feel lucky to be in working situations with two people that I admire so much."

A short representative roster of others whom Claire has worked with, either in a free-lance capacity or as members of her own groups, includes Howard Johnson, Carol Sudhalter, Virginia Mayhew, Patience Higgins, Jerry Dodgion, Tommy Newsom, Billy Taylor, Allison Miller, Roberta Piket, Nicki Parrott, Eli Yamin, the late Tom Chapin, and score upon score more.

"In the late 1990s, I was gonna make my own CD, pick a bunch of tunes that I love, and just record them, even if I'm the only one that ever hears it. So that's when I made my first CD, *Swing Low*, in 1999. To my surprise, it was well received, way beyond my expectations. And then, by taking that leap into being a leader and actually putting something out under my own name, life started shifting around a little bit. I'm still just pluggin' along from gig to gig, but now I feel like I'm a free-lance baritone player who gets gigs as a leader.

"I had done the Mary Lou Williams Women in Jazz Festival with Diva in 1997 and I met Billy Taylor then. In 2000 I did the festival with my group and that was a tremendous opportunity. Then the next year Billy invited me to play with his trio in the Jazz at the Kennedy Center series. Now those, you know, are huge breaks and I say, with zeal, 'God bless Billy Taylor.' In fact, Billy is a hero of mine, as one who has helped so many people and elevated the exposure of the music in such a conscious way. It's so intentional, so absolutely brilliant.

"For me it was always about the music. I think anybody who's involved in jazz and in the jazz world has been so touched in their soul by the music that they do this because they have to. It's a lifetime of a labor of love. You might not attain that much materially but you get such a heart full, a soul full, of experience and depth in this music. I feel like I've just scratched the surface. I feel so lucky. I feel so thrilled that I have this in my life."

René Marie listened to singers as a youngster, and in her twenties she got hip to the instruments. Since then her major listening has been to horn players, guitarists, and bassists. That taste for instruments was one of the aspects of her art that impressed me several years ago when I caught her at the Washington, D.C., Blues Alley, for she came across as another member of the band, not as a singer added on. The combo she brought with her for the gig consisted of saxophonist Addae Jahi, pianist Bruce Barth, bassist Elias Bailey, percussionist Brian Jones, and drummer T. Howard Curtis.

The next day, at the hotel where she was staying, I asked René Marie to talk about her life and career.

"My earliest memory of music," she began, "is when I was about four. I was lying on the sofa watching my dad act out the music to Ravel's *Bolero*. He would tell me to pretend that he was an African hunter, spear in hand—only it was a broomstick—and he would crouch rhythmically in the living room and act like a warrior or a hunter looking for his prey. At the climax of the song, he would push the spear in the air like he had killed the prey. And I just remember being thrilled by that and by that music.

"This was in Warrenton, Virginia, where I was born in 1955. We were very poor. There were seven kids and my parents were both teachers. In black families, especially back then, it was expected of the children to know how to do something artistic, such as singing or reciting poetry. As a child, I was exposed to a lot of music: Mitch Miller, Burl Ives, Hank Williams, Sr., Harry Belafonte, Odetta, Aretha Franklin, Nina Simone, and bluegrass music. Before I turned ten my sister and I were listening to the Beatles and Simon and Garfunkel. We never listened to any jazz. Music was a big part of our family but I was the only one who did anything with it extensively.

"My mom's father was a preacher and there were six sisters in her family. One sister played piano and the other five sang. They would travel with him and sing in the different churches. The black churches shared preachers. If one congregation couldn't afford to take care of his needs, he would visit other churches, the same churches all the time, just locally. We went to church every once in a while but I didn't have any strong ties to church as a child. I know a lot of singers start in church and I did sing in church and I played piano and conducted the choir there, but it wasn't *heavily* and it was only *briefly* that I did that.

"My mother bought a piano and my oldest brother, Claude, was taking lessons. I would sit in a chair behind him while he practiced at home and watch the notes that he touched on the piano and look at the music on the chart. And when he would get finished I would get up and play what he had just played. I asked him to write the notes down on the keys, a, b, c. So I kind of taught myself how to play a little, with his help. When my mom saw that I wanted to learn to play she got me piano lessons, which was a real struggle for her financially. I started taking lessons in the fourth grade

"My parents divorced when I was ten and I moved to Roanoke, Virginia, with my mother and two of my siblings. We left in such a hurry that we couldn't bring the piano with us. I had my brother mail my music to me and I taped some sheets of paper together and drew a keyboard and set my music up and just kind of practiced that way, 'cause I missed the piano so much. At school, in the fifth grade, I had a teacher named Mr. Ray Ebbitt whose daughter took piano lessons. Every time we'd go into the lunch room, which was also a multi-purpose room where there was a piano, I'd play whatever I could whenever I'd get a chance. Mr. Ebbitt noticed that I could play and he asked my mom about it and she said that I had taken lessons. So he introduced me to the woman, Kiss Eskelund, who was giving lessons to his daughter. Her hands were bent from arthritis, a very sad situation, but she could still play wonderfully.

"About a year after we moved to Roanoke, my brother Claude rented a U-Haul truck and brought the piano to Roanoke during a blizzard. That was my Christmas gift. I was eleven or twelve. I took lessons from Mrs. Eskelund for about a year. She exposed me to some beautiful classical music and I fell in love with it and continued teaching myself. She played Franz Liszt's 'Hungarian Rhapsody' in its entirety for me and I said, 'I've gotta have that! *Please* let me have it!' And she said, 'No, it's too difficult for you.' I said, 'I promise you, I will learn it!' And I did! She also gave me 'Meditation' by Jules Massenet. I still have that and the 'Hungarian Rhapsody' and all the exercise books she gave me. I treasure those! She died and I didn't take lessons any more.

"There was a man giving a Halloween party for the kids in my neighborhood in Roanoke. At the party there was going to be a talent show. I was about twelve and I didn't know anybody but I went to the party because my mother encouraged me to and the kids were getting up singing these little *kiddie* songs. The song that was popular at the time was 'House Is Not a Home' and I knew the song, completely, so I got up there and people were whispering, '*Who* is *that*?' I don't know what gave me the nerve to do it but I got up there and sang the song from beginning to end. It was real quiet and I was singing my heart out, really pushing. I wasn't scared of holding back, I was just *belting* it out. When I got through I just ran down the steps and ran all the way home. I was scared then, like, I couldn't believe I did that! But I also had this feeling, 'Oh, my God! That felt so-o-o *good* to *do* that!'

"'Okay, I have the ability and when I sing people listen,' I said to myself. Not only that, I loved it; I loved that feeling of singing that song from beginning to end and touching somebody else with it. I think that's why I had all that energy in me after I left the talent show and just ran all the way home. I didn't even stick around to see what people were saying, I was so scared and nervous; but I felt really good, really good.

"Before that I hadn't done any singing in public, only at home with the family, harmonizing to Peter, Paul and Mary and stuff like that. I had a cousin, Marc Robinson, who played guitar, and he and my

Don Byron, DC Free Festival, Freedom Plaza, Washington, D.C., July 4, 1992. Photo by Michael Wilderman.

Jane Monheit and Joel Frahm at the Blue Note, New York, December 17, 2002. Photo by Enid Farber, © 2002.

Gianni Basso, Nicholas Montier, Carol Sudhalter, Gustle Mayer, Jim Galloway, Marc Richard, Engelbert Wrobel, and Frank Roberscheuten, "The Sax Night Session," Stage Torre, Jazz Ascona, Switzerland, July 1, 2003. Obscured are pianist Olaf Polziehn, bassist Lady Bass Lindy Huppertsberg, and drummer Shannon Powell. Photo by Naclerio Gerardo.

Carol Sudhalter and Stefano Benini at Osteria del Porto, Settimo del Pescantino, Italy, December 29, 2002, playing "Scrapple from the Apple." Off camera are pianist Andrea Tarozzi and bassist Enrico Terragnoli. Photo by Maurizio Brenzoni.

Billy Taylor at the International Association for Jazz Education Conference, Sheraton-Washington Hotel, Washington, D.C., January 10, 1991. Photo by Michael Wilderman.

Luluk Purwanto, South Bauer Plaza, Claremont McKenna College, Claremont, California, October 12, 2002. Photo by Ronald Teeples.

Facing page, top
Jazz advocate Cobi Narita, pianist Billy Taylor, and trumpeter Ingrid Jensen at the Mary Lou Williams Women in Jazz Festival, Kennedy Center for the Performing Arts, Washington, D.C., May 1, 1996. Photo by Ken Franckling.

Facing page, bottom
Lisa Sokolov and Ellen Christie, Vision Festival, The Center, New York, May 26, 2003. Photo by Michael Wilderman.

René van Helsdingen, Essiet Okon Essiet, Luluk Purwanto, and Marcello Pellitteri, South Bauer Plaza, Claremont McKenna College, Claremont, California, October 12, 2002. Photo by Ronald Teeples.

Nora York, Makor, New York, December 2001. Photo by Enid Farber, © 2001.

Sonny Rollins and Carlo Pagnotta, Umbria Jazz, Perugia, Italy, July 2003. Photo by Giancarlo Belfiore.

Pam Bricker and bassist Steve Zerlin, Lewie's, Bethesda, Maryland, May 1998. Guitarist Chuck Underwood is off camera. Photo by Jim Saah.

Above

René Marie, Tribeca
Performing Arts
Center, New York,
June 20, 2003.
Photo by Enid Farber,
© 2003.

Right

Claire Daly, Nola
Recording Studio,
New York, May 31,
2001. Photo by Enid
Farber, © 2001.

Shaunette Hildabrand, "At Last the 1951 Show," Stage Torre, Jazz Ascona, Switzerland, July 2, 2001. Photo by Neale Stokes, © 2001.

Evan Christopher, Grove FM Stage, Pori Jazz, Finland, July 14, 2003. Photo by Erika Else, © 2003.

Patrizia Scascitelli, Fifteenth International Jazz Festival, Bologna, Italy,
November 15, 1974. Photo by Roberto Masotti.

Facing page, top
Howard Johnson, Harold Land, Johnny Griffin, Steve Lacy, and Phil Woods,
Teatro Morlacchi, Umbria Jazz, Perugia, Italy, July 20, 2000. Photo by Giancarlo
Belfiore.

Facing page, bottom
Uri Caine, Sala Podiani, Galleria Nazionale dell'Umbria, Umbria Jazz, Perugia,
Italy, July 13, 2002. Photo by Giancarlo Belfiore.

Leonard Gaskin, Allen Tinney, and Eddie South, Chicago, February 1947.
Photo courtesy of The Leonard Gaskin Collection.

Above
John Firmin and Kim Nalley, Monterey
Jazz Festival, California, 1999. Photo by
Stuart Brinin Photography.

Right
Ray Gelato, 1990s. Photo courtesy
of Ray Gelato.

Danny Moore, Walter Barns, Sarah Vaughan, George Botts, Dempsey Combs,
Club Bali, Washington, D.C., 1949. Photo courtesy of George Botts.

Art Blakey, Philharmonie, JazzFest Berlin, Germany, November 1987. Photo by
W. Patrick Hinely, Work/Play © 1987.

Above

Monnette Sudler, HR 57, Washington, D.C., September 13, 2002. Photo by Tyler Neyhart.

Left

George Botts, Westminster Presbyterian Church, Washington, D.C., October 17, 2002. Photo by Tyler Neyhart.

Armen Donelian, West Orange, New Jersey, 1999. Photo by
Judy Benvenuti.

brother Eric, who was the one just older than me, wrote this song when John Kennedy was shot; we learned it and my sister and I would sing harmony on it. But I never sang out in public. That was my first time. And I got such a thrill, and when I went home I told my mom, 'I just sang "House Is Not a Home"' and she wanted all the details.

"Maybe a year after that I started a band in the neighborhood with some teenage boys that played different instruments. It was called The Majestics and we did rhythm and blues, whatever was on the radio that was in my key and that they could figure the chords for— Aretha Franklin and Carla Thomas and Roberta Flack.

"When I was fourteen or so my uncle was the host of a public TV program and I was on it a couple of times. That was a big thing. Then there was a family friend who was a waiter at one of the country clubs and he got me a couple of gigs there, me just singing and playing the piano. Then I got a job at a cafeteria and they had a big grand piano in the lobby and it was Christmas time and I said, 'Is anybody gonna play Christmas songs?' The manager said, 'No,' and I told him I could and so he gave me that job, instead of working behind the line. Also, there was a YMCA and they would have young bands or local bands come and play. Our band was *pretty* good. I don't remember gettin' any money. If we got any it was minimal, fifteen dollars each, *maybe*. But I didn't care; it was just for fun.

"There was an *adult* rhythm-and-blues band called the Randolph Brothers. Their sister normally sang but she was having a baby; they heard me sing and they wanted me to sing in her place, so I did. Now I was singing in clubs that I was really too young to go into, so my mother would go with me, and they put all this makeup on me so I'd look older than I was. I was probably fifteen by then.

"Also, at that time, there was a Miss Black Teenage Roanoke Valley Pageant, and four of my friends and I entered it as a lark, just to see what it was all about. I sang a song by Miriam Makeba called 'Liwa Wechi' and won the pageant, much to my surprise. That was in the newspaper and that's when I started becoming known as a singer.

"I was singing more in the church, directing the choir, and I was still singing with the neighborhood boys. People were coming up to me and saying, 'Did you know that you have a new piano player?' And because I hadn't been to band rehearsals I'd say, 'No, I don't know it,' and they would tell me who he was. His name was Brion Croan and we married three years later when I was eighteen.

"But before I married I became a Jehovah's Witness, at seventeen. And when I did that I stopped singing in public. Brion stopped playing and I stopped singing. I got pregnant three months after we married and our first son, Michael, was born twenty-seven days before our first anniversary. I loved being a mom, I really did. And two-and-a-half years later his brother Desmond was born. We would sing and play at wedding receptions of Witnesses, only of Jehovah's Witnesses. Somebody's always gettin' married and we were able to get back into our music just a bit. It was hard because the kids were so little, you know—trying to nurse them and change diapers and so forth.

"My first introduction to jazz was when I was seventeen and the movie *Lady Sings the Blues* came out. I kept hearing about this woman Billie Holiday, but of course Diana Ross played the role and that's why *I* wanted to go. The soundtrack came out before the movie did and I remember hearing some of the songs on the radio. Wow! I loved these songs! Billie Holiday was singing 'Lady Sings the Blues' and I just *had* to see the movie. And the very next day I went out and bought a songbook of Billie Holiday's tunes and took it home and learned 'Good Morning Heartache.' And after that I started looking for her and Sarah Vaughan and Ella Fitzgerald."

Once she became a Jehovah's Witness, René Marie "concentrated on these spiritual things that I was learning and on my family. There just wasn't much room left for music. I sang a lot to my babies and made up lullabies. I listened to the recordings that I had of Billie and Sarah and Ella, but I didn't do much singing the first three or four years after I married, other than singing at weddings. I started writing music, which I had never really done before—several songs, one that's on my first CD entitled 'Hurry Sundown.' I would sing the songs and play them on the piano for relatives and friends. 'Tell me what you think about this,' I'd ask and they would like it and say, 'You should sing that,' and I would go, like, 'Where? How can I sing it? I don't have any outlet for it.'

"I would sing in the morning, and I would wake my sons up by putting on Aaron Copland's 'Fanfare for the Common Man.' I wouldn't blast it in the bedroom, I'd turn it on in the living room, and that's how they would wake up every morning. I played for them the same stuff my dad played for us and exposed them to the same wide variety of music, including jazz. And I sang all the time; I couldn't stop singing. Music is always going inside of my head. It's maddening, almost, sometimes."

Years went by before René Marie reentered the world of professional perfoming.

"In 1995, when I was forty, my oldest son was in college. He came home for a Christmas break and went to a restaurant in Roanoke; he called me from there and said, 'Mom, you need to come and hear this jazz that's playing. There's a woman singing here and she's *terrible*. She can't sing at all. I know you can sing better than this.' So out of curiosity I went up there and we sat across the table looking at each other and listening to her and I said, 'You are right, I can sing better than that. And she's getting paid for it, too, Michael!' He says, 'Mom, you should start singing again.' By that time, I was playing Cleo Laine and would just be prancin' around in front of 'em. They would join me in harmony 'cause Michael played trumpet and drums and Desmond played guitar. So we still had a lot of music in the family."

That night the family discussed whether René should begin singing in public again and they all, including her husband Brion, agreed that she should. With the help of her piano-playing sister-in-law she got six tunes together and went back to the restaurant and asked if they could play during the break. They were granted permission to do so and their fifteen-minute set garnered them strong applause, which encouraged René to sit in at a club with the combo of a fellow Witness. This became a regular weekend gig for her. Her earnings supplemented the salary from her part-time job at a bank.

In October 1996, a half-year or so after René had resumed performing, Brion Croan decided that he no longer wanted his wife to sing in public and demanded that she live up to their agreement that if it "interfered with the marriage," she would cease doing it. She dropped out of the band.

"It was the most miserable time. I missed it so much. By March of '97 I went back to him and said, 'What can I do to go back into singing but still be pleasing to you? What can I do?' So he listed some things he wanted me to stop doing and some standards he wanted me to meet and I said, 'Okay, I'll do that.'"

Although she felt these new rules were unreasonable, she never-theless agreed to observe them because she "wanted to sing so badly." What her husband insisted upon was "just silly," says René. "He didn't want them putting their hands on me, not even to touch me on the shoulder or the arm, nothing. So I had to tell them, 'When we're in performance, please don't touch me. It offends my husband.' They said 'Okay, whatever it takes,' because by this time they were wanting to play with me."

Taught how to hold a microphone and how to scat by the combo's drummer Bob Peckman, René soon became a local sensation. "I started singing in little places outside of Roanoke, but my marriage started to deteriorate. I think when I started singing, a facet of my personality that I had suppressed was coming back to the surface." She laughs. "I was asserting myself more as an individual. And that didn't fit in well with the way we had been living and the way our marriage had been going. I was speaking out more about things that I wasn't going to tolerate.

"In December 1997 Brion issued an ultimatum to me. He knew we were getting ready to record our first CD, *The Renaissance*, and I was upstairs working on the music. He said, 'If you go to rehearsal to-morrow, don't come back home. But if you want to keep on living here, you call the musicians tonight and tell them you're not going to sing any more.' I said, 'I can't do that.' So I left; I moved out of the house. In April '98 I went to Richmond and moved in with my mother.

"We were still recording in Roanoke, at Flat Five Studios, and I was driving back and forth every weekend to do the recordings. I was doing gigs there that I still was committed to and I was working full time at the bank in Richmond. The album came out in September '98 and I sold the CDs out of the trunk of my car and went to music stores in Richmond and put them on consignment. I met some people who were deejays at some of the radio stations and asked them to play the album. Between September and December I was trying to figure out, 'How do I go from working my day job to doing what I really want to do?' And I couldn't figure out how to make the transition.

"So I took the problem to my brother Claude and he said, 'Just quit your job and somehow the family will figure out a way to look after you while you get on your feet. Jump and the net will appear.' So I quit my job in December on a Friday. And three days later I got a call from Theater Four in Richmond saying they needed a vocalist for the next ten weeks to go on the road for a production and they needed one *immediately*. That was what I needed, a regular check. I didn't have to worry about hiring musicians. I just had to learn my part. And then I started getting gigs in the Richmond area and things took off for me."

René's late-blooming career was encouraged, and to some considerable degree set in motion, by three individuals who early on recognized her extraordinary talents. They were John Fechino, a young jazz enthusiast who frequently came to hear her sing and became her manager for a year or so; the jazz scholar, the late Joel E. Siegel, one of whose special areas of knowledge was jazz vocalists; and Rich McDonald, president of the record label MaxJazz. Fechino got her out into the club scene. Siegel saw her at D.C.'s Blues Alley a couple of years before I caught her there and urged McDonald to check her out. On seeing René in action, McDonald asked her to sign with MaxJazz, which she did. René Marie soon went on the road.

"St. Louis, Chicago, New York, Mississippi, Florida, Maryland, Detroit, San Francisco, and L.A. Where else have I been? Panama City in Florida. New York, at Birdland and the Blue Note. Massachusetts. Hartford, Connecticut. We were at a jazz festival there. We did the East Coast Jazz Festival in Maryland. I did a couple of jazz festivals in Virginia, one in Charlottesville. Oh, the Atlanta Jazz Festival. Next month I'm going to the Dominican Republic, then to Puerto Rico, then to Seychelles, Portugal, and then to Paris to the JVC Jazz Festival. We open for Freddie Hubbard in the Sunset Café."

Since our conversation of several years ago René Marie's domestic and global itinerary has increased many fold. Her CDs have won prestigious awards, including one from the Association for Independent Music and another from the French-based Academie du Jazz.

"When I'm singing a song, it's as if I'm the person that the song is talking about. I *become* that person. I *know* I'm feeling it. As for my body language, I *know* I'm doing that, I feel like I'm standing like it, moving like it, my facial expression is like it. And I've often, in the midst of the singing, asked myself, '*What in the world are you doing?*'" She laughs. "But I can't stop it! I tried for a while, because one time a musician who took me under his wing said, 'Just watch videos of Ella singing. She's not bending over and making these contortions with her body; she's just standing there singing.' And I thought, 'He's right! So I'm gonna stop! I'm not gonna do that!' And I tried it for about two-and-a-half gigs and I just gave up, because there was no way that I could just stand there and sing without moving my hands and my body.

"Maybe it's the twenty-three years of suppression that's coming out, Royal," said René Marie, laughing. "Although I've always sung with a lot of enthusiasm. I have a lot to say. Sometimes I don't even know what it is I have to say until I start singing a song. And then there's always the question of how much do I expose myself while I am singing. You can stand there and sing and look pretty and it sounds okay, but when I do that I don't feel like I'm really going anywhere. If I want to get the most out of the music, I feel like I have to expose myself to the audience, and once I do that it's like undressing, in a way. Your face gets these expressions that, you know, are not very photogenic." She laughed again. "But if that's what it takes to get the notes sounding like that, well, what else can you do? So I would rather do that than just stand there and be a stage ornament. I don't want to do that. I don't like standing there and feeling like I'm separate from the band, I like feeling like I'm a *part* of the band. And I like communicating with the musicians on the stage, even if it means turning my back to the audience occasionally. I'm willing to do that in order to communicate with my accompanists, because I want to be a part of what they're doing and I want them to be a part of what I'm doing. I know I feel very strongly the songs that I sing and I don't pick or choose the songs lightly.

"I feel like I'm still discovering who I am. Like I said, there was so much suppressed when I was one of Jehovah's Witnesses and I find out new things daily about my likes and dislikes. So it's okay to go there or to feel a certain way or express myself in this way."

"My father was a student at Howard University," said Billy Taylor, pianist, band leader, educator, producer, author, radio and television host, and ubiquitous and articulate spokesman for jazz, as he began an interview with me a year or so ago. "My mother was going to teacher's college in Washington, D.C. They met at that time, but before they got married, he moved back to Greenville, North Carolina. He was born in North Carolina and had friends there. His best friend was a doctor and my father was a dentist and they started an office together in Greenville. So my earliest recollections are of Greenville, a small tobacco town in North Carolina. My family moved to Washington, D.C., when I was six.

"When I was very young I'd found that many people in my family played music. I had uncles and aunts who played the piano. Everybody seemed to take a turn at the piano every now and then, both on my mother's and father's sides. My father was the son of a Baptist minister and everybody on his side was highly trained in music, playing and singing. My dad had a wonderful baritone voice and led his father's choir at the Florida Avenue Baptist Church in D.C. when I was a kid. And I had uncles and aunts who played for the choir and on other occasions, too. When I was growing up I could hear them practicing at home and at the church, so I heard a lot of music.

"I had this one uncle, Bob, who was the middle brother of my father, who had five brothers and two sisters. My grandfather just really rode herd on everybody. This one uncle was kind of a maverick; he didn't do what the other brothers would do. He liked to play a different kind of piano. He played jazz. I didn't identify it as jazz but he played stride piano. He was very good at it but he didn't study; it was just something he picked up by himself and liked to do for fun. I told my dad when I was very young, 'Dad, I want to play like Uncle Bob.' He said, 'Aw, you gotta study. Don't do what he did. You study music and you play better.' So I said, 'Yeah, yeah, yeah, yeah!'" Taylor laughs.

"I went on and followed my uncle Bob and tried to learn some things that I could get from him, but he said, 'Look, I taught myself, but I'm not a good teacher. I know a few things but you need to learn for yourself. Do what I did: learn for yourself.' That sent me right back to my dad and I said to him, 'Well, look, maybe I should take some piano lessons.' So Father said, 'Well, that's a good idea if you're gonna play music,' and he sent me to a music teacher. By this time I was six or seven years old and I began to learn a little music, but I kept fooling around, 'cause I wanted to hurry up and play jazz and it wasn't happening. The teacher was a little annoyed and she said, 'Doctor Taylor, your son, he's got some talent but he just won't apply himself.'

"My uncle Bob also turned me on to people that were coming to the Howard Theatre and to other places of entertainment. There were a lot of restaurants where people performed and there were bars that I didn't know too much about at that particular point. My dad's office was right around the corner from the Howard. The matinee only cost fifteen or twenty cents. So I'd go to hear these wonderful artists. I often heard people on the radio as well as in person. Fats Waller was the one that *really* came across to me in those days. I heard him on the radio and I heard people like Earl Fatha Hines, I heard Claude Hopkins, I heard the Mills Blue Rhythm Band, Don Redmond, Fletcher Henderson, and lots of Duke Ellington.

"I ended up studying harmony with Henry Grant. He was one of the people who really turned me on to understanding a little bit more about Ellington." Grant was bandmaster at Armstrong High School and a charter member of the National Association of Negro Musicians, of which he was president in the 1920s. Ellington had studied with him.

"When I was very young, ten or eleven years old, I was really interested in music. I wanted to play and I thought the guitar would be easier than the piano. It wasn't. The guy who lived next door to my aunt played guitar very well and we used to play together; we went on an amateur show at the Howard Theatre and won because he was so good. I didn't contribute very much 'cause I couldn't solo or anything like that; I could just play chords.

"That kind of hooked me on show business—the applause and all was pretty nice. Then I got to know other musicians who were playing around the neighborhood. This one musician was a little older than I but he was a great player. He was very attracted to Ellington and he ultimately played with Duke. His name was Billy White, an alto saxophone and clarinet player. He was the best musician that I was gonna meet for a while because this guy was better than any other musician that I was fooling around with and he taught me a lot.

"We had a player piano and I used to put my fingers where the keys went down but that was hard. I realized that I better really just buckle down and try to learn where notes were and learn many things I had been just sluffin' off. And I did and began to play a little better. The person that I was studying with then, my first teacher, was Elmira Streets. She taught me to read and really got me started.

"I played my first gigs when I was about eleven years old. There was a club on U Street, Republic Gardens. It's gone but there is a

Republic Garden right in the place where I played my first gig. It was just me and a singer. I was playing at little parties and I knew a lot of young players and one of them turned me on to this lady: 'You know, she wants somebody for tonight.' It was too late for an eleven-year-old to be up. I don't remember how I got out of the house. Maybe I stole out. Anyway, I played the gig and made a dollar.

"There were a lot of us who played piano by ear and listened to records and went to hear all the great artists who came to the Howard Theatre. And at Howard University there were a lot of people who played classical music, which by that time I began to get interested in. I wasn't interested in studying classical music but there were several people there who played *beautifully*, and I heard a couple of concerts there, 'cause it was only a couple of blocks from where I lived at that time.

"My family had records and I had a little record collection from when I was very young. I sold papers and saved my money and bought 78rpm records. They only cost about thirty-five cents apiece. I liked my old wind-up player 'cause it was portable and I could put it in my room and listen all the time. My dad had an electronic one and that was nice. It was easier than winding my thing up. My uncle gave me my first Art Tatum record and said, 'If you want to hear somebody play, listen to this guy.' It was 'The Shout'"—issued in 1934 by Decca—"and it was wild; it was all over the piano. I said, 'Well, I really want to play like that.'

"I don't think I had really decided that I wanted to be a musician. I liked the idea of being able to play the piano. I was really hooked on the instrument. I was studying, teaching myself, and learning from other people. When I was at Shaw Junior High School there were people there who were very good; they played better than I did, and they made me want to play better. So I said, 'Why, I can do that,' and I worked at it.

"Dunbar High School made a big impression on me. I went there because my family expected me to go on to college. I was on that track from grade school. My parents figured that this jazz thing would pass after a while as soon as I got some sense and realized that there were better things for me in terms of earning a living and so forth. So they were very tolerant. They knew I loved music and they liked the fact that I played pretty well at the time, for a kid.

"By that time I was playing lots. Just kid stuff. We were playing parties. Then there was the Tommy Miles Big Band, ten or twelve pieces. I wasn't good enough to play in it, but a little later I played in one of its competitors, Bill Baldwin's Band, an even better known band that played all of the dances at the Lincoln Colonnade."

Billy Taylor and saxophonist and flute player Frank Wess enrolled at Virginia State College in Petersburg in 1938. Wess dropped out after a semester. Taylor would be granted a bachelor of music degree in 1942. Among the professors he studied music with there was composer, curriculum innovator, and widely traveled lecturer Undine Smith Moore. In 1975 Taylor earned a doctorate of music education at the University of Massachusetts at Amherst.

"Frank and I had been very good friends in high school. I always wanted to play the saxophone until I heard Frank play it and then I decided that, well, maybe I'd better go back to the piano," Billy says with a laugh. "He's still one of my best friends and a wonderful artist. I learned a lot from him. We used to listen to records and he had a fantastic ear back then. He could pick out the keys of things. 'What is that?' I'd ask and he would say, 'Oh that's so and so.' And then he'd play it! 'Oh, yeah, okay,' I'd say.

"My freshman year I played with a local band in Petersburg, Benny Layton's band. I actually had a radio and there was a country and western band that came on every day. There wasn't a lot of jazz on radio, but there was some. I had heard some other people play country and western on national radio where they sounded pretty good. I wasn't crazy about the style but it didn't offend me. But these guys, I said, 'Man, this is just ridiculous; they're terrible,' and I badmouthed these guys so much in my group of friends that the guys said, 'Well, man, if you're so good, why aren't *you* on the radio?'

"So I said, 'Oh, man, I probably *could* get on!' And so, after shouting my big mouth off, I went down to the local radio station and I told the guy I wanted to play on the radio and he says, 'Come on over here and lemme see what you can do. Can you play?' I said, 'Oh, yeah, I can play'—'cause I was playing in bands at that time. I sat down and played and he said, 'That's pretty good. Okay, you can start on Tuesday.' I didn't mention money to him and he didn't mention money to me, so I never got paid for it. But I was on the radio for a couple of months. Then the gigs that I was doing and my lessons were getting in the way of it so I said, 'I made my point,' and went on to something else.

"While I was in college, the Count Basie band came to town. That was the only time I can remember in the four years that I was in college that they ever played Petersburg. And so we all rushed down to hear the band. I'm standing around like everybody else and the guys in my band kept telling them, 'Why don't you listen to our piano player? He's very good; you should hear him play.' And I said, 'Man, get outa here! That's Count Basie's band, I don't want to take his place, get outa here!' They were talking with Jo Jones and he said, 'Well, maybe right after intermission Basie'll let him sit in.' And he did! He let me sit in with the band. And that was one of the most wonderful experiences I ever had because this was the great Basie band, with Freddie Green and Walter Page and Jo Jones and Count Basie. I was about twenty years old and it was fantastic! Jo Jones was wonderful, and in later years, when I met him again he became one of the really big influences on me and introduced me to Coleman Hawkins and a lot of the people who worked on 52nd Street in those days."

Taylor was playing so many gigs by his sophomore year that his father "decided that if I was gonna waste my time on music then I'd have to send myself to school. So in my junior year I changed my major to music and he told me that I was, from that point on, sending myself to college—which I did for the last two years. And that was all right 'cause I was working at night. I couldn't drive, so I would have to take the bus over to Richmond, which was about twenty minutes away and where most of the gigs were. I was fooling myself into saying, 'Well, I'll study on the bus or at the bus stop or something,' and sometimes I did and sometimes I didn't. My grades were kind of a heartache, but I graduated."

After a year of hanging out in D.C., Billy Taylor took off for New York, arriving on a Friday night.

"I dropped my bags at my uncle's house, where I was gonna stay 'til I got myself together. I wanted to go to 52nd Street but I didn't know where it was and I went to Minton's Playhouse instead, because I knew where that was—it was in Harlem. I figured I'd meet some guys and get to 52nd Street sooner or later. The main thing was, I wanted to be heard and the place to do that was, I thought, some place like Minton's or one of the other clubs in town.

"Ben Webster was there and he was a *big* hero of mine. He had been working with Duke Ellington and I had always wanted to play the tenor and I wanted to play it the way *he* played, that big sound that he got. So it was just a double thrill for me to walk into that club on my first night in town and he's there jamming. He didn't hear me play very much because the bandstand was so crowded by the time I got on, but he said, 'Well, okay, come on down on Sunday and sit in with my group, and if you sound all right, we'll talk about it. Maybe I'll give you a gig.'"

So the twenty-two-year-old pianist took the subway down to 52nd Street and located the Three Deuces, where Ben Webster's combo was alternating with the Art Tatum Trio.

"It's two nights later and I really was totally intimidated by seeing all the names—Billie Holiday was next door—of people that I'd heard about who were on The Street. I didn't think I would get a job like that. I said, 'At least I'll get the audition and they'll get to hear me.'

"I went in and there was a young lady who was from Washington, D.C., a piano player, and as I made my way to the piano to make this audition—I was just going to play a couple of tunes—this woman stopped me and said, 'Billy, what're you doin' in town?' And I said, 'Well, I'm going to go up and play for a minute. Ben Webster asked me to play.' And she said, 'Oh, really? Hey! I'd like you to meet a couple of people before you go on.' And I said, 'Yeah, well, fine.' So I'm still walking as I'm talking and she said, 'This is so-and-so and so-and-so and Art Tatum,' and I didn't hear any of that until I got on the bandstand and I said to myself, 'Wonder if she said—I thought she said "Tatum"?'" Billy bursts out laughing at the memory. "I hadn't even looked outside, at who was working in the club! All I knew was I was going to the Three Deuces and it was the first club that I got to from the subway and I just walked in at ten o'clock or whatever time it was that I was supposed to play and I just got on the bandstand and played. I gave it my best shot, did all the things that I was supposed to do, and got the gig. And I got the chance to work opposite Art Tatum.

"Jo Jones by this time was back in New York and he came in to see Sid Catlett, who was the drummer with the band when I joined, and he and Sid took me around to the White Rose Bar, which was right around the corner, and all the musicians were there. Coleman Hawkins and Charlie Shavers and a lot of people like that who are always in places like that. It was just a wonderful thing to be in the company of all these great musicians and they were standing around talking, you know—shooting the fat."

In the course of working at the Three Deuces, Billy and Art Tatum got to know each other. "It was the beginning of what was for me a very important friendship," reminisces Taylor. "He was just a marvelous friend. I didn't realize at the time that he would tell people from time to time, 'Hey, there's this kid that plays piano and he's pretty good; you ought to give him a job.' He never told me. I found this out from other people."

Billy would go along with the nearly blind keyboard genius to after-hours clubs. "When he finished work he liked to go and hang out a little bit and listen to other players and singers and just drink beer and have fun. There were some sessions that would take place at the Hollywood, a bar in Harlem. Every Monday night piano players would start gathering about nine or ten o'clock. Tatum wouldn't show up until maybe one or two in the morning and by the time he got there all the heavies would be shootin' their best shots. So after a while, after everybody had played, Tatum would get up and play and give everybody a master class on how it should be done. Tatum was the acknowledged boss in those days. No one in his right mind was going to dispute that.

"That was a wonderful club, the Hollywood. You could hear any number of people there just because Tatum used to go there. They'd hang around on the outside chance he would show up, and he showed up quite a bit." Among those Billy recalls seeing there were the Lion and the Lamb—Willie the Lion Smith and Donald Lambert—and Marlowe Morris, three of those "heavies."

"When I was working at the Three Deuces, Dizzy opened at the Onyx Club, which is just across the street, with the first bebop band on 52nd Street. In the band were Oscar Pettiford on bass and Max Roach on drums, both of whom I'd gotten to know. Bud Powell was supposed to be in the band but he wasn't there. Don Byas was on tenor. They didn't have any piano player. This was 1944. I would go over and sit in with the band when Dizzy would have rehearsals in the morning after the club closed and check out his harmony and all that sort of stuff. It was a wonderful opportunity to learn from guys who actually were creating the music right there."

Since those days Billy Taylor has continued to grow artistically as a pianist and combo leader. A roster of the jazz artists whom he has performed and recorded with since those 1940s 52nd Street days would take up many pages and amount to a veritable *Who's Who* of jazz greats of the past six decades. He has also for many years been a chief spokesman for the art form of jazz, utilizing the print media, radio and television, the lecture hall, and his gigs and productions with consummate skill and a talent for communicating to audiences of all levels of jazz interest and knowledge.

One of the great jazz educators, Billy co-founded—with drummer and administrator Dave Bailey—Jazzmobile in 1965. "We wanted to get some things started in Harlem," he explains, "and one of the things that we wanted to do was to take the music back to the community. So we came up with the idea, 'Let's update the New Orleans tradition and play bebop on a mobile bandstand in the various neighborhoods.' And it was wildly successful. Young people would come up and stand around the bandstand and hear Buddy Rich or Max Roach or Dizzy and they would say, 'Oh, wow! What is this? Wonderful!' It gave them an image and a sound that they could emulate.

"Let's go back, just for a moment, because the whole idea of teaching and really talking about jazz to people and to music teachers, I started back in the '40s. I wrote the first book on how to play bebop in 1948. I wrote it because I had been working with Dizzy and Bird and I was very upset with them because they were two of the most articulate musicians I knew when it came to expressing what their music was about, yet when a newspaper person or somebody would ask them, 'What is bebop?' they wouldn't answer. So that was really why I got involved in it. I said, 'Here are guys who know all about the music and, for whatever reason, they choose not to talk about it.' So I said, 'Somebody ought to be doing it.'" Dr. Taylor has authored a dozen jazz manuals along with a 1982 study, *Jazz Piano: History and Development*.

For a decade now, Billy Taylor has been Artistic Advisor for Jazz to the Kennedy Center. I wanted to hear him speak about two aspects of the programs that he has developed there. For my first query, I observed that his feeling about this music spreads across the entire spectrum of it and he has expressed that sentiment in his choices of bookings for the several series that he has inaugurated and hosted at the Kennedy Center.

"I was brought up with the idea that the music built from one style to another and that you could connect those styles in many ways even though the players who were famous for those particular styles often did not choose to do it that way," he said. "I thought that I would try to get musicians who were adventurous and who were excellent musicians, despite the fact that they were not household names, on television, *CBS Sunday Morning*, and on the shows that I produced at the Kennedy Center. And it worked like a charm.

"People on many occasions left those Kennedy Center sessions saying, 'I never heard Jane Ira Bloom play like that' and 'I never heard Charles Lloyd do that kind of thing when I heard his group play.' It was a matter of showing people very graphically that here is a continuum of the music itself. This music is not an aberration; it is a part of the mainstream, despite the fact that many people treat it as though it is not. I was very anxious to make this point and I was delighted that so many people—as long as they were not challenged by someone saying, 'You *gotta* learn this, you *gotta* like this'—could just see these musicians perform and then listen to the musicians talk about what they were doing, how they were doing it, why they were doing it. And it seemed to work."

I reminded Dr. Taylor of a conversation we had had backstage at the Kennedy Center several years before on the evening when the baritone saxophonist Claire Daly joined his trio for a performance that was taped for his radio program *Billy Taylor's Jazz at the Kennedy Center*. I had brought up the subject of his vigorous support over the years for women instrumentalists in jazz, pointing out that he had earlier invited other women instrumentalists to join his trio in concerts taped for his radio show, including trumpeters Ingrid Jensen and Tanya Darby, saxophonists Carol Chaikin, Sue Terry, Jane Bunnett, and Bloom, and violinists Regina Carter and Karen Briggs. I reminded him that on that earlier occasion I had asked him why he had done that and also what prompted him to found the annual spring Mary Lou Williams Women in Jazz Festival at the Kennedy Center in 1996. He had replied that he believed women jazz instrumentalists were "a great and underutilized resource."

"Two things," he hastened to add as our interview neared its conclusion. "First of all, for each of the series that I've started at the Kennedy Center, I have tried to come up with the name of someone who is significant in the music that the Kennedy Center is presenting. So I used Art Tatum Piano Panorama as the title to one series because his approach covered the whole spectrum of jazz from before he started 'til the time he died and even past that time. The idea was similar in the case of the Mary Lou Williams Women in Jazz Festival because Mary Lou Williams in many ways was an example of someone who presented perfectly a continuum of the music from early barrelhouse and ragtime right up 'til the time *she* died. She was as modern as anyone that *I* ever heard at that time because she had played with Cecil Taylor and many other people just to demonstrate her perspective on how those things came together.

"And I was very anxious to make sure that women got an opportunity to be heard. I think this is something that we have shorted, that we have given nowhere near the kind of attention that we should have. Many of the women who could have made *enormous* contributions to music were not given an opportunity to do that, and we're trying to correct that as well as we can at the Kennedy Center. And so far I'm delighted that we have been able to do it. When I first started, I brought a hundred women in for the first Mary Lou festival that I produced and I said, 'This is just a smattering of the women who are available and should be heard at the Kennedy Center and other places like it. I would like to see much more of that in other places.' It's getting there and people are really getting an opportunity now that they didn't get prior to our doing this at the Kennedy Center."

3
Visionaries and Eclectics

"The power of music is much vaster than what this culture in America has pigeonholed it into."   Lisa Sokolov

"I don't think about jazz and Armenian music as having boundaries. It's all music to me, and I guess the challenge of my life has been to try to integrate it all into a seamless style where you don't hear any boundaries."   Armen Donelian

"I learned from the beginning that any kind of music is interesting and serious."   Luluk Purwanto

Of the several times that I have caught Don Byron in performance, one of the most enjoyable was in the mid-1990s when, in the Smithsonian's Baird Auditorium, he and a half-dozen of his musical associates offered selections from his CD *Bug Music*, which features the recorded music of Raymond Scott, John Kirby, and small group Duke Ellington.

I went backstage with my brother Bill after the concert and presented Byron a copy of my recently published *Swing Era New York: The Jazz Photographs of Charles Peterson*, inscribing it to him on the spot and then opening it to photographs of Scott, Kirby, and Ellington. He thanked me warmly for the gift.

131

Don Byron in the past decade or so has emerged as one of the most innovative performers and composers on the jazz scene, taking first place in the clarinet category and placing near the top as composer in poll after poll. And it is not just in the polls but also in reviews of his performances and of his recordings that he has enjoyed the consistent praise of critics. His popularity with his fan base surges impressively.

I caught up with Byron a couple of years later when I attended a concert of his in the Library of Congress. Drawn from his CD *A Fine Line*, the evening's program illustrated well the range of his musical tastes, for it included covers of tunes by Stevie Wonder, Sly and the Family Stone, Ornette Coleman, Stephen Sondheim, Roy Orbison, and Robert Schumann.

I interviewed Don in his Manhattan hotel room the morning following his guest appearance in the 2003 JVC Jazz Festival's Clarinet Legends at the Iridium Jazz Club. It featured clarinetists Tony Scott and Buddy De Franco, who together headlined the week-long series. I had attended Don's appearance the night before. Surely one of the most eclectic of artists in the entire history of jazz, Don Byron speaks of his many musical interests and his participation in a number of seemingly disparate genres in the discussion that follows.

"I basically grew up in the '60s," Don began, "and my dad played bass in a kind of calypso band that did a lot of jazz stuff. My mom was into what I would call the soul singers of the period, like Dinah Washington and Nancy Wilson. My dad loved Oscar Pettiford, he loved Oscar Peterson, he had a lot of Arnett Cobb records, Cannonball Adderley. I remember"—Byron chuckles—"I used to love to listen to Philly Joe Jones's 'Blues for Dracula.' That's probably the first record that I put on voluntarily.

"After that I listened to a lot of rock and roll and Motown. I mean, in that period, it was really unusual to even see any kind of black music on TV. James Brown or Aretha Franklin or somebody like that—we're talkin' about the kings and queens of black music—were the only people who would go on Ed Sullivan or anything like that. So it was always a big deal when those people got some air play and some of my earliest memories of seeing music on TV were about watchin' Ed Sullivan. I remembered seein' Rahsaan on Ed Sullivan, all kinds of people, James Brown, all those Motown acts. I loved *Shindig*"—a British television program. "That was my favorite show, especially when you see Billy Preston playin' on there. Just to see a black musician in the business makin' money, doin' somethin' important. That was really meaningful to me.

"And that is kind of a theme for me. I don't really consider myself, like, this avant-garde musician. Until I got into this kind of big-name jazz thing, I was just a working black musician and I wanted to do things that were meaningful in lots of different kinds of ways. That kind of model of seeing Preston in the middle of the Beatles and seeing him in the middle of the *Shindig* show—that made a lot of impact on me.

"Then, going to calypso gigs with my dad. His group was led by a clarinet player, a guy named Fats Green, who was a fantastic improviser. Still, when I hear him I think he's great. He was somebody that I saw; he was a clarinet player. He played a little bit of alto, but only to read stuff, and he led the band from the clarinet. People wonder how I can lead the band from the clarinet. The reason I don't think it's a corny instrument and I'm not wimpy about it is 'cause the musician that my father thought was the best musician *he'd* ever played with was his clarinet player, and when he took out his clarinet and started playing, there was no question who was leadin' the band. So that was really important.

"My first clarinet teacher was a guy named Lou Clyde. There was a YMHA in my neighborhood and I must've been about six or seven when I started taking lessons on a clarinet that my uncle had played when he was a kid. It was a wooden clarinet, a nice clarinet, and immediately people could tell I had a good sound. That kinda has been my trademark, that I had an unusually professional sound for a kid. I didn't have a lot of technique but I could play in tune and sound kinda like close to professional pretty early on. I could read music and stuff like that and at that time in elementary school they had somethin' about bands. Now, when some junior high schools don't have any music, our elementary school had a good band. I was the only kid in first or second grade playin' in the band. There are a few kids that were in that band that are still playing. It's a funny thing about growin' up in New York. You play with kids and they're still playin'—like Steve Jordan, the drummer that used to play on the Letterman show; he was in that band with a whole bunch of us. I've known some of these people a long time."

I asked Don to speak in some general and specific terms on how he feels about music as being expressed in everything from classical to re-creating Raymond Scott, Duke Ellington small groups, and John Kirby to avant jazz to klezmer to hip-hop and so forth. I asked if he has some kind of philosophy of music that persuades him to approach it in this fashion.

"Well, it's not so much of an approach. I do things in an artistic way when I do them, but there's nothing artistic about wanting to do different music, and there's nothing avant-garde about it; it's just that *I* do a lot of music without waiting to be asked to do it —like klezmer music. Even if I had started playing klezmer music two years later"— when klezmer had begun to attract a wider audience than its traditional one—"no black musician would have ever been allowed to learn klezmer music and become a major player in it. It was an accident, but people react to that like there was something weird with me. 'Why is he so crazy that he'd *try* that?' The truth of the matter is, I wouldn't be asked to play classical music or a lot of these musics. I *do* them because *I* feel like experiencing them"—he chuckles. "It's just really simple. I have expertise in a lot of these areas and if I didn't do them myself, they wouldn't get done at all. Also, if somebody had been puttin' together a Mickey Katz tribute ten years ago, I might have been the best person, genetically and skill-wise, to do that. But I would've never been asked.

"It was just an accident. I fell in around some people who were not the usual klezmer types and who had other aspirations in other musics and we did lots of music together. But the truth of the matter is, even in the same band, if I had auditioned for the band two years later, they would have looked at me like, 'What the hell?!' When I started playing klezmer music nobody was makin' money at it. And nobody in klezmer music was playing their first instrument. Andy Statman—clarinet is his third instrument. The Klezmorim guys, that's all their second instrument.

"There was a real musicianship gap. Once I started playing, all of the unemployed clarinet players in New England were all of a sudden playing klezmer music. If it had been more of a thing, I never would have been asked. And people need to admit that their orientation about what black musicians are capable of doing and want to do is fairly fixed. People expect black musicians to be perfecters of their own self-cultural thing. There's a group of musics and *instruments* that they don't expect to see black musicians in or playing. They don't expect to see black musicians in a symphony and they don't expect to see a black musician in a klezmer band. If Liza Minnelli's puttin' together a big band and there are no black musicians, nobody cares.

"Along with that, the clarinet and black musicians are not somethin' that people put together. It's not like, 'Oh, yeah, Buster Bailey.'" Byron chuckles. "That's not what people think; people think, 'Benny Goodman, Artie Shaw,' and then they see me and they say, 'Oh, look at him, he's got dreadlocks!' But that's their assumption; it's not mine.

"All this time, I've just been a versatile working musician. Before I was signed with a record label there were periods when I was playing with downtown cats like Marc Ribot, playing with Mercer Ellington, playing with Mario Bauza, playing shows, just a working musician, and then once I got signed, some of the more small group things that would showcase my clarinet started happening all of a sudden. That was my entire workload. Up 'til that point, I was doin' all kinds of things.

"It's just that the clarinet takes you to a different type of work than people are accustomed to seeing black musicians play. Okay, you want to play classical music, you can do that on the clarinet. You want to play Indian music authentically, you can do that on the clarinet. You want to play all kinds of Eastern European, not just the Jewish stuff, but Macedonian, Romanian, Bulgarian, all those things are part of the legacy of the clarinet. Clarinet is a very international instrument and people just don't expect *me* to do it. If anybody else does it, 'Oh, he's just doin' that.' But people don't expect me to do it. And that's *their* thing. It's not *my* thing.

"Whatever opportunities there are to play clarinet, I'm just gonna play 'em. Aside from all this stuff that I mentioned, when I was a working musician I was reading New Music pieces, classical pieces, some completely through-composed, some with a little improvisation. I knew I wasn't gonna get into the symphony but I knew I was playing clarinet at that level, so I got attached to a lot of New Musicy kind of things and that's remained a part of my work—now more as a commissioned composer. I'm dealing more with groups like the Kronos String Quartet and Bang on a Can and stuff like that. But that was a part of my work. Those people know me from working with me.

"What makes these conversations difficult is two things. There's definitely a lot of racial issues to be discussed about people's assumptions, and also it's not just about jazz; it's about being a working musician, and being a working black musician has its own set of problems that are different from being a working white musician. If I play in a mixed big band with black and white musicians, the white musicians and black musicians are all going to *completely* different kinds of gigs. And yet people don't want to talk about that or *admit* that. But I *have* to deal with that because I play an instrument that people's basic assumption is why would I want to play it?

"Like, when I was seventeen years old I get into this fancy school and immediately every semester I'm there I get a transcript that says that I'm not a clarinet major, I'm a saxophone major, and I have to change it back. I wasn't even playin' any saxophone and, at one point— I just found this out a year ago—the president of the school called my father in to try to convince him to stop me from playing clarinet. This isn't 1940, this is 1979. 'I don't think he's that good, I don't think he can really make it. So why don't you just tell him to get a saxophone,' and just leave this shit alone. I just found this out this year!" Don says, laughing. "And it was shocking to me because it gave me that whole feeling of having to convince people that I was really a clarinet player. It wasn't even about what they'd heard me play; it was just like, 'No, you can't be that, you can't be *tryin'* to be that, you can't be *assumin'* that you're gonna play any clarinet in the world.' So I have just tried to stay with it and make as many opportunities or *take* as many opportunities to play the instrument as I can.

"I think, to a certain extent, what I did after I left New York, I completely checked out of wanting to convince the clarinet community here that somehow I was gonna come in and I was gonna play the ballet and opera and shit like that. What I did was I just said, 'Well, I'm interested in all this music and while I'm learning it I'll learn it all on the clarinet. I may play some saxophone, I may play some piano, I may get my writing together, but whatever it is, I'll learn it on the clarinet. And then, over the course of time, I got into some different kinds of music that were clarinet specific, and then, on the other hand, I played lots of music on the clarinet that was not usually for the clarinet. When I was playing with Vernon Reid—or, recently, I've been playing with people like Me'Shell N'Degeocello—nobody's doing that on the clarinet.

"It's just the hipness factor you need to be around situations like that, and not that many people have it on the clarinet. Just the idea that this is not a lame instrument; you just have to make your language contemporary. If your language isn't contemporary then you don't sound right in a place. If people are playing funk and you're playing swing, that doesn't sound right—it's not the instrument. That's one of the major concepts that I've tried to keep in my mind: there's nothing wrong with the instrument. And yet there are times when I wish I could just play a lot of tenor and make a lot of money and do more things idiomatically and it doesn't have to be an amazing thing. I have a kind of funny relationship with it 'cause now I'm really studying tenor and thinking that I want to do more normal things and I am really feeling for the first time in my life like there's another instrument that I want to achieve things on besides clarinet, 'cause I've *never* wanted to achieve anything on any other instrument until a couple of years ago—not even bass clarinet. I just love playing clarinet," he confesses, laughing. "Did that answer your question? That was a long answer."

I commended him for his answer and asked him to talk a little bit about his interest in Raymond Scott, adding that Raymond Scott, along with the classic boogie-woogie pianists, was the first music that I really listened to as a twelve-year-old in the early 1940s.

"When I made that record *Bug Music*, I had just come out of doing *Kansas City*, the movie, and I have to say I was really frustrated with the lack of preparation that we had making that film. Like, 'Okay, so we can just show up.' In fact, the whole time I was making it I said, 'Whyn't you call Herb Pomeroy or one of these cats that could just do some shit like this in their sleep and have them write out something that sounds like that Kansas City stuff orchestrationally?'

"People make a mistake thinking the Basie band didn't have charts. There were charts! They just didn't write 'em down! I think that's really funny! There's something very Eurocentric about that assumption, that because people didn't write stuff down, it wasn't arranged! And they had a *sound*! This kind of tight-voicing sound that those bands had.

"The orchestrations for *Kansas City* were actually supposed to be conductions by Butch Morris—that was the original plan—and Butch Morris did show up to the thing, but some of the more conservative people in the group just wouldn't even swing that way. They weren't gonna look at a guy with a stick and play the right notes; they weren't down with that.

"So it was completely frustrating for me because I'm just really detail-oriented about stuff like that. So after I came out of that I was ready to do a repertory thing. I'd been studying Raymond Scott just for myself and then I read about the connections between Charlie Shavers, Raymond Scott, John Kirby, the Ellington thing. Once I started researching that, I just couldn't believe the dissing that Kirby got in academic stuff like Gunther Schuller's book," that is, *The Swing Era: The Development of Jazz, 1930–1945*. "I mean, this was a band that people would've *killed* to be in. Ben Webster wrote his own part to be in that shit. I was just talking to Kenny Davern about it. He can sing the solos in that shit! This is a thing that musicians thought was at a very high level, and for people, years after the fact, to diss it, it just didn't seem right, didn't seem right.

"And it also seemed that here was a group of black musicians who were juggling the same kinds of influences that I was juggling. That's just what they were. It *seems* cute but it's *not* cute. If you like a Chopin nocturne, you play it. And it's not the jazz, it's the notes, it's the notes that Chopin wrote, the little hanging, voice-leaning type of stuff that's the piece, and that's why you play it, because you want to. I understood that completely

"And then, Buster Bailey, he's just such a bad cat. It's obvious that he was a Benny Goodman type of guy that was workin' both sides of playin' the stuff. He never got too much recognition for that but it's obvious when you hear somebody like that. I mean, he was a ridiculous player. And so there was that.

"Then there was the Raymond Scott stuff, which I was studying for content in the past few years. Even the Kronos Quartet, they've been playing Raymond Scott tunes. People study these tunes 'cause there are some interesting approaches to writing harmony in them. Those tunes are just really rich compositions, they're really smart, and he has a real orchestrational command of that small group. Just listen to some of the pairings. If one person's playing, two other people are accompanying him. He'll get stuff out of the tenor and the trumpet in weird octaves and it sounds really full. Scott had it together, and that's what that writing is about, really sounding full, because you really know what the tendencies of the instrument are in terms of filling out a chord.

"Then the early Ellington stuff, that's my favorite period of Ellington, always will be. It's the most interesting period. It's just completely explosive, and he's inventing what he's doing from tune to tune, sometimes based on some girl's shakin' her ass or whatever. Whyever he wrote the piece, these pieces are completely revolutionary and often quite different from each other. Even some of the harmonic moves he makes, there's no precedent for a lot of them." He pauses and hums a phrase. "The move between those two chords, I've never seen that anywhere, never. I'm not even sure why it works. How did this cat come up with this shit? How does this work? I've looked at it up and down and I understand what it is but I don't understand how someone will come up with it. He's just a bad cat. I don't think people really understand how rigorous Ellington is as a composer, and when I say rigorous, it's like there's a way that you can be a composer and what you're doing is writing things that people have heard before, and then there's a way of writing that's like you're just on a tight rope, you're just doin' what you're doin', maybe you're being matter of fact about it to yourself. Not that many people write like that, and this cat, in about a ten-year period, *everything* sounded like that.

"And then these cats, they're just *playin'*. I mean, the way that Harry Carney is *playin'*. These cats are playin' like *wild* men. There's that film *Black and Tan* and they play 'Cotton Club Stomp' even faster than it is on the record. Just up and down the horn. It's just impressive. It's an impressive period of an impressive person's life. It's not what Wynton and them are about. That's too buck-wild for them, that music. They're really about the classic five saxes, Jimmy Blanton on, that's what their group is about when they're talkin' about Ellington. I like the other thing," he concludes, laughing.

"Just like last night, there's Buddy De Franco, there's Tony Scott, and it's *natural* for me to gravitate towards Tony 'cause he's crazy, you know what I mean, he's a wild man, and yeah, I can relate to people in their wild period or in their wild mode, that's easy for me to relate to. So that's my period of Ellington.

"I just put 'em all together; I just put the three things together. *Bug Music* could've been, if I was in graduate school, a nice paper. Some footnotes, you know, all fleshed out. A couple of my records would've made nice papers, but that one in particular. That's a dissertation—that and the Mickey Katz CD. They're not academic sounding records but the *idea* of them is academic."

I observed that it was a minute or so before noon and that he had established that as his time of departure from the hotel.

"Well, I got ten minutes if you have more questions."

I proposed that he speak about his compositional methods.

"It's not like I write melodies and try to set them, although sometimes that happens. I decide what kind of compositional elements a thing should have. Maybe it's based on another kind of piece that I've heard or a certain kind of writing that I've studied. There are some pieces that we play in *Music for Six Musicians* that are really from my study of Second Viennese School music, of Schoenberg and Berg and Webern, and when I say 'study,' I mean that I've performed a lot of that stuff, besides studying it, so I'm really familiar with it.

"So it may be a certain kind of technique, especially when I'm doin' film, which is for me the most inspiring thing. It's like, while listening to some Brazilian music, I say, 'Well, this kind of thing, this needs some Second Viennese music, this needs something with string quartet, this needs this, and that needs that.' So I start with the technical idea of what I want to do and that also may get down to, 'Well, I think this should have contrary motion; there should be a fugue; there should be unison writing in this spot.' I may have the feeling for a technique, as opposed to just saying, 'Well, hey, you know, I'd like to write something nice, it's pretty, it sounds good on the clarinet,' and that kind of writing. Because, again, I've prepared myself for doing a whole lot of stuff.

"In the course of a month I may spend some hours of my day goin' through the Rimsky-Korsakov orchestration book or something like that. I'm prepared to do a lot of different *sorts* of things. I may get a commission, an opportunity to write some music for an occasion. Just like recently I'm gonna have to write some music to accompany an author. So I decided to put together a string and wind kind of sextet with string quartet and piano and clarinet. That's a technical decision in terms of orchestration, and then what kind of music it'll be, that'll be another kind of technical decision, and then I'll have to flesh that out.

"When I've written a certain kind of technique I think there's a thread that makes it sound like something I wrote. Like Stravinsky wrote in a lot of different kinds of styles, but there was a kind of thread about intervals and a sense of music and a sense of rhythm that kind of tie things together. So I would hope that there's that in the totality of what I've put out.

"There isn't one kind of way that I write. Sometimes I admire people who can stick with one thing and perfect something—someone like Harry Partch or Steve Coleman, someone who's in one mode of writing. 'Okay, we're gonna refine this, perfect this, blah, blah, blah.' That's just not my personality. As a person, it's not my personality; as a musician, it's also not my personality. It's more my personality to say, 'Okay, I want to do this, lemme try to do this well, I want to do that, I want to try to do that well.' I want to do a few things and lemme try to do it well and personalize it and individualize it, and yet still have it be in the pocket, for whatever it is.

"So if I write a string quartet, I want it to be competitive; I don't want it to be, like, the jazz guy they gave a chance to. I want it to be competitive with other string quartets. I'm gonna play some legit clarinet, I want it to be competitive with other legit clarinet players. If I write some Latin jazz, I want it to be competitive, and yet individual.

"It's kind of a concept that I really feel I borrowed from Stravinsky and Eddie Palmieri, that you can be in the pocket of something and be outside of it at the same time. You can individualize and be in the pocket, and you can think for yourself and think within a thing. And sometimes that means you kind of fluctuate between those extremes, which certainly someone like Eddie Palmieri definitely does. One minute he sounds like an old guy in Cuba and the next minute he's got his elbows all over the piano and it's completely dissonant. That kind of fluctuation I think is a part of what I do. I don't feel like I do it exactly in the violent style that somebody like Eddie Palmieri does it, and I say that with all love and respect. He's one of my greatest heroes of all music. My particular style of fluctuation, I think, is a little softer than that."

I asked Don Byron to describe the actual mechanics of his composing. Does he use the clarinet?

"I definitely do not use the clarinet. There's no clarinet involved. I play a lot of piano. At one point I used to play gigs on piano. Now, I'm not saying that I have any piano technique right now, but I can write in a certain kind of way; I use a lot of the theory that I got from people like George Russell. It's definitely something that happens at the piano.

"At this point I have computery kind of stuff to help me, which most musicians now use. I can't remember the last time I went to a rehearsal and got a handwritten chart. That's a thing of the past. Some people's software is better than others', but, yeah, everybody's using some kind of thing. Some people have stuff that's more involved in recording and notation than I have. I am just strictly notation.

"When I'm actually composing something, I like paper, but it's easier to save and keep stuff, move it around, expand on it in software. And the *best* thing about software is you can hear stuff back that you can't play. It's really important that if you're doin' things that are structurally complicated, where even one pianist might have a hard time playin' it himself, you can get it played back—that's the greatest thing about the software, for me. Sometimes I've had things that I had to play and I just put the accompaniment in the software and then I typed it in. Now I can slow it down, speed it up. I remember I was working on this Copland thing and it was really kind of tough, so I can play it at half speed, three-quarter speed. The software stuff is really useful in a lot of ways. So I do use it. You get one more question."

"Let's see. What are your travels like these days?"

"Longer than I like. And most of it has been in the States. I have a couple short European kinds of things, like a couple weeks at a time. And I'm tendin' not to like that so much. Last year was ridiculous. We went to China," he says with a laugh. "Oh, my god! Yeah, this is not the part of what I do that I really enjoy. I think everybody around my age, we had our period of lovin' doin' stuff like that and I think it's changin' as we get older and our backs don't like it any more, legs don't like it any more, lungs don't like it. And I've traveled through all the worst shit that's happened, through 9/11, through Ebola, through SARS; I've been in all those high-risk places. I've seen and done some shit I'd rather not be doing," he says, chuckling. "When the Ebola thing was happening? They would hand you cards saying, 'If something happens to you, please give this to a doctor.' Then the last time I traveled to De Gaulle, all the handlers for Air France were wearing those masks and I'm thinking, 'What the hell am I doin' here? Why do I need to be here?' You know, it's not like I don't like playin' in Europe. I love Italy especially. It's just that the mechanics of travelin' are really difficult on the body. I grew up with all this asthma stuff and I have to admit, even now, even after my yoga and whatever, I'm a frail person, and I would rather be home. It's not a musical thing.

"People ask, 'Why should you get thousands of dollars for playin' one gig?' The reason is that getting *to* the gig is what you get paid for. And then playing a professional performance on not enough rest, not enough sleep. There's always gonna be something that you have not enough of. That's what local musicians don't have to deal with that traveling musicians do.

"It's ridiculous! I mean, every jazz musician knows how to do laundry. Whenever we get to a hotel and there's a heated towel bar, I can bet you, within five minutes of seeing that, everybody in our band will have laundry up. Everybody does it. They got the soap. I mean, these are people that can't even pick up things in their house, but they get on the road, it's the survival skill.

"I don't really enjoy the travel. I like playing. That's why I have been focusing on trying to get involved in writing things."

I was attracted to the idea of including Lisa Sokolov in this collection of profiles after listening to several of her CDs a couple of years ago and concluding that she was one of the most innovative singers presently working in the jazz idiom. Gifted with extraordinary range and control, she does things with her voice that, frankly, I had never before heard. I put her on my list of potential interviewees and we exchanged several e-mails.

In New York taping interviews a year ago, I called her and made arrangements to meet her in the Student Café of New York University, where she has been on the faculty for more than two decades. We chatted over coffee for a half hour, which was as much time as she could spare from her professorial duties that day.

I caught Lisa Sokolov not long ago at the 55 Bar, which is a few steps from Sheridan Square in New York. The experience of seeing her in action fully met my expectations after previously knowing her art only from her recordings. It was a stunning performance. She has a way of seeming to sculpt her sounds from the air. As for the emotional impact of her voice, I have seldom been so moved by a singer. In Lisa's program that evening were visits to the Delta blues, gospel, and standards more than a half-century old that she had updated to reflect her sensitivities to John Coltrane and other modernists. Laura Nyro's "And When I Die" took us to the edge of emotion in a way that only a Laura Nyro—or a Lisa Sokolov—could do. Her original "Hard Being Human" revealed her as a compositional talent to be reckoned with. Accompanying Lisa with brilliance were keyboardist D. D. Jackson and bassist Cameron Brown.

A visionary improviser and a strikingly original innovator who applies her flexible voice and extraordinary range to song with a unique passion, Lisa Sokolov is in the first rank of a growing band of musicians who can truly be said to be pushing the envelope of the jazz idiom into the postmodern era.

Several months after our initial meeting at New York University, we had a mid-afternoon lunch of turkey sandwiches on rye at the Omega Diner on West 72nd between Columbus Avenue and Amsterdam and she talked about her life and career for two hours.

"I was born in 1954 in the hospital in Manhasset, Long Island, to Bernard and Helen Sokolov, who were born and raised in Brooklyn. I was the second of two children and grew up in Roslyn, Long Island.

"My grandparents on my father's side were Russian Jews. My great-grandfather, Harry Sokolov, was from Pinsk or Minsk, around there. He came here as a stowaway on a ship after a run-in with the town bully. He thought he had killed him but he hadn't. My great-aunt, Fina Sokolovskaya Koushpeil, then moved to St. Petersburg with her mother, my great-grandmother, and came to the United States after the Russian Revolution. She was a singer in the Jewish theater, in theaters on Second Avenue around 12th Street. We used to sing together. I loved her very much.

"My grandmother on my father's side was a dancer. She had studied with Isadora Duncan and Martha Graham and was in the thriving theater and intelligentsia scene in downtown New York. I remember stories from my dad about the Café Royale in what we call the East Village.

"My great-grandfather on my mother's side, Moisa Liza Singer, was also a singer, and a poet as well. In Austria he had begun to study to become a cantor. He left synagogue training there and moved to New York in 1885. I just did my first cantoring this past holiday. It was deeply satisfying. I guess it is in the blood.

"My father played stride jazz piano, purely as a love. I remember hearing him play tunes like 'More Than You Know' and all sorts of stride piano. He was a great devotee of Art Tatum. I remember hearing records of Art Tatum from a very young age. And he was a great devotee of Mabel Mercer. So I listened to a lot of Mabel Mercer as a young person, which probably has influenced my devotion to diction. I remember jazz in the house through recordings, and also a lot of classical music. I remember when Stan Getz's 'Girl from Ipanema' came out and my father played that nonstop. And I remember some big bands. But mostly it was Tatum through my growing years, my elementary school years. As a kid, I listened to a lot of Ray Charles and Al Green. I remember as a child going to Leonard Bernstein's Saturday concerts for children, and that was very influential.

"I sang from the minute I was born and I was admonished for singing nonstop. I remember in first grade there was an assembly in which the whole school sang 'Do-Re-Mi' from *The Sound of Music* and I sang the solo, my first memory of singing alone in the midst of many. I studied piano, violin, and flute as a young child. I did violin 'til fourth grade and I stopped the flute by the time I was in seventh grade. I continued piano. I had a music teacher named Mr. Fuller, who was an influential, wonderful man. I sang choruses from the age of seven and always loved that.

"I started studying piano, classical piano, with a man named Marshall Kreisler, who I believe lives on the Upper West Side still. I studied with him throughout elementary school. There was a school called Fiedel School that was run by a man named Ivan Fiedel. His son Brad Fiedel is a very well-known composer for film now. Ivan had a big estate and he was a composer of children's opera and a great pianist. His wife is a wonderful dancer. And every Saturday I would go there and study with them. I went to a school after Fiedel School where I would go every Saturday and all summer and we'd do musical theater and piano.

"In sixth grade I chose to stop piano for a year, and then in seventh grade I snuck into the auditorium one day and heard the music teacher playing 'An American in Paris' and I was bowled over by that experience. That was the moment when I went back to my mom and said, 'Now I really choose to study,' and I continued to, first with Mr. Tagalino and then back to Marshall Kreisler. So music was always my love. It was always a way that I found a space around myself where I could communicate with other levels of things, the invisible. I always felt that way.

"In high school I started a trio with a pianist named Michael Capobianco and a trumpet player named Jim West. We played mostly tunes. There was a teacher who taught music, Harold Gilmore. I studied conducting with him. He turned me on to Coltrane. Also in those years I listened to a lot of Judy Garland, a lot of American classical show, theater, and cabaret music. I remember listening to a lot of American theater music.

"The pop music of the time that got to me would've been the Beatles, Aretha Franklin, Laura Nyro, the Isley Brothers, and Sly and the Family Stone, that sort of thing. I was very much into Parliament Funkadelic. Any kind of soul and any kind of funk music I found very compelling. I was also into Jefferson Airplane and that world, as well. I was intrigued by Janis Joplin but I kept a bit of distance. Aretha was played nonstop. I was a devotee of Laura Nyro—her capacity to incarnate emotion and also how she moved time. In my later life I have realized how influenced I was by that. I would say Laura Nyro was a very powerful influence. And Aretha. And I listened to a lot of Ella Fitzgerald at that point also.

"When I went to college I became aware of Betty Carter, who I just completely loved and was completely called to. I followed her around and went to many, many, many of her concerts. I also remember hearing Meredith Monk when I was in college, and reviewers will mention sometimes that they can hear these influences, Meredith and Betty, in my singing. I remember hearing Thelonious Monk for the first time, certainly an influence, and I would go hear Sun Ra a lot and was a great, great fan of that world—and of Eric Dolphy.

"When I was in high school, I went to a place in the summer called Amherst Summer Music School, a music camp in Raymond, Maine. I studied opera there. I was very big into choral singing. I sang in many all-state choruses. I was the president of the choruses in high school and I remember being called in by the principal, who told me that there was a child who had developmental problems and they asked me to work with this kid. And so I started to go to this child's home once or twice a week and work with him through music, because that was my language. That was the first time I worked with another person in what became a career in music therapy. So that was a very important moment.

"I was always playing classical piano, I was singing opera, I was singing choral music, and I had my jazz groups. That was through high school, where my conducting teacher Harold Gilmore told me about Coltrane and Bennington College, where Coltrane's bass player Jimmy Garrison was teaching. I applied to Bennington and went there, in 1972. When I got to Bennington I learned that Jimmy Garrison had left the college, so I actually never met him. But it was his music that had brought me to that place. And I discovered faculty there who each had a great influence on my work, including Milford Graves, Bill Dixon, Jimmy Lyons, and the great voice teacher Frank Baker, who had sung in the Metropolitan Opera." Garrison had taught at the college the school year of 1970–71 and he died in April 1976, several months before Lisa left Bennington.

"Bennington was unusual because many people came there who were not students but who wanted to play with Bill Dixon and to be involved in the music that was going on. It was a very big music scene at the time.

"Bill had the large ensemble and I was a bit timid, I was a little afraid of him. So it took me a while to really get my courage up to approach him and say, 'I want to be in the large ensemble,' which was half professional musicians and half students. Bill Dixon went on sabbatical and at that point Jimmy Lyons came to take his place—a great saxophone player with Cecil Taylor and just a dear, dear, dear man who was very approachable. I went to him and said, 'Jimmy, I want to sing.' And he just embraced me and wrote the most magnificent music for me. That was a very formative experience. Jimmy wrote such interesting, intricate music. He wrote me a beautiful, beautiful solo.

"Six months before I got there Frank Baker had a massive stroke and lost his capacity to speak or to sing. He was a brilliant teacher who would just sit and radiate. The fact that he didn't sing for me really gave me the chance to develop my own sound. He taught me an enormous amount. I also was still playing classically, with Lionel Novak, and I studied composition with Lou Calabro and, for a short time, with Vivian Fine. And I studied with Milford Graves, who is also a very big influence in my musical life. We did a lot of experiments with rhythms and how they affect pulses and things like that. He would hook me up to machines and play rhythms and I'd tell him what I noticed and we had a lot of fun.

"There was a lot of free jazz going on at Bennington and a lot of interest in how energy is moving in the body. In high school I had been drawn to knowing that the power of music is much vaster than what American culture has pigeonholed it into. That's always been deeply interesting to me.

"I always loved languages. I speak French rather well, I speak German not so well, I speak Spanish less well. When I was at Bennington I was a double major of what they called Music and Black Music, two separate departments, and I did both. I had a minor in philosophy; I was always very into philosophy. I was a great lover of Plato and Empedocles and that whole classical thing, which was really a place of love for me. At the same time, Steve Paxton, who had developed a form of dance-movement improvisation called contact improv, was teaching there. A whole postmodern-movement world was being birthed there. My mother sculpted large stones and so art was always, and still is, a very big part of my life. I studied art, drawing, and sculpture at Bennington. So all those influences were always there and there was a lot of collaboration. At one point I had to sit down and say, 'Which way am I going? Am I gonna really devote myself to art or devote myself to the music?' I remember the day of making the choice."

After the four years at Bennington, 1972 to '76, Lisa moved back to New York and helped form a ten-piece band with Henry Letcher, a drummer who was Duke Ellington's nephew. "The band was basically made up of mostly uptown New York guys who'd never been out of the States," says Lisa. "I had a trio at the time with a violinist named Derrik Hoitsma, whose professional name now is Derrik Jordan, and a pianist named Peter Dembski. When they heard we were going to Paris they decided to come along.

"We supposedly had a gig in Paris but when we got there, it turned out we had no gig and everyone was a bit overwhelmed by, all of a sudden, being in Paris with no money and no work. The band stayed together for a short period of time. I could speak French and I proceeded to get a job taking care of children, which gave me an apartment. Then the band members went back to the States, but my trio stayed. Peter and Derrik and I did a couple of gigs, and then they left and I hooked up with a dancer named Harry Shepard, who connected me to a project that Steve Lacy's wife, violinist and singer Irene Aebi, was doing at the Musée d'Art Moderne. I started singing for her dance pieces and did a couple of performances there. I wound up staying in Paris for four or five months.

"When I came back to the States I decided to pursue my interest in music therapy. So I enrolled in a master's program in music therapy. There was always this question of whether I would just sing and wait tables, like my friends, or find a way to use music as service to support what I was doing musically.

"When I was leaving Bennington in 1976, Bill Dixon told me to go see Sheila Jordan when I got to New York. So after I got back from Paris I was living on Second Avenue and 9th Street and in my head I heard him say, 'Go see Jeanne Lee.' Now, I didn't know who Jeanne Lee was but I called her and said, 'My name is Lisa Sokolov. Bill Dixon told me to call you.' Later I realized that I'd called the wrong person but obviously I called the right person, though it would have been wonderful to have met Sheila at that time.

"Jeanne invited me to come to see her. It turned out she lived three blocks from me. She had a guest, dancer Patricia Nicholson, bassist William Parker's wife, and Patricia was listening to us sing together. At the time Patricia and William had a big ensemble and were working on a very large piece called 'A Thousand Cranes.' When she heard me singing with Jeanne, she said, 'Well, my husband would like to hire you; come to rehearsal tomorrow.' That was a very big moment 'cause the whole world opened up for me. Jeanne and I became close from that point forward. She was a mentor; she was older than me, she had kids, she'd been doing it for a longer time.

"That night I had a concert singing for a choreographer—I sang a lot for choreographers at the time—at the Merce Cunningham Studio. It was a two-part show. The other singer and dancer went on first and I heard this woman sing and I was blown away, 'cause I heard someone who came from the same planet as me. There's no other way to say it; I'd never heard anyone sing like me, speak the musical language that I speak. And I was bowled over. When I went to the rehearsal with William's band the next day, there she was—Ellen Christie. So the trio in the big band was Jeanne Lee, Ellen Christie, and me. The three of us worked together for many years from then on. And once things opened up with William, I've continued to work with him to this day. That was 1978.

"In terms of gigs in those early years, there were a lot of them with William Parker and that whole group, a lot in Studio Henry and in St. Mark's Church working for choreographers. I accompanied dance classes and watched a lot of bodies go by. And I began also working as a music therapist up in East Harlem at Northside Center, which was the school of Dr. Kenneth Clark. I worked with kids who'd been born junkies or had very fundamental problems.

"I was invited to come and teach in Switzerland. Right before my first gig there—this was about 1980—I broke my back in a riding accident. I was really committed to doing this gig"—she laughs, recalling it—"crazy as it was. So I got them to make me a brace and I lay on the floor in the airplane and flew to Zurich. And did a concert there, a solo performance. I was into doing a lot of solo work at that time. I remember standing in the theater and singing these long tones and hearing my heart beat; it just crashed through my tone.

"It was during another one of those trips to Zurich that there was a woman named Stacey Wirth Hinton in the audience. She's a choreographer with a small theater and she invited me to come perform there pretty regularly. I did a solo concert there and the newspapers went slightly nuts. I mean, they just loved it, and on the cover of the paper were these headlines, 'The Amazing Sokolov' and just these fabulous reviews. I had a friend there, Peter Wydler, whose mother's name is Othella Dallas. She sang with Duke Ellington and he wrote a lot of music for her. She danced with the great choreographer Katherine Dunham. Peter's mother was on the road a lot with

Ellington and with Dunham and his father was a very elegant Swiss man who did a lot of managing for her.

"After this concert Peter said to me, 'Well, let's go to the Montreux Jazz Festival, let's just go.' So we went. He had brought along the papers with the banner reviews and we were in the lobby at the Montreux festival and he said, 'Just wait here for a minute.' And he went into the theater to one of the producers and said, 'There's a world-class singer from New York who's here and this is the review she just got for her concert last night.' And they took a look at it. I instantly bought a pack of Marlboros, 'cause I knew something was up. 'What'm I gonna do, guess I'll smoke a cigarette, ha!' And that was not normal for me.

'Peter came out and said that it was Singers Night and they wanted to hear me. So I went in and they were all working to get this set together; it must have been three or four o'clock, and Dave Brubeck was there. The producer said, 'Would you like Mr. Brubeck to accompany you?' I said, 'No, thank you, I'll do it solo.' And that knocked everybody off their chairs, that I'd turned down playing with this great, great musician, Dave Brubeck. I said, 'Thank you very much. I'm honored, but I'll do it by myself.' They were bowled over. And then I started to sing and the minute I—I don't mean to sound egocentric— but the minute I started to sing the whole place hushed. I sang for about five minutes, and I heard from the sound booth, the producer is saying, '*You go on at 8:30!*'

"I had no clothes—I was wearing jeans and a t-shirt. I had just come from Zurich and all my stuff was still there. I had three hours. So we ran in the pouring rain with a credit card and went from store to store and threw some clothes together. I still have the shirt.

"It was just one of those great moments of life, the great gig highlight of my life, just completely thrilling. It was magical, it was beautiful, it was just this great, great moment. Montreux Jazz Festival, 1987."

During these early years in New York after college Lisa studied Tai Chi with Jean Kwok and they would now and then drive to Montreal to see her teacher, Sefu Lee. Lisa left a tape of her trio with Lee on one of these visits and she soon got a phone call from Chris Slaby, who wanted to hire her for a gig at his club L'air de Temps in Montreal.

"I went up and did a gig there; it was a great hit and for the next few years I would go up once a month. That was a place where I was really able to learn my chops in terms of what it was to do three sets a night, five nights in a row. I learned an enormous amount there. That was very formative, my real training ground of just hardcore gigging.

"I would do little gigs here and there in New York: the 55 Bar, Roulette, Joe's Pub, the Knitting Factory. I keep sort of regular things going as a way to keep evolving. I was invited back to Montreux the next year and things kind of went from that. I go to Europe about twice a year—Switzerland and Germany; I was in Tomperei, Finland, this year, and I've been to Iceland, Norway, and France."

Sokolov lists drummer Gerry Hemingway; bassists Cameron Brown, Mark Dresser, and Mike Richmond; and pianists Jim McNeely and John DiMartino as some of those she performs and records with. She has worked in the ensembles of William Parker for years. "I had the honor of recently working with Cecil Taylor," she says, "and we've become great cohorts. I look forward to continuing working with him. I worked for many years with my husband, David Gonzalez, on guitars." Other musical associations include Badal Roy, Irene Schweitzer, Andrew Cyrille, D. D. Jackson, and Butch Morris.

Lisa Sokolov, it should be noted, is also a prolific composer of her performance materials. I asked her to say something about how tunes come to her.

"They come mysteriously and at their bidding and in their own time. My students are used to me, in the middle of class, just stopping and saying, 'Excuse me, I have to go write something down.'

"I write musically a little bit like Cecil Taylor. First, I'll just write lines and then I'll write notes, just as ways to sort of hold on to things, and then I'll go to the piano. But most of them come at their own bidding—phrases, arrangements—and then I try to sit in them long enough that I know I can come up from the ocean and bring some of it with me. My better pieces come pretty whole. I don't get a phrase and I don't sit at the piano and work and try to figure out where it goes. I don't have that.

"I started working for Hospital Audiences Incorporated in long-term chronic psychiatric settings. I would go to these places with people who were at the end of the road, many of whom turned out to be quite remarkable musicians. I have played music in some very

altered settings for many years, in terms of *really* using music to exca-
vate souls of people and bring them back into a relationship. I train
therapists and physicians in the nature and the power of the voice. I
do a lot of performances in nontraditional settings with physicians
and at big conferences and community sings, things like that. My
work as a music therapist is a very big piece of what I do." Lisa Sokolov
is a Master Teacher and head of the voice faculty at the Experimental
Theater Wing at New York University's Tisch School of the Arts.
She has been teaching at NYU since 1981.

Usually, when interviewing singers, I ask how they see themselves
in terms of their art.

"I would say, certainly theater is involved in what I do and there is
musician-vocalist as instrument involved. I always felt like there were
many singers to continue the lineage of traditional jazz singing and
that wasn't my job. I am interested in the expanded range, the possibilities of an expanded timbre and emotional range. I am not so interested in the narrow tonal range often found in singing. And it would
certainly seem, maybe in correlation to this idea that the role of music in this culture is narrow, that the role of music is far wider in, for
example, Indian or African traditions, where the role of art and the
power of music in daily life is much larger. I've always subscribed to
that; I've always felt that music was really a haven for me, a vehicle for
me to touch on things that were not so mundane.

"As far as lineage for my work in terms of jazz singers, I think it
would be Sarah Vaughan, Betty Carter, Jeanne Lee. I'm a great lover
of Ella Fitzgerald. I think you can still hear the influence of Meredith
Monk along with Laura Nyro. Then there was the playing of Roland
Kirk, which was very influential, and Sun Ra, Miles, Coltrane, and
Nusrat Fatah Ali Khan, and this idea of voice being a wider phenomenon and not being narrow, to really explore the cra-a-zy expanse of
what this human expressive instrument has always been—that's what's
really held me.

"In those early ensembles with Bill Dixon and with Jimmy Lyons I
was one of the instruments; I wasn't in the role of the girl singer. And
so, having to come up to that and being able to keep up with twelve
saxophone players and not have microphones, I thought of myself
that way, as an instrumentalist.

"At the same time, I have always had a real interest in the phenomena of vowel and consonant, maybe starting back from that early experience of listening to Mabel Mercer as a child: the power of these things that I call the phonemes, or essentials, of singing and of music. What vowel is, what consonant is, what text is, the basics of interval and time, I'm into these very small things and trying to go deeply into them and to realize, as a singer, that we're dealing with the most human of instruments. We're not just physical bodies; we are energetic beings, we are emotional beings, we are thinking beings, we are great souls. What is it to become an embodied voice? What is the process, the journey of becoming embodied? How does this, through resonance, then affect the listener? To hear Coltrane call out, the calling out of singing, those things have always called me forward. What it is to stand and open your arms and let that really full being, entire alive primal cry to the invisible come forward, I'm interested in that.

"My son, Jake, was thirteen in August. He plays cello and a mean improvised piano. And my daughter, Raina, is nine and she has been singing since she came out of my belly. It's incredible how she sings. She's quite good. My husband, David Gonzalez, is a fine improviser also. We all improvise together. Both of my children speak from their hearts through music. It's our family's second language. It's in the lineage.

"So nowadays, when I have a free moment, I sit down at the piano and play through repertoire. Bach, Chopin, and Beethoven are the regulars. I stop after each piece and I improvise, having been informed by what I have just read. And then back to another beautiful piece of written music and then back to freedom. That's what I consider a good time."

Because I was unfamiliar at the time with Uri Caine's deconstructions of the works of European classical composers, I was riveted by his eight-member group's performance of Bach's *Goldberg Variations* at New York's Jazz Standard several years ago. With keyboard bows faithful to the composer's score, across-the-spectrum jazz improvisation, gospel singing, and wry emanations from a turntablist-sampler, the uninterrupted hour-and-a-half set was truly a mind-blowing tour de force.

A year or so later I caught up with Caine at Umbria Jazz. In the Galleria Nazionale Dell' Umbria, he was performing a solo recital on a late July afternoon for three hundred rapt fans—a rich display of this eclectic musician's art. Underlying the dense, sometimes thunderous passages, the earth-quaking movements, and the races against time that Caine's fingers can execute, I heard stride, blues, boogie woogie, boppish lines, Earl Hinesian trumpet notes, balladry, on-the-edge Cecil Taylor-like clusters and leaps, and echoes of the European classics. He even drummed with his knuckles on the piano lid and added a coda of "Shave and a Haircut" to one selection. Notwithstanding these evident sources of inspiration, it all came out Uri Caine.

The following spring I got together with Uri at the Omega Diner on 72nd Street on New York's Upper West Side and he talked about his life, his career, and some of his musical projects.

"I grew up in Philadelphia," Caine began, "and there was always music in my house. My parents were Americans who were very into the Hebrew renaissance, speaking Hebrew to my brothers and sisters and me, probably because they wanted to move to Israel. Some of the first music I heard was Israeli music that consisted mostly of Sephardic music of the Jews from countries like Yemen, Iraq, and Iran, which was very popular. When I was a young kid we used to sing around the table on Friday nights after we would eat, so that was a very communal music experience, singing Hebrew songs. Then I was also hearing the cantors singing in various synagogues, especially on the high holy days. It was very dramatic.

"I remember my parents sitting down and listening to classical music on the weekends," Uri continued. "It didn't really make much of an impression on me. I remember them also listening much more actively with us as children to these Hebrew records, because they were teaching us Hebrew through this music. That would be the dominant type of music that I was aware of as being my parents' music. I also remember when my mother got into the Beatles and we went to see *Hair*, the musical. She also listened to Aretha Franklin. I started to hear all that when I was in grade school from listening to the radio. But it was reinforced in my house. I was happy that my parents liked that type of music. They were very open-minded. They didn't listen to jazz at all. I think they just didn't know about it.

"I'll tell you an experience that made a big impression on me. I had a cousin who was eight years older, a pianist named Alan Marks. His wing of the family grew up in St. Louis but he came to our house to practice during the summers because my parents had a piano and they were very open to that. He was in his teens and I was just starting piano lessons, at seven or eight, with the neighborhood piano teacher. I was sort of an indifferent student. I was into music in a very passive way and I remember thinking that it seemed very boring.

"Alan came and practiced all one summer, seven or eight hours a day. That was a revelation to me, that somebody could sit and work so hard on something. Plus I was hearing the music and pretty much it was becoming internalized. I would hear how he would go over and over and over again certain passages. I wasn't thinking that I was going to be a musician but when I look back, it made a strong impression on me. When he moved to New York I remember coming up and hanging out with him when I first started coming here. Then he moved to Berlin, saying he didn't want to deal with the commercialization of the American music culture. So he was somebody who was already in the world of music and it was a different world from mine. Alan passed away about three years ago in Berlin. He made some great records. He was an interesting person. When you look back on your life and reflect on certain encounters, you see that they were really influential.

"I also had an uncle, Abraham Wechter, who was much closer to my age. He was my mother's younger brother by twenty years. He gave me my first Miles Davis and John Coltrane records, 'Round Midnight and Crescent, when I was about twelve. He's a guitar builder; he built John McLaughlin's guitars when he was using the scalloped finger board. That's what started me, at least from a recordings point of view, and I became fascinated. Miles Davis and John Coltrane were sort of my entrance into jazz.

"Some friends at school told me about a French pianist in Philadelphia named Bernard Peiffer who was a virtuoso. He had moved to the United States in the '50s. I started studying with him when I was twelve or thirteen and that was a real turning point for me because he was the sort of teacher who showed that music encompassed a whole broad range of things, everything from studying the history of it to trying to build up a technique on the piano through studying harmony and composition. I would have lessons with him that would go on for hours. Sometimes I would bring in pieces that I had written and I would see him rework them. It totally expanded my mind. Plus we would all go to hear him every week. He played at a place in Philadelphia called the Borgia Tea Room. A lot of musicians went there.

"When I got a little bit older I started to try to hang out. I would go to the clubs in Philadelphia and that's when I started to see other musicians who were living there and playing local gigs—people like Philly Joe Jones, Johnny Coles, Hank Mobley, Bobby Durham. You could see Sun Ra play, Pat Martino. There was a very diverse thing going on in clubs, and as younger musicians we could go to these places and, if we were lucky, they would let us sit in and play a tune. I decided to try to focus 'cause I wanted to get into that; it seemed like the most interesting thing for me to do.

"I met a group of friends in junior high school and we started playing as a group. I don't know how it really sounded. We were playing in functions in the school—the school play, things like that. I remember when my friends told me, 'You can make money playing music!' It astounded me. There was one club in Philadelphia in particular then called Togetherness House—sort of this hippie folk club—and even as young guys we were playing there. Once you are on that path and you see that it gives you the opportunity to delve into a lot of different things, it gives you that spark to keep on going.

"As a young pianist I was very conscious of trying to blend in, to play in a group situation. I saw how important that was. People like Philly Joe would always talk about that, how when you're in a rhythm section you don't have to overplay, just sort of, like, do things in a minimalistic way. You're sort of hearing with a third ear what's going on and responding to that rather than cluttering things up. For instance, how to play behind singers, or how different horn players had different styles that you in a way have to adapt to for this person.

"I spent a lot of time in a record store called Third Street Jazz where, especially on the weekends, people would go to hang out. They would save records for us because they knew that we were saving all the money we were making at these little jobs to buy more records. So the fanaticism grew. And it seemed to be in a certain way supported by the people around us, which is a nice feeling. The musicians were very supportive in Philadelphia if they saw that you were serious. We were about fourteen and our parents thought, 'At least they're not hanging out on the street, getting in trouble; we know where they are, and they're working on their stuff.' I never had the problem of going through a family rebellion to be a musician. It was encouraged—even though I don't think my parents really understood what it was about musically.

"I had another really important teacher whom I met when I was around fifteen. His name was George Rochberg, a composer. I started studying with him because Bernard recommended him. He started me on a whole different pathway which was more this exercise of coming in every week and writing pieces based on styles of classical music as a way to learn form and harmony. I did that with him for about three years, and through him I learned a lot of musical skills such as score reading, rudiments of orchestration, and ideas of form.

"I was very into what I thought was avant-garde music at that time, like Boulez and Stockhausen and late Stravinsky. But the world where that music was played was a lot different from the world where I was growing up in Philadelphia. There was a certain disconnect even though the music spoke to me. Maybe that type of listening also had an effect on me.

"I bought many, many, many records. Through Miles and Coltrane I started to study the piano players that they had. I was really into people like Herbie Hancock and McCoy Tyner, early Chick Corea, Keith Jarrett, those styles. But then I also moved backward. And this was really from Bernard's influence, because he would say, 'Better check out Art Tatum. You have to check out Fats Waller; these guys are incredible.' And of course, as soon as I heard them, it was like, 'Wow!' I really started to enjoy listening to them and was always sort of shocked by how out it was, how original. And I was very influenced by them because I was noticing that a lot of the more modern pianists weren't playing with the same type of left-hand action.

"I love Jelly Roll Morton and I remember listening to Otis Spann with my uncle and he said, 'Man, you gotta check out the older styles.' The older guys that he was hanging out with were listening to things like Cream and Jimi Hendrix, which I liked too, and they would say, 'Listen to the people that these guys are coming out of,' and that made a lot of sense to me. Even at that young age I realized that there is this thing that's called tradition, or development, or it's a progression. It doesn't mean that it gets better. It means that things move from one person to another and from one era to another and that in this whole thing of really studying records and trying to create a personal chronology in your mind—how did that get to this?—you start to see how music is connected in that way, which is really interesting. When I would read about conflicts, that these guys couldn't get along with those guys, and this music as opposed to that music, I understood that people's egos get caught up in what they do and they see other challenges as challenges to them. And that's not really the way it is. It's much more that music is there for that expression and aggression and contradiction and development, and people themselves can go through all those different dialogues with the tradition.

"I went to college at the University of Pennsylvania, in Philadelphia. I studied music there. The composition teachers I had were really good: George Rochberg and George Crumb. I didn't have a minor but the other courses I took were liberal arts courses, and I took a great course in Shakespeare, which I really loved; some American history courses; French—and we had to take courses in how to read German and Italian.

"It was a very academic music department. They didn't sanction any of the playing I was doing; they didn't even know what it was about. Unlike a lot of musicians who go to music school to become jazz musicians, I didn't have that experience; that was totally what I wanted to do on my own, my own thing. I thought, I don't want to enter that world immediately. There was this insane test that they gave where we had to identify any piece from 1500 to the 1900s. They would let you listen to it for about twenty seconds and you would have to write an essay about it. Then they would give you a piece of score and say, 'Who wrote that piece?' To study for that test I had to listen to stacks of records every day, and after three months of that, I really started to enjoy it. On one level it's like a trivia test, but on another level it was one of these things where your head is just bombarded with music and what seemed like a torturous project actually turned into something I really enjoyed. So I had some good experiences in college and I met a lot of interesting musicians. In a way, it inspired me to go out there and try to be a player, and it convinced me that you can be a composer and do all these other things without having to be a teacher in a university—at least I could see it's possible.

"I started playing with this saxophone player in Philadelphia named Bootsie Barnes and that's when I really started working with a lot of these older musicians, because he would have them on his gigs—people like Philly Joe and Mickey Roker. I started working with Bootsie pretty steadily when I was about eighteen. At that point I had moved out of my parents' house and was going to college in Philadelphia and was playing almost every night, playing in many different parts of Philadelphia, sometimes outside of Philadelphia. I saw that my playing started to get to another level because I was playing so much. During that period I started to practice a lot, too. I had been practicing in high school, but then being able to live by myself I could get more intense with what I wanted to work on. That was sort of between the periods when I was about eighteen and when I graduated from college. I was basically living in Philadelphia in that period, playing a lot; also at that point there were gigs in Philadelphia where people from New York started to come down to play—Joe Henderson or Freddie Hubbard. Sometimes I would be in a local rhythm section, and that also started to broaden my horizons

"I had been coming up to New York pretty steadily, trying to move to New York, but it took me a while to do that. After college I thought, 'I'll try to move to Israel and see what that's like.' I knew Hebrew and I had been to Israel. Even though the political situation there is very complicated, it's an amazing country. I found that knowing Hebrew in that environment really gave me a very strong feeling. But I ended up thinking, 'If I'm gonna move, I really should try to move to New York instead of here. I love Israel but I need to find what I'm trying to do as a musician.' I stayed three or four months. I was also sort of traveling around. I went and played in the Caribbean. I was trying to figure out what to do. Maybe I was procrastinating about moving to New York.

"I moved to New York in 1985 and got an apartment. I had been coming up to New York and sleeping on people's floors. I had been used to playing in Philadelphia every night and there were different types of music there. New York was a different experience because, even though I knew a lot of musicians, as many musicians will tell you when they first move here, it's very hard to make money. I went through a bit of scuffling and played in many different types of situations where I would not have been playing in Philadelphia. But gradually I started to fall into different groups and get gigs and by the early '90s I was working with Don Byron, who had a number of different projects and I was involved in many of them. Much of it was touring in Europe. I was working with Sam Rivers and Buddy DeFranco. I was playing with a lot of different people. I wanted to taste as many of these different scenes as I could, pick-up gigs, and I was also playing keyboards. I played in a group with Kevin Bruce Harris that was much more like an M-base style of music"—that is, a jazz-funk style that came into being in New York in the mid-1980s and is characterized by austere harmony, rhythmic dislocation, and dissonance. "I played with singers—Annie Ross and Jean Carne. I used to play at a place called Augie's Pub and I met a lot of musicians there, even though we were playing for no money, basically. But it was just the experience of again throwing yourself into it. I was a little surprised at how hard it was at times, different groups being totally unaware of other groups in the city. I understand that more now because there are so many musicians in New York; at times it can seem like a very big place, at other times a very small place. I started to see that many of the groups I was playing with were playing more in places like the Knitting Factory than at the Village Vanguard. There were all these different scenes and I would try to do what I could to keep in contact with all the things that were happening here. Once I started working more, things changed subtly, because then you're on the road, you're not even in New York much of the time. But you see that there's a wide world out there for music and that there are people who are appreciating it and that also becomes another opportunity.

"I've been doing a lot more gigs with my own projects and not as much as a sideman, although I still enjoy being a sideman and have been playing special projects with Don Byron's or Dave Douglas's groups."

Caine's records under his own name over the past decade include jazz deconstructions of Bach's *Goldberg Variations*, Beethoven's *Diabelli Variations*, and some of Mahler's works, the latter released as *Urlicht: Primal Light*; *Blue Wail*, which reflects the influence of Herbie Hancock, McCoy Tyner, Keith Jarrett, Cecil Taylor, and other jazz pianists. He also released *The Sidewalks of New York: Tin Pan Alley*, an exploration of the early music hall repertory that influenced Fats Waller. All of these were recorded for the German-based Winter & Winter label. Caine performs these projects in concert here and abroad, his musical travels taking him to jazz, classical, and New Music festivals and concerts in Europe, South America, and Asia and all over this continent, keeping him on the road for an aggregate six months a year.

"It's definitely a good opportunity for us to go to all those places because in many of them, even though it would seem they wouldn't know about your music, they do know it and follow it; they know about all the musicians, and the audiences are very enthusiastic. There's a certain group of fanatics in many parts of the world and those are the people that come out and see us. You can have a good contact with the audience that way.

"What I was trying to do," Uri pointed out about the Mahler project, "was relate certain aspects of his music—for example, his inclusiveness of many different styles, from folk music to high art music—to different dance forms and sort of play it through the refracted lens of the type of music that we were playing, and do it in different styles coming out of improvised music and jazz. Also, it gave us something different as a form to play on rather than just standards, and added a sort of autobiographical component, a commentary about Mahler's life that you're doing through music. So it's music about music. It's an idea of transforming something that for me sounds very much like klezmer music and making that reference explicit. For instance, taking the heartbreak of one of his songs where he is talking about children dying and then reading in his biography that his children in fact died after he wrote the song. This is very haunting. Then to play that with the heartbreak of a bossa nova, just trying to make these parallels that then are expanded upon musically, not through talking theory but through real music making. And I saw, especially when we took that project out on the road, that it was very affecting, that it had a strong resonance with the people who knew about Mahler.

"Something like the *Goldberg Variations*—the idea of theme and variations—is very close to the jazz idea of taking a standard and improvising on it, in the sense that the composer is taking a theme and then using the changes, the harmony of the theme, as the underpinning for a new piece. And that's what a lot of improvisation does when it's based on those fixed harmonic patterns. It's in the same sense that Bach, in an almost encyclopedic way, put all these different types of music in these thirty variations called the *Goldberg Variations* that he wrote at the end of his life—from dance forms to very intense counterpoint to keyboard writing that was almost in other people's styles. I thought I could create a piece based on that same thing that would tie all those things together; the musicians can use the changes to play a lot of different types of variations—dance forms like mambo and tango or different jazz styles, everything from ragtime to a much freer type of jazz—and intersperse that with playing Bach and improvising over the Bach. And so, in a way, it sort of ties in all those ideas. Some people didn't like it at all. They didn't get it or they thought that somehow it was disrespectful of Bach. But to me, I really wasn't looking at it that way. There were certain aspects, maybe, that were experimental or didn't work out and that's always part of music making for me so that's fine. But the idea is to somehow use the improvisational aspect that we're all developing and sort of set it loose on these other forms.

"I still enjoy playing more conventional, straight ahead jazz—but in my mind not so conventional—in a trio with acoustic bass and acoustic drums. That's something I've been doing since I was a teenager, so I want to keep on developing that.

"I just see all these things as feeding off each other. It's a way to explore something and study it from a lot of different angles and then let your imagination loose and use your musical instincts. It doesn't have to be heavy-handed in the way it's delivered. Because it's about music first, which is different, it's mysterious, and you have to dance with that aspect of it.

"When you realize that a lot of the music we're doing is group-oriented music, you realize that there's a certain group dynamic that is important in music and that touches on many different aspects of music making. When you play with different people and they all are doing different things that pull you in different directions, this can be good or maybe sometimes not so good, but you have to deal with that. I want to give the players a chance; I don't want it to be so scripted. I prefer a looser, open style because I see how it keeps people on their toes when they're playing and also allows things to develop. You sort of go with the flow and see where things are going. It's important to try things that people might seem skeptical about and evaluate how it goes. It's not that you're your own worst critic but you sort of keep a realistic view of what's going on and try to improve it, more by letting the music evolve on its own.

"I used to compose at the piano, but I got a laptop two or three years ago and I use that a lot, especially when I'm on the road. You can hear what's happening and it saves a lot of labor of copying out parts, which was a problem for me. I would constantly be rearranging. I use Sibelius, which is a software program for creating scores and plays back the music. It makes parts and keeps all your music in the computer, so when you're doing different projects and the saxophone player says, 'I lost my part for this piece,' *bingo*, there it is! It's a life saver.

"There are many ways to generate ideas. You get ideas from improvising and then listening back. You can do that with a computer. You can play into it and then see what comes back and adjust it. I like writing away from the piano because when I was writing at the piano, it was based on where my fingers were moving, and I had to get away from that. This is especially important if you're writing for groups or an orchestra. On the other hand, many composers check their work on the piano, and I do that too. I'll take the music and just try very slowly to hear what's happening, because there's always that process of endless revision, listening to it one day, and then going, 'Hmm, it needs more of this' or 'It's too long here' or 'I don't need this anymore.' And that's one of the fun aspects of it. I mean, you do have to write the final bars at some point, and maybe that comes for some people because there's a deadline. At other times people have the luxury, especially if they have a group, of keeping on writing, changing it. It comes down to very little things, and that's when you're getting into that aspect of music which is really interesting."

In that final sentence Uri Caine alludes to the balance, and tension, that the jazz composer/bandleader strives for between the working out of the details in his or her notated form and the musicians' individual and collective interpretation of that form. This, for Caine, constitutes one aspect of the jazz art that provides him great satisfaction.

Having witnessed the result of the joint effort that evening at the Jazz Standard when Uri's combo improvised in such cooking fashion on his brilliant arrangement of Bach's *Goldberg Variations*, I can attest to the great enjoyment provided the listener as well.

I first saw singer Pam Bricker perform on a 1983 Thursday evening at the Shoreham Hotel in Washington, D.C. Drummer Eddie Phyfe had put together a quartet for a series of concerts in the hotel's Marquee Ballroom, where the big bands appeared during the Swing Era. In a review that I wrote for the *Washington Post* I observed that the foursome—vibraphonist Lennie Cujé, guitarist Paul Wingo, bassist Steve Novosel, and Phyfe—had "the combustibility of dry timber" and added, "An unexpected bonus was a brief sit-in by singer Pam Bricker, who scatted 'Doodlin'' all over the place in a voice of remarkable range, excellent control, and impressive rhythmic surety." Bricker at the time was twenty-eight and a year or so into her Washington, D.C., jazz years.

During the two decades that followed, I saw Pam in a number of different formats and contexts at many of D.C.'s jazz venues. In early 2003 I spent a couple of hours audio- and videotaping her life story at my home in Silver Spring, Maryland.

"Piano lessons at age four," Pam began. "My father was a research psychologist and he moonlighted as a classical musician, a trombonist. He was a classical musician in pit orchestras for local productions of musical theater. He would get little ensembles together with us. I played clarinet, my brother Tom played trumpet, and my sister Lisa Day played flute.

"My mother, sadly, was stricken with manic depression, bipolar disorder, when I was maybe six years old. She left the family about that time, never really to return. She married another trombonist, Henry Southall, who played with the Woody Herman band in the '60s. His recording of 'Watermelon Man' is the Woody Herman original of the tune.

"I had classical piano training. I remember being maybe six years old and sort of camping out in the back yard in New Jersey and my father just set me up with a blanket and a scratchy transistor radio. For many years I remembered the melody of a jazz tune I heard on it"—she scats and snaps her fingers rhythmically—"and I kept that melody in my head. That was my first *jazz* that I ever heard.I finally discovered in my thirties that it was 'Gravy Waltz' by Steve Allen, and there are nice lyrics.

"I grew up in New Jersey and my parents would take me into New York to the ballet. *The Firebird, Swan Lake*. I loved those things. And they took me to see Peter, Paul and Mary as a child and I loved them.

I saw *Oliver* on Broadway and Jimi Hendrix at the Filmore and the Chambers Brothers at a community concert.

"I switched to clarinet when I was nine. I was already dropping out of piano. I never really had the passion for it and wasn't a particularly good piano student. At school they were starting the instrumental music program at that age and I tried a few different instruments. They said, 'Well, you have a good chin for playing clarinet.' I sort of realized later that I was duped 'cause they needed a lot of clarinets. But I dutifully went with it and quite enjoyed it. I always studied privately. By the end of high school I was taking the Erie/Lackawanna train, then getting on the subway and going up to 125th Street to study with a classical clarinet hippie dude with an American flag on his cap.

"I was a serious clarinet student through the end of high school and loved classical music—sort of the classical hits. Camille Saint-Saëns's *Organ Symphony* I remember being a big one. Loved Broadway musicals. *Man of La Mancha* was a big one for me. This is what was on the stereo at home. I listened to classical music at night for a while on my bedside radio, New York stations, and I remember a classical music program that had 'Eine Kleine Nachtmusik' as the theme. Loved that ever since.

"Meanwhile, the Beatles came to town in '64, I'm in fourth grade, and that galvanized me. The Beatles were a *huge*, *gigantic* influence on me. Grade school up through high school, yeah, for me was all about the Beatles, watching the Beatles go from 1964 to '69 and the world of music that they traversed and created. My brother and sister and I, we all gathered around the phonograph and listened to the Beatles together, just listened so intently, and because our mother had left the family and eventually divorced my father around that time, it was something that we clung to.

"They created pop music, the pop music that's still in place today, and, yeah, I was right there watching it and wanting to *be* it. That's what I felt I wanted to do as a musician, something *that* creative. The vocal harmony, the arrangements, and the way they sang and the way they blended. My brother and sister and I would sing the harmonies together. That was a lot of ear training for me. I was just learning their simple, but magical, songs.

"I was quite a loner as a child; I didn't have friends 'til I was a junior and senior in high school." Of her teachers, Pam names "first and foremost Joe Loretti, Summit, New Jersey, who was the band director in junior high and he switched to high school the same year that I did. So he just carried me right along with him and really encouraged me to join the stage band. That was my first jazz singing. I sang 'A Lot of Livin' to Do' and Cole Porter's 'True Love.' First time I ever got up and sang.

"In the school band I rose to second-chair clarinet, maybe held first chair at some point. The big coup was a youth orchestra when I was fifteen. It was run by the Finkels. I see David Finkel now coming to town, the cellist. His parents ran this young artists' chamber orchestra and I was invited to audition. That was a very strong experience for me. We did Ravel's *Le Tombeau de Couperin*, which is very jazzy in a way. It was just such a deep thing for me to play that kind of music. Then, when I was sixteen, at a music camp run by the Finkels up in Massachusetts, I got to play some chamber music, Hindemith's woodwind quintets. I loved playing clarinet in a woodwind quintet, which is French horn, oboe, flute, clarinet, bassoon. Whew!" She, laughs, remembering the experience.

"On my father's record player in the '60s was Don Ellis, *Electric Bath*, with a lot of odd meters, tunes in seventeen and five. I was able to count odd meters and found that kind of thrilling. I remember my father being envious of my ability to play in odd meters. My father gave me some pointers, just sort of as a beginner clarinetist, about breathing. He said, 'Squeeze the air out from the bottom like a tube of toothpaste,' also giving me a little domestic advice at the same time. And I probably have squeezed the toothpaste from the bottom ever since I had that breathing tip from him."

Pam attended Hampshire College, a free-form school in Amherst, Massachusetts, arriving there in 1973.

"At Hampshire there were two faculty members in the music department, the classical guy and Jim McElwaine, clarinetist. He was a gigantic influence on me. I fell in love with him. Several of my first songs were about him. He showed me the Leonard Bernstein *Sonata for Clarinet and Piano* and gave me Jobim's 'Wave' and Duke Ellington's 'Do Nothin' Till You Hear from Me' to sing. We worked on classical music but he also really started me listening to jazz—first time I ever heard 'You Can Leave Your Hat On' by Randy Newman. The sort of perverse sexuality of that tune, for me as an eighteen-year-old, that was the cat's meow."

Researching a paper on utopias her second semester, Bricker joined the Twin Oaks commune, half way between Charlottesville and Richmond, Virginia.

"The commune had about about a hundred members, most in their twenties and thirties, mostly white, having in common a great desire for intellectual freedom and individuality, not a natural situation for togetherness because everyone was so independent-minded and all trying to live together as well.

"I played my clarinet a little bit, would get together with other instrumentalists and read through some duets, did some free improv. I remember doing some modern dance free improv with a couple other women 'cause I came up in modern dance from age nine. I'd taught myself guitar when I was sixteen and I played it there. I had already started writing tunes and wrote a couple more in the two-and-a-half years that I was at Twin Oaks. That was a big period for me, listening to Loudon Wainwright III and old timey music like the New Lost City Ramblers. I learned to play spoons at that time and we'd go into Charlottesville and give concerts with a fiddle player. I was playing fiddle tunes on soprano recorder. My boyfriend at Twin Oaks was a banjo player. From age sixteen on, that's when I had become a folk singer. My repertoire was Joni Mitchell, Bob Dylan, and my own tunes. During the time that I was there is when I just finally decided I didn't have a place to put clarinet anymore. I did my first professional job singing in 1975 in Richmond at Poor Richard's, on Cary Street next to the Salad Bar. I was playing acoustic guitar.

"The cottage industry of Twin Oaks was rope hammocks. They had headphones dangling from the ceiling at the stations of the different processes of making a hammock and one day after I had been there a couple of years and was weaving, taking the shuttle and going like this"—she moves her hands back and forth in simulation of the process—"and weaving the rope hammock, somebody said, 'Here, check out John McLaughlin!' and I put on the headphones and that was just another pivotal experience. I said, 'Okay! Right now, I'm leaving the farm! I gotta go and do music full time, that's it, period, that's what I have to do!'

"I just kind of abruptly packed my bags, in the rain of course, and I went up to Amherst, Massachusetts, where I found a group house to live in and started hanging around the campus and auditing classes for free. I was very much in love with the music professor, but he had already settled down with another student and so was not available as a boyfriend. But we actually worked together a couple of times, and maybe the first job that we did was at the University of Massachusetts, just duo with his Fender Rhodes piano and I played guitar and sang. We did one of the duets from *Porgy and Bess*, and the person who hired us is now a gigantic bigwig in the jazz reissue scene, Steve Berkowitz, with Columbia Legacy. He was staying in the Four Seasons hotel in Georgetown when I was singing there, with Louis Scherr on piano, about two years ago, and said, 'I gave you your first job twenty-five years ago,' and we had a good old time reminiscing.

"So I just landed back in Amherst and that's when I started music full time. I'm listening to fusion, jazz/rock fusion, which was such a new thing then, and it was so soulful and intellectual at the same time: Emerson, Lake and Palmer and the Mahavishnu Orchestra; Weather Report was later.

"I took my guitar and started singing in coffee houses as a solo. My posters said, 'Folk Rock Blues Jazz' and I drew a picture of myself in a little 1940s-looking dress holding my guitar." She chuckles. "Soon after that I was invited by a rock guitarist to join his band and that was my first rock band. We met at a club in Northhampton, Massachusetts, called the Lazy River. In 1975 that club was booking rock and fusionist kinds of groups. I saw Oregon there and I saw Sheila Jordan there. And that was the first club, the main club, where I played with my first rock band, Jim Kaminsky, otherwise known as Jim K.

"Soon after that I stole half his band and made my own band, which I called the Bricker Band and we had a fabulous reign of a little over two years, a meteoric rise to local notoriety. We played all the beer joints in Western Massachusetts and a lot of colleges in Massachusetts. The band was electric keyboards, the guy very much into Joe Zawinul and Chick Corea; the guitarist was more of a James Taylor country rock; there was a mad dog drummer, as always; and the bass player was very much a Paul McCartney fan. I brought my own tunes, played acoustic guitar on a couple of them, but mostly just sang. So it was rock. We did Little Feat's 'Two Trains Runnin',' 'Five Hundred Miles High' from Chick Corea, and Horace Silver's 'Doodlin',' and some friends of mine were writing, so I did some of their originals."

The band broke up in 1978 due to "dissatisfactions and grumbling and artistic differences." Pam felt she was "ready to make the big time" and "wanted musicians with more chops." She had begun to listen to jazz seriously "and wanted better players to take with me." For a while she worked with her guitar in a trio format with a bassist and percussionist, her notoriety from her rock days getting her work as far away as Boston.

"And, some time in there, I hooked up with a producer in New York who said, 'Okay, I can get you a record deal.' Whoever he knew in the biz, he would take me, just myself with my guitar, into the office of, say, the vice president of whatever big label—but never got me a record deal, never got much of a response. He tried to get me a gig writing a jingle. It was just such a farce.

"We went to Motown in L.A. to record an original song by a friend of mine for a movie with Susan Sarandon and David Steinberg, *Something Short of Paradise*. I sang this song, 'Spring Fever' by Steve Stone, over the closing credits. While we were out there he took me over to the L.A. Motown office and I did my schtick and they had no interest. But we did ride the elevator down with Marvin Gaye." She laughs. "So that was a big moment.

"But that year that I was with the producer was a big heartache for me, because I had already pretty much stopped writing songs and I felt this tremendous pressure to write, 'cause at one of the labels they said, 'Well, we got plenty of singers, we need material, we need songs.' So I said, 'Okay, I'll write,' and then they said, 'We like your songs but we need a *hit* for the album, show us the *hit* song that's gonna be on your album.' One of the record label people said, 'You're twenty-four and that's a little bit old to be starting a career in recording.' And that was even worse pressure.

"So I'm thinking, 'Ah, great!' And by the end of it, no record deal. And that kind of sent me down the path to pretty much my good old nervous breakdown at age twenty-five. Between 1979 and '80 I went insane; I tried to kill myself. I had moved to Boston, living with my boyfriend, the bass player from my trio. Whole life fell apart. I tried to stop performing to get myself to write. And it just backfired completely. I didn't write, I was broke, and kind of reached a state of desperation.

"That was an interesting time in my career because I really didn't have much interest in music during the period of my insanity. I hated music and *all* art. In fact, to me it seemed just nonsensical. Nothing touched me, nothing made any sense, it all seemed full of holes. I just couldn't even listen to music for a while. When I started to come back I was into whatever was the pop music on the radio and thinking, 'Well, okay, I gotta get back in music, and get back in the clubs and start earning a living again. It was a survival thing.

"So I started playing my guitar again. Just before I left Boston, I had my first job as a jazz singer, at the Copley Plaza Hotel, with some bass player student of Miroslav Vitous. Teddy Wilson was in the big room at the Copley Hotel at that time and I was out in the lounge. I learned a night's worth of standards. I already had an interest in singing standards, partly because I had writer's block and didn't have my own repertoire to offer and thought that some of the pop music magic would rub off on me if I started learning Gershwin and Cole Porter and Harold Arlen.

"I remember the first-chair clarinet from high school that I'd had a crush on, he showed up at the Copley one night. To just walk into my gig, it really freaked me out, 'cause it was this blast from the past. I wasn't taking LSD but I think maybe he was tripping. He was talking all kinds of crazy stuff like, 'I'm the fifth Beatle!' We sang Beatles songs. Oh, wow! It was just insane! I mean, I had some wild times as I was losing my mind. I was flippin' out.

"I ended up going back to the commune, to lick my wounds and try to recover. I stayed at Twin Oaks for another year-and-a-half, just long enough to sort of come back to life and get myself back together. I got in a relationship with my future husband, Gareth Branwyn, there, and then, in 1981, we moved to Arlington, Virginia, at the invitation of the real Patch Adams, a very close friend and the doctor in Northern Virginia whom Robin Williams made a movie about." (After twenty-two years of marriage, Bricker and Branwyn separated in 2003.)

"In that first year or so in Washington I played at Food for Thought, a health food restaurant on Connecticut Avenue. Solo guitar, pass the hat. That's where I met Mary Chapin Carpenter, who had just recently been doing the same thing, playing there. We got together a few times to sort of jam and pick and grin and then she became the world's most famous folk and country crossover artist. David Jernigan, the great bass player, was at Food for Thought one evening and I was still doing, from my Amherst days, 'One Note Samba' on guitar and singing it and 'Do Nothin' Till You Hear from Me.' Those were the only jazzish things that I was doing and all the rest of my repertoire was my folk/rock/pop. I got to David's table and he says, 'Yeah, sounds great, Hon, but when are you going to start playing jazz and drop all the boring folk music?'" She laughs. "And that's the story that I've told three million times since then, much to his chagrin.

"Where else did I play? Whitey's, in Arlington. I was living just three blocks from there. It was a rock dive"—she growls the word "dive"—"and I played solo there quite a bit. I became their darling for a little while. I would play, like, every Thursday night, doing my eclectic solo acoustic guitar act. Starting from scratch, you know. I'd been famous in Massachusetts and now I was just back to starting over again, which I had already done, so I just did the same thing, went to clubs, met musicians.

"At the same time that I was making my first forays out and trying to become a musician again, I had continued my interest in jazz. I went to the jam sessions at the One Step Down, Lawrence Wheatley presiding, and got right up and sat in, probably not the first time I went, but eventually, after persevering. You know about the cold shoulder from the anti-vocalist jazz thing. But they let me up there and they liked what they heard. Who knows what I was doing? I just went to the open mikes. I remember doing the folk scene and then suddenly I was sitting in at the One Step Down and Charlie's Georgetown. And Charlie's Georgetown was where I met Rick Harris, and very soon after that he said, 'I've got some arrangements; do you want to get together and do some vocal jazz harmony in my basement on Church Street?'

"And that was how Mad Romance got started. The original four voices were Rick, Pam, Steve Hilmy, and Jamie Broumas. We rehearsed for a year before our first performance. Our debut was at Blues Alley of 1983. We did the Kennedy Center, Constitution Hall,

Wolf Trap, and other Washington venues and, just before we broke up, Monterey Jazz Festival. Our last performance was at the Blue Note in New York City in '87."

Pam and Rick also did the 1993 North Sea Jazz Festival as a singing duo, enjoyed a four-year engagement at D.C.'s Henley Park Hotel with a rhythm section of pianist Louis Scherr, bassist Tommy Cecil, and drummer Tony Martucci, and released two CDs. Pam stayed on at the Henley for another year in duo with pianist Dave Kane. Pam has been supported in performances by the late Emily Remler and such Washington-area jazz musicians as saxophonist Buck Hill, pianist Larry Eanet, and the late Charlie Byrd. She has been at the U-topia on U Street for ten years.

The several-hour conversation having taken Pam into the 1990s, I asked her to talk about how she thinks of her role as a singer, the vocalists and instrumentalists who have influenced and inspired her, and her current performance schedule.

"For many years I was a very straight-laced mainstream jazz singer. I think I even did an interview and talked about how I didn't like to mix pop style with my pure jazz sound." She chuckles. "And I took an interest in cabaret. Oh, a big singer revelation at that time, from Rick, was Irene Kral, and I just flipped for her, a bunch of us did at that time. But as the '90s wore on, I felt an urge to break out of such a straight-laced jazz frame of mind and repertoire. I said, 'Jazz, like crime, doesn't pay; you have to mix it up and modernize it.'

"That's when I got the job at U-topia with pianist Wayne Wilentz and drummer Jim West. Wayne's mainstream jazz playing is informed by the whole jazz history, but he also comes from the blues and he has an encyclopedic knowledge of pop music. Our taste in *both* jazz *and* pop music is very similar. It's as if we were separated at birth.

"I wanted to get out of jazz jail; I was ready to break out. In fact, I returned to my pop and rock roots. I got a job to sing an evening's worth of dance/rock music. Patch's old group of hippies out in West Virginia gave an annual party which they called Rock Stock and they asked me to sing and be the band one year, so I recruited some of my people that swing both ways. We went out to West Virginia and rocked the party and that just gave me such a jolt of inspiration. I wanted to *rock out* again." She laughs. "All my pop music influences, all my non-jazz background, I *missed* it.

"All this time, since 1978, I did have a once-a-year job in Nantucket, Massachusetts, at a restaurant called the Brotherhood of Thieves, where I played my guitar; for many, many years that was the only time I ever played my guitar, two weeks on Nantucket. Gave me terrible problems with calluses. A year would go by and then I pick up the guitar and my fingers are bleeding. When I started at U-topia, that gave me a chance to blend in some other styles of music besides jazz. To this day it's billed as a jazz night, but I *never* do exclusively jazz, I *always* throw in Stevie Wonder and Aretha Franklin and the Beatles.

"I also started playing guitar duo with Chuck Underwood, maybe two summers ago, and we do a lot of jazz in our duo, and I also play a lot of percussion. Some of my originals have a very jazzy feel on acoustic guitar, some Steely Dan that nicely spans jazz and rock; and then we do our version of the Rolling Stones' song 'Wild Horses,' which to me has a very Norah Jones kind of a thing, a little jazz flavor. And of course I've been checking out Cassandra Wilson over the years. What she's done as far as bring contemporary pop music into a jazz context has been great for me, an encouragement to be eclectic. And now it's all the rage; everyone's doing it." She chuckles.

"We do Luther Vandross, a lot of Brazilian music, some bebop heads, like 'Billy's Bounce' and 'I Mean You.' I recently learned 'Save Your Love for Me' from the Nancy Wilson and Cannonball Adderley album. Then, from the pop world, Chaka Khan's 'Through the Fire' and 'Sexual Healing' by Marvin Gaye. We do a blues from Dave Frishberg, 'Can't Take You Nowhere,' and we make the audience sing along, like an echo, a shout call response. We'll do 'Anthropology' and I just scat the melody, and I'll even trade fours with my drums. It's pretty wild. We do U2, Elvis Costello, the Pretenders, Jimi Hendrix. When I play my guitar it tends to be more kind of alternarock. 'Cause all during the '80s I loved the alternative rock scene and collected a bunch of those singer-song-writers that had kind of a punky influence. I have a lot of those in my repertoire.

"And that's sort of my post-jazz period. The years from when I met Rick, who was a huge influence on me, through Mad Romance and then the Pam and Rick Duo, that was a lot of years. And then the Henley Park with Tommy Cecil on bass, Tony Martucci on drums, and Louis Scherr on piano. When I wasn't at the Henley Park or with

Mad Romance I did solo work or worked with other bands. I got to play with just the greatest Washington mainstream jazz players during those years. After the Henley Park I worked with George Colligan. We did a little tour of Chile.

"I spent several years as a rock and roller in bar bands in Massachusetts and people were starting to put pressure on me," says Pam in response to my query as to influences. "'You gotta listen to jazz, you have to check it out.' I think it was probably a potential suitor who put Carmen McRae on and at that time I just couldn't relate to her; the style was so radically different from the pop and rock that I was listening to. I just didn't like it and dismissed it. It was another couple of years before I rediscovered her. Lambert, Hendricks and Ross was an entrée for me into the world of jazz, and also the Pointer Sisters, 'cause they were doing Lambert, Hendricks and Ross–style recordings at that time in the '70s. But then, finally, I broke down and listened to Ella Fitzgerald. I had some big double-album compilation anthology and, of my own accord, I listened to her a lot.

"But I have never listened to Billie Holiday. I'm sorry; I know it's blasphemy. I'm also not that into Mozart—go figure. My thing about Billie Holiday has to do with how I eventually came to feel about Joni Mitchell. It seemed to me, as a young person, that they both kind of wallowed in their pain. I wanted more defiance in the face of misery. I certainly acknowledge that Billie practically invented the kind of jazz singing I do, and I'll hear her recordings here and there and be knocked out by them. I just never had a Billie Holiday phase, not yet. But I did go right to Sarah Vaughan. Sarah Vaughan and Carmen McRae, and Carmen became my queen over Ella and Sarah. Her interpretation: she never forgets what the lyrics are saying. Carmen can wring ten shades of meaning from a single word that you never thought to notice before. I got to see her perform in Washington two or three times. And I got to see Sarah Vaughan also.

"Joni Mitchell *was* a huge inspiration to me. I always say that's why I am a singer today. Her first album I listened to right when it came out. I heard it on the radio, and hearing her made me want to switch from being an instrumentalist to singing. Bette Midler was someone that I listened to. A lot of times her versions of standards were the first time I heard them. 'Skylark' and 'In the Mood.' From the world of rock I liked Gracie Slick. And rock was very important to me after the Beatles. I never stopped listening to rock 'n' roll and I like progressive kinds of art rock." She names as favorites Jefferson Airplane; Ten Wheel Drive; Blood, Sweat and Tears; Cream; Eric Clapton; and Blind Faith. "I had a definite Dylan phase. I loved The Band and Crosby Stills and Nash. I learned finger picking from a Joan Baez record. I wasn't a big Joan Baez fan but my finger-picking style that I have to this day very much comes from one of her tunes, 'Barbrie Allen.' I also started collecting some obscure folk music, like Jean Richie, the Appalachian singer and dulcimer player. My father made me a dulcimer and I played it at that time in high school. That was so cool. And I had a boyfriend who was a guitarist and a big Dylan freak and we listened to country blues: Mississippi John Hurt and Howlin' Wolf. I saw John Hammond, Jr., at Max's Kansas City in New York. And we were listening to bluegrass, which was also a guitar influence on me, since I wear metal finger picks, like a banjo player does."

Not to omit the influence of string and horn players, Pam names guitarist John McLaughlin, who provided her the reason "why I do music full time." She adds guitarists James Taylor and Bonnie Raitt. She names again, as "a huge guitar inspiration," Joni Mitchell.

"Thinking back to my first encounters with jazz, I remember finding Miles Davis's *Birth of the Cool* album in my father's record collection when I was a junior or senior in high school. I listened to it many times and to this day I find I know most of the solos and arrangements by heart. It remains one of the most important recordings in my life. Weather Report was a big listening event for me in the '70s.

"When I sing, I feel the influence of my three musical 'homes': classical, pop, and jazz. From my years as a classical clarinetist, I take accuracy of pitch and rhythm and general musicianship, as well as emotional interpretation of other composers' music. From pop music I take a kind of no-holds-barred, deeply personal expression and my ongoing identification as a singer-songwriter. My years in jazz I feel have expanded my musicianship greatly. I tend to treat the songs of the Great American Songbook with a classical reverence, at least on the first chorus, then of course feeling very free to improvise after that. Because of the emphasis on improvisation in jazz, I try to listen very closely to all of the other musicians on the stand and to respond to them throughout every song. That exchange is very stimulating, especially with good jazz players, of whom there are so many in this area. I do most certainly think of each song as a three-minute play and myself as an actress getting into and staying in character for the duration. I try to study each lyric for meaning and subtext and to portray the passing emotions as vividly as possible. On songs that have some connection to my own life, I allow myself to relive emotions freely, and for the rest, I use my imagination. It's very satisfying to me.

"From my years of restaurant singing, I've learned to sing for my bandmates and for myself, no matter the size of the audience, but also to be ruthless about establishing and holding eye contact as a way of drawing the attention of the crowd. Feeling emotionally connected to much larger crowds is a whole other skill, which I'm getting a chance to hone in my work with Thievery Corporation. I very much enjoy all of these aspects of singing, and my audiences tend to respond to my enthusiasm.

"My current schedule goes something like this: I teach jazz voice at George Washington University about twelve hours a week from September to May. I also teach at home a few hours a week. I currently have four steady jazz gigs a week and miscellaneous concerts and performances throughout the year. I sing with a society band three or four times a month. I also do some jingle singing for local radio and TV, mostly car dealers and home builders and real estate companies. Lately I've been making some guest appearances on other musicians' CDs. Those with Al Williams, Wayne Wilentz, the Kennedys, Tony Gil, and John Bergin are some recent projects."

Bricker has CDs under her own name, including *Lookin' Good* and *U-topia*, two others with Rick Harris, and an LP with Mad Romance, all on her and Harris's label Madro Records. She contributes vocals to CDs of Thievery Corporation, Walter Salb, and L'Atome.

"I consider myself a singer-songwriter at heart," says Bricker. "One of my songs, 'You Can Tell,' is on my CD *All the Things You Are* and another, 'It's Not Too Soon,' is on *U-topia*. I am currently right in the middle of writing and recording my next project, which I plan to make 90 percent original. Also, I'm very proud of my collaborations with John Bergin, which have been a shot in the arm for me as a composer. I did co-write one tune with Thievery which was released as a vinyl single, 'Halfway Round the World.'"

Pam has been a twelve-time Washington Area Music Association nominee in the Jazz category and a winner five times, for Best Contemporary Vocalist in 1999, 2000, and 2001 and Best Contemporary Recording in 2001 for her CD *U-topia*. She shared the 1993 Wammie for Best Duo or Group with singer, pianist, and trumpeter Rick Harris.

"The band I've been touring Europe and the United States with, Thievery Corporation, is a dance-oriented, electronica, world music, trip-hop kind of band. I've been recording and touring with them for the past five years or so. We started with one- or two-week tours in Europe and have been steadily increasing our tours there and now here. In the fall of 2002 we toured the United States and Canada in two two-week tours. In May of 2003 we toured Europe, twenty-four shows in thirty days, including Athens, Thessalonika, Naples, Florence, Milan, Rome, Brussels, Fribourg, Utrecht, Zagreb, Luxembourg, Lisbon, Oporto, Moscow, and St. Petersburg. Touring time has slowly increased over the last few years. Venues tend to be either rock clubs or alternative rock clubs of about a thousand capacity and festivals."

Clarinetist Evan Christopher has for several years been attracting attention as an inspired virtuoso on his instrument. His tone, somewhat reminiscent of the great Edmond Hall, yet thoroughly individual, is wonderfully woody, and his seemingly effortless ease with startling turns of phrase marks him as highly inventive.

I saw him in performance at Switzerland's Jazz Ascona several times and then at Finland's Pori Jazz 2003. In fact, highlights of the Pori festival for this long-time lover of early jazz styles were the several sets I caught of Evan with trumpeter Duke Heitger's Steamboat Stompers, who turned up on one stage or another every day of the festival and were clearly an audience favorite.

Having caught Christopher in two different New Orleans–style groups at Ascona and then another at Pori, I assumed that this was his chosen niche. However, while he by no means intends to desert traditional jazz, the interview that follows clarifies that he belongs in this chapter by virtue of his varied tastes, the disparate musical sources he draws from, and a musical vision no less imaginative than any of the others included here.

We got together one morning in an alcove off the lobby of my hotel in Pori and talked for a couple of hours. I asked Evan to begin at the beginning.

"Ah, the beginning. I've thought of this recently, actually. I didn't pick up the clarinet until I was about eleven. From about the age of six, there were piano lessons. I had always been interested in ragtime. Maybe that's what made me want to take up piano a little bit. There were recordings from my father's collection, but before that, there were a lot of my mother's collection—folk records from the 1960s and '70s, from that folk revival that manifested itself in her playing amateur guitar and my father actually trying to learn how to pick a little five-string banjo. I was thinking about this recently in terms of its relation to skiffle, gospel, and blues, and what for me seems to have been an orientation toward musics that are a little harmonically simple.

"My music education started with bebop and went forward, but after I finished my college education I quickly started going backward. I went so far backward exploring the New Orleans music, which encompassed a lot of forms, that it made me recently pause to wonder if my orientation for that music was because of the crappy Peter, Paul and Mary records that I'd been subjected to," he says with a chuckle. "And Kingston Trio and Pete Seeger records and things of this nature."

I point out that he jumped forward quite a few years and ask that he go back to early musical influences from family and others.

"Well, I had to jump forward to jump back," Christopher explains. "I don't have memories of my parents listening to music for their own pleasure and I didn't have friends or family members who were interested in music, until they learned that I'd developed an interest in music, which wasn't until I was about eleven. So, no, music was, for the most part, pretty absent except for these occasional little sing-alongs that maybe my parents would have for family friends, and these were few and far between, thankfully. I remember things like 'MTA' and 'Hang Down Your Head, Tom Dooley' and 'Down by the Riverside.'

"My parents were transplanted mid-Westerners who ended up in California for my father's work. My dad's name is Robert Kunst; he and his first wife raised me. Her name was Paula and she hailed originally from Kentucky. He was born in Chicago and then lived in Illinois and Wisconsin. When he finished his doctorate in education—I guess back then it was called industrial arts or industrial education and then changed to technology education and later became obsolete in the university setting—he had two job choices. He was given California State University at Long Beach or somewhere in South Carolina. Thankfully, he chose California, so I wasn't raised in South Carolina.

"I was born in August of 1969 in Long Beach, California, in the hospital just a hundred yards from the university where I finished college. Robert and Paula Kunst adopted me in December of 1969. What little I know is from a letter written to me by a social worker who handled the adoption. I found it pretty interesting. The social worker indicated in this letter that my natural mother was Thai and about nineteen years old at the time she came to the United States. It was sort of a strange situation. I don't know what part of Thailand this was. I would only presume the city.

"Someone from the air force probably intended to marry her and bring her back to the United States. She'd be about eighteen and I think she was working in a bar, essentially to raise money to help her mother who had tuberculosis. She dated the customers. I think this isn't so uncommon. So this probably very young man from the air force decided he was gonna bring her back to the United States, but in the time that the paperwork was being arranged for this to happen she became pregnant with me. Meanwhile, this fellow was in the United States trying to bring her over.

"I was born in the Veterans' Hospital and, since I wasn't his child, they gave me up for adoption, which was, for the most part back then, done in anonymity. I haven't done any research to find out if there are any juicier details to the story, but it's pretty fascinating. I can't assume anything. My birth mother wasn't very forthcoming with the social worker about details, which was clear from this letter. I think it was a little embarrassing for her and she didn't speak any English, really. My natural father could've been Thai; he could've been anything. There's really just no way of knowing. It seems like a pretty good story, though.

"My given name was Evan Christopher Kunst. It became important for me to be my own person. It was really my career in music that showed me what things were worth pursuing. I would be reluctant to give too much credit to my childhood. So my name became, in 1993, after I finished university, just Evan Christopher. The family still lives in California; my father is married to his second wife. I have one sister who is about a year-and-a-half younger than me and is living in Southern California, married, with a couple of children—living actually in the suburb that we used to as children make fun of. You know, 'Who would live in those suburbs?' My sister was adopted also, a couple of years after after I came home from the hospital.

"Piano lessons until I was about twelve, relatively informal situations. I don't suppose there was any point where I took any of it very seriously. I lacked self-discipline or motivation and never got very far with it. I still use the piano for composition and as a tool for learning music. I guess it helped me learn to read and it's a good foundation for the arranging things that I do, for the writing. But I was a pretty crappy piano student.

"In the school band, where you switch from clarinet to saxophone because you want to be in the jazz band and there aren't any clarinets in the jazz band, I switched to tenor because it had the solos. Then I got to college and realized that there were too many saxophone players, so I went back to clarinet, which led me down a wonderful road back into the early beginnings of the music that are woefully unrepresented in the university setting."

Curious what kinds of music he was listening to during the high school and college years, I asked Evan to provide me some details.

"In terms of popular music? I did my best not to not listen to any of it. I gravitated more toward classical music, which was available in my local library—classical piano music. Remember the Joshua Rifkin recordings of Scott Joplin, which are quite classical in nature? I wore those out, whistled along with all of them. I really enjoyed those. That would have been about the time I picked up the clarinet. Also, I had to find some recordings where the clarinet was represented. So a couple of first recordings that I found in my father's collection were some nice early Artie Shaw records from the late '30s and a little bit of Benny Goodman.

"What happened then is some friends of *his*, some colleagues who actually had extensive record collections, were quite pleased that I was picking up the clarinet and they wanted me to have all the wealth of the West Coast Dixieland recordings, as well as all the Louis Armstrong, the Hot Fives and Sevens. They were sending me post-cards with names for my future band and they were quite enthusiastic about it and so that was part of it. My father knew all these songs; he remembered spending time with his mother, listening to the radio. In his memory he had a large repertoire of the songs sung by big band singers. I don't think there's a standard I learned that he didn't al-ready know.

"When I started college my orientation had to change to the jazz after World War II, because that's where the university setting makes you start. But before I began college there was something significant. I ended up taking my last year of high school at an arts boarding school in California, the Idyllwild School of Music and the Arts. It was in an area of the San Bernardino Mountains, just a couple of hours east of Los Angeles. That's where I actually had my first classi-cal clarinet lesson, since I came as a clarinet student. They didn't have any jazz there. I had gone to some summer camps for jazz of-fered by different universities, and the University of Southern Cali-fornia was one of the summer programs that I attended in this area of Idyllwild.

"After I finished at Idyllwild, I didn't know what I wanted to do for college. I went back to those people I'd met in the USC summer program, who thought I was younger and didn't realize that I had finished high school, and they said, 'Well, we'd like you to do the Commercial Music Program here,' or Jazz Studies, whatever they called it. The person involved in getting me into that program was Dr. Thom Mason, my first saxophone teacher, first *jazz* teacher, re-ally. I stayed at USC for about a year-and-a-half. The scholarship money got a little funny so I left school and went down to San Diego to reacquaint myself with some musicians whom I had met when they played a concert in Idyllwild, and among those was bassist Marshall Hawkins, from Washington, D.C., who was living at the time in Idyllwild. He was coaching tennis and basketball at the school and playing a lot of bass. He was going down to San Diego and Palm Springs and he was working all the time.

"I'd broken into a classroom at Idyllwild to use the piano and Marshall caught me in there banging out chord changes to some-thing, maybe 'Just Friends,' and we sat down at the piano for half an hour together and we've been friends ever since. I was his first piano student. This would have been early in 1987. And we agreed to get together more for piano lessons when he was available to do it, if he wasn't having to go down to San Diego to work with Joe Henderson or Richie Cole or someone.

"Marshall produced a concert at Idyllwild and brought up some musicians from San Diego, including Jimmy and Jeannie Cheatham and the Sweet Baby Blues Band. These were the musicians I wanted to acquaint myself with a couple of years later in San Diego, and so I moved there and began working as much as I could with Marshall and the musicians that I met through him. At this time I was playing alto saxophone mostly. Clarinet I was playing as a double. In San Diego, one of the musicians that decided to help me out a little was Flip Oakes, a wonderful multi-instrumentalist. He gave me a couple of fake books of mostly Dixieland-type tunes and I started learning a lot of these, sort of the Top 40 Dixieland tunes. And when I say that, I don't mean traditional jazz; I mean Dixieland in the connotation that we think of as playing with sort of straw hat commercial-type bands that I'd had a *little* bit of experience with because clarinet was always a strong double when I was at USC.

"A part of my scholarship at USC had been to go on jobs for other departments of the school; for example, the dean of the Architecture Department would have a reception, and instead of paying money for outside musicians, he would just transfer money from his budget to the Jazz Studies Department, and this would then become part of my work-study scholarship. For some work-study, you sit at a desk and staple papers together. Well, my work-study, many times, was small, casual receptions on different parts of the campus, where I met a lot of outside musicians. Sometimes we'd get on these little jobs where we'd play dance music or a little Dixieland, instead of them bringing in the college combo that's gonna play a bunch of bebop. They needed something more functional.

"I liked that, I enjoyed those things, and I enjoyed learning about that type of music. At the time, my orientation was a little more the small swing groups of Barney Bigard and Ellington's small groups and, of course, Artie Shaw's Gramercy Five and Benny Goodman's small groups. I had a friend in college, Chris Dawson, who's about my age and he was exploring Sonny Clark as much as he was exploring Teddy Wilson. He and I had an interest in the earlier styles that most of our peers *didn't* have, and we're *still* friends because of that. But by the time I got to San Diego I was just familiar enough with the genre to be interested in it, and Flip Oakes got me work with some of the local Dixieland bands of San Diego. I was working with Conrad Janis frequently in that sort of Dixieland band.

"At this time I met Jack Sheldon for the first time and a trombone player named Mike Fahn. I think that's also when I met George Segal and a fair number of modern musicians who actually played a lot of these casual jobs. This time was important because it gave me a reason to explore some of the earlier styles outside of what I was learning in the university. I was getting these work opportunities. Stylistically, it probably wasn't very good. These are modern musicians playing 'Bill Bailey'; they weren't very serious about the idiom. What was more significant than anything was that I was meeting some older musicians I'd heard on records, and I started to feel like a real musician hanging out with these guys. That was more important than what I was actually gleaning from them musically.

"The two most significant people I met in that period, people who were interested in that music, were Larry Wright and George Probert. Larry was a multi-instrumentalist from California, and he introduced me to George who was a soprano saxophone player. They opened me up to all sorts of things. This was when I got my first recordings of early Fletcher Henderson and little blues groups. It was the first time I'd heard Edmond Hall, the first time I'd heard Bix, the first time I'd heard the things with Bix and Tram, and early Ellington, first recordings I had of groups like the Harlem Hamfats. These were the kinds of things they introduced me to. All of a sudden, the most important thing wasn't harmony, which seemed to be the orientation of the education I was getting at USC; it was what these guys were showing me about rhythm and melody."

I suggested that he was interested in this old music because it must have meant something to his sensibility. That is, he found himself responding to it in a more emotional way than to any of the styles he had encountered before that time.

"Two things are working here. I was developing a sensibility and the music appealed to it, but fundamentally, I was being pulled into it by the clarinet because I could work playing clarinet. There were too many saxophone players and nobody was calling up the Jazz Studies office looking for people to give concerts playing modern jazz; they were saying, 'Hey, we need a little straw-hat band to come play outside for this reception, this poolside thing.' What I was realizing about the whole shaping of the early history of jazz was that the music evolved the way it did *less* because of people's sensibility and *less* because of people's artistic desires, and *more* because those early players were just working musicians changing the music because the demands for the music changed first.

"These are things that I'm interested in and that spoke to me, that's one part of it. But the reality is that when Flip in San Diego was teaching me these tunes, immediately I could have work with little trios and quartets playing clarinet. I went down there to hang out with Marshall and these guys, and we could get together at the house and make music, but we weren't working; I wasn't working *nearly* as much playing bebop alto saxophone as I was playing Dixieland clarinet.

"Switching back to clarinet after USC was much more a function of too many damn saxophone players and too many unrewarding situations; if you want to play jazz saxophone, that's one thing, but I would rather make fun music than stand up with some of my colleagues and stare at our tennis shoes and rehash old Charlie Parker heads. That just didn't seem as interesting to me, and it didn't seem relevant, it didn't seem functional. So that's really what happened in that transition after USC to San Diego. It was clear that it was going to be easier for me to pay the rent with the clarinet.

"I eventually started to work my way back up toward Los Angeles and I moved back to Long Beach and enrolled at Golden West Junior College, did a bunch of General Education courses, just hammered it out straight through in about a year so that I would have nothing but music classes left at the end of it. At Golden West I met Tom Kubis who is one of southern California's most excellent arrangers; he plays great clarinet and saxophone, too. He was involved in a couple of crossover groups that he wrote arrangements for. I studied arranging with him for about a year and transferred after Golden West to Long Beach State to finish my degree, went back to taking classical lessons with Gary Bovier at Long Beach State, and just started being more serious about getting the degree finished. It was important for my father; he was going to help me finance a car if I finished." Evan chuckles. "So, from 1990 to '93 I hammered out the degree. I got a car out of it, and right before I was finishing the undergraduate degree at Long Beach State I started getting involved with some musicians in San Diego again, including a singer-songwriter named A. J. Croce, the son of Jim Croce. He remembered that I played clarinet when I was living in San Diego and worked at his mom's club, Croce's, a few times.

"I got back to my apartment one day and had a bunch of phone calls from A. J. saying, 'You gotta get up here to Ocean Way, we need you for this recording.' Well, I raced up there and in the studio was Robben Ford on guitar, Ron Carter on bass, and it was just silly, just doing this funny little pop tune that needed a little clarinet for it.

"Right after I finished school I started touring with A. J. for this record company, Private, and promoting that first album that I got on almost by a fluke. Those are some of my first trips to Europe. Through A. J. a lot of great things came. That was the first time that I went to Rome and met Tony Scott and that was very interesting. I'm still friends with Tony and went to Rome for his eightieth birthday a couple years ago. We just took him to the airport a couple of weeks ago to send him to New York for his concerts. We practice together in his house and go have pizza together and stuff and it's fun to hear stories about Billie and Bird and just be in his presence.

"Those touring opportunities also led me to New Orleans for the first time. In the summer of '94 I told A. J., 'Okay, after this season I'm quitting and moving to New Orleans.' And that's how I got to learning about clarinet players like Big Eye Louis Nelson—Louis Nelson Delisle—and Louis Cottrell and Raymond Burke, Albert Burbank and Willie Humphries, and more of these New Orleans cats who are a little bit in the cracks. I mean, all of a sudden, there was a whole new wealth of clarinet players that I hadn't been exposed to, these New Orleans guys. That was on and off in New Orleans, until I got offered the job by Jim Cullum's Jazz Band in San Antonio, Texas. I moved away from New Orleans to San Antonio for about two-and-a-half years—six nights a week, did some radio things, and was involved in some of Jim's projects.

"Once I got back down to New Orleans, everything started to normalize again and that pretty much brings it to the present. It's been about two-and-a-half years that I've been back in New Orleans more permanently. On returning to New Orleans, I confirmed that what is very exciting to me are these Creole music projects, exploring the French West Indies music and the biguine music and starting to be more serious about composition. I began to write a lot more and started to find like-minded musicians to help me out with these projects. Now we're getting somewhere. I'm beginning a master's program in the fall at Tulane University and that will be my excuse for staying in New Orleans for two more years, and then I'm hoping to get back to New York.

"I think there's a way for me to stay very firmly in the New Orleans style and find a different way to speak that language—instead of doing what may seem more natural, instead of going from, 'Okay, I'm at the beginnings of jazz, now I go to swing, now I go to bebop, now I go through these different stages.' You ask me, what would be the result of my musical philosophy? Instead of being something that follows that continuum that already exists, I'm trying to find almost a parallel continuum that stays more geographic in nature, meaning more relevant to those Caribbean rhythms, to the language of the clarinet as it evolved first in New Orleans. I'm trying to stay where my roots are and keep my voice consistent. Then the construction will change relative to the stories I'm trying to tell, relative to the ideas and values that I'm trying to communicate.

"I mean, I developed a strong desire to do it correctly. I'm thirty-four and only now am I almost feeling like soon I can be finished with old music, in a way. I'm still trying to get it right. Not that in two years I'll say, 'Oh, I've now got this right,' but I'm starting to see ways I can make a departure from it. But I'm not quite done with old music, and it has been fifteen years."

I interrupted to express my puzzlement at his intention to "make a departure from . . . old music." I asked what will happen after he reaches that stage—that is, when he feels that he has mastered it.

"It's not a question of mastery; it's just a question of having the confidence or having the objective knowledge that, 'Okay, now I know where my roots are, now I can move forward and try to make something a little more relevant for the year 2003.' In studying the music, I'm developing some serious problems with the application of the old music and its having been divorced from function for a half-century, in terms of why it was created at its inception, which was as a dance music.

"I think that once you've figured out the beginnings, that's when it's time to start figuring out, 'All right now, you're going to create a music around a set of values and represent it in a certain way. Well, what's that gonna be?' I mean, you can't just do museum pieces; you don't want to be one of those secondhanders or necrophiliacs that sits there and plays transcriptions of solos and arrangements that were done seventy-five years ago. You gotta do something else."

"Can you define what that 'something else' is going to be?" I asked.

"I'm starting to, Royal, I'm starting to. The language—which is really strange for me to say—is becoming a little more abstract. It's encompassing some rhythms that were always present in early New Orleans music but really seem to have their roots in the Caribbean. My direction right now seems to be going back to larger forms, like the ragtime forms and the forms of the Brazilian choros and Cuban danzón, where you have three or four themes. The model I keep turning to is sort of what Astor Piazzolla did for tango. I would love to see myself as being able, with the roots that I've chosen, to not be so hung up on the parameters and the initial construction of early jazz, but instead find applications that are expressive in a more contemporary narrative. How? By getting away from the trappings of this box called the jazz standard, getting away from a little box called the six-piece jazz band. Basically, what I need to start doing is getting out of these little boxes."

I asked Evan to cite some musicians whose work has inspired him to think along the lines he has just described.

"The depth of pianist Brad Mehldau's trio, the sense of program, the programmatic elements that come out of Mingus, that you find in the projects of David Murray or Don Byron. Maybe not so much the free improvisation, which in itself hasn't really interested me so much, but the sense of program or storytelling. Guitarist Bill Frisell has had some very beautiful projects that actually seem less like ja-a-zz to me than, like I say, some way of telling little stories, giving us pictures, presenting us with themes that are representative of an idea or a value or a value object. And there's the Tin Hat Trio and scores of others, I'm sure. All these are the kinds of musicians who are becoming more interesting to me.

"I don't know what the connection will eventually be to New Orleans music. I know, for me right now, we're not done with old music yet, but we've expanded. The musicians that I'm choosing to work with in my groups now, we've expanded the context to encompass more sort of pan-Creole musics of the Caribbean and Brazil. I'm starting to explore Mexico and Cuba more now. I'm starting that master's program to these ends. All of this is to help me be stronger in the idea that I can justify an approach to the roots of my music through the contributions that clarinet made, not only in New Orleans but also in the Caribbean.

"Those are the clarinet players who always fascinated me more when I discovered them. They were the ones who were just technically brilliant on their instruments and were right there in that transition from written music to improvised music. And I'm finding their sound in musics that seem to have one thing in common, that the instrumentalists themselves had French classical training and that the areas in which they developed their music were urban centers related to the African Diaspora: centers of trade, like the clarinet players of the French West Indies; like Eugene Delouche and Alexander Steele, who made their first recordings in Paris playing biguine and have a remarkable similarity to the approach that the New Orleans clarinet players had to the instrument itself. I found early recordings of Carmen Miranda, and the clarinet players have that same remarkable sound. The clarinet as a substitute for violin starts to appear in Cuban music as early as some of the Cuban danzón things from the teens and twenties. There's a way to tie them all together and be able to justify whatever I do next. The roots are here," he says, chuckling, perhaps with the excitement of discovery awaiting him in his musical explorations. "And the clarinet is kind of omnipresent, more so than saxophone. In some ways, even more so than trumpet. So, just to find a language for it, that'll be the harder part.

"It's starting to take a little bit more of an abstract shape, because I think there are so many trappings with the more conventional constructions of melody and harmony, to the point that you have to avoid them because they're almost cliché. The music will have to be constructed to overcome these things, much in the way that Piazzolla managed to overcome the trappings of traditional tango. I don't think everything he did was necessarily tango, but the roots were in tango and he was a virtuoso on his instrument, the bandoneon. I would love to be able to not have the trappings of being a traditional jazz clarinet player or an avant-garde clarinet player or any —I just want to be a clarinet player!"

From 1978 to 1987 when I was the *Washington Post*'s jazz critic, I would every so often review gigs of pianist Armen Donelian at the One Step Down. This was a major jazz club in Washington, D.C., for three decades until several years ago when it closed its doors. I recall one memorable occasion about twenty years ago when Armen was accompanist, along with bassist Tommy Cecil, for trumpeter Chet Baker, who was absent for the opening set because he arrived nearly two hours late.

Armen and I were out of touch during the '90s. Then he contacted me in 2001 to tell me that he had been awarded a Fulbright fellowship for a three-month jazz professorship in Armenia, the land of his ancestors, and I decided to include him in this collection of profiles. Last year I had the opportunity to see Armen in performance at the Armenian Embassy here in Washington. He presented a program of Armenian folk materials and his own compositions for the Annual Armenian Christmas Open House. Some of the songs were sung by mezzo-soprano Maro Partamian. The next day Armen dropped by my home in Silver Spring and we taped the interview from which the following is drawn.

"I was born in Jackson Heights, New York, on December 1, 1950. My parents were both of Armenian descent and my father, Khatchik Donelian, was born in a village in Turkey called Burdur, about three hundred kilometers southeast of Izmir on the west coast of Turkey. Izmir is sometimes called Smyrna. My father was two years old when my grandfather, Ohannes Donelian, left Turkey in 1915 to come to the United States. My grandfather left a handwritten diary in Armenian, which we have as a family heirloom and have had translated. It documents his whole early life and his father's life, so I know about my father's side, going back to my great-grandfather.

"My great-grandfather's name was originally Kevork Donelian. His first name was changed in 1867 to Khatchadour upon his being ordained as a priest in the Armenian Orthodox Church. According to my grandfather's diary, Khatchadour and thirty-five members of his family were deported from Afion Karahissar, a large rail junction near Burdur in a region where carpets, poppies, and grains are produced, and force-marched into the Syrian Desert during the 1915 Turkish campaign of ethnic cleansing of Armenians, never to be heard from again. My distant cousin in Armenia, Aghavni Badikyan, relates a story passed down through my grandfather's sister, Aghavni Donelian, that during this march Khatchadour was forced by Turkish soldiers to carry a sack of stones on his back until he dropped dead. Whether this can be corroborated is uncertain.

"My grandfather Ohannes was a designer and manufacturer of oriental carpets. He left Turkey in 1915 to avoid the Turkish massacres of Armenians. And when he left, basically, he had to leave his whole business. He had many people working for him in factories. He came to the United States—didn't speak a word of English—bringing with him my grandmother Elizabeth, my father, my aunt Armenouhy, and two uncles, Don and Hrant, who died in his teens of leukemia. The ship's manifest containing Ohannes's name is recorded in the online archives of Ellis Island. He reestablished his carpet business in New York as an importer, but his business failed during the Great Depression never to revive.

"My father and his brother and sister grew up in Mt. Vernon, New York, and my father went to Columbia University, studied electrical engineering, and eventually became involved with nuclear technology during World War II. He worked on the Manhattan Project, although he didn't know it as such because all the scientists were kept in the dark about what they were doing. But he knew that he was doing important work and he had to be screened by the FBI. When they read in the news that the bomb had been dropped on Hiroshima, of course he was completely shocked, but by the same token, he knew that they had been struggling to develop this before Hitler did. At any rate, after the war my father got involved in peaceful applications of nuclear technology and started a corporation called United Nuclear.

"My father was a lover of music. He played violin as a child. He was a big fan of Mozart and Beethoven; Chopin was one of his favorites, and Bach, of course, was always around. When we were growing up we had the sound of Armenian records in the background at family get-togethers. My father was a brilliant man; he did quite a bit of reading and was kind of a daunting figure in my life," Armen recalls, chuckling. "Put it this way—he was a very hard act to follow in some ways.

"My mother Lillian was born in this country. Her parents were Armenians from Damascus, Syria, and came here around 1905. My mother's father, Gabriel Sarkisian, was an artisan. Her grandfather, Sarkis der Michaelyan, who was born in Malatya, Turkey, was an artist and jewelry maker in Damascus. In order to make a living here my mother's father got into photo-engraving. At that time, photos had to be etched and he worked in that part of the process. My mother had a sister and three brothers, and one of those brothers, Bart Sarkisian, was a kind of amateur pianist and played club dates and weddings and social events. As a child, he gave my brother and me a copy of the old Number One fake book, which had all the standards going back to 1915, and we would learn these tunes. I have two brothers and a sister, John, Gary, and Margaret.

"The earliest musical recollections I have are when I was around five or six years old; I remember playing melodies by ear on this piano that we had in our basement. It was an old beat-up piano with broken keys and strings missing, but there were enough notes in the middle of the keyboard that I could make some music on. Whatever I was hearing, I would just sit down and play it. My oldest brother, John, played clarinet and my next oldest brother, Gary, played guitar. My sister at the time was still quite young, around three years old. Once in a while, on family occasions, my father would pull out his violin and play a few creaky notes.

"We grew up in a town called Armonk, about forty miles north of New York. We were the only Armenian family in the town and there was no Armenian church for us to attend. My parents enrolled us in the Episcopal church. I remember singing the Episcopal hymns at quite a young age. I started piano lessons when I was around seven-and-a-half. I was playing from the John Thompson books. My brother was playing clarinet and learning some of the Mozart concertos and he was also into Pete Fountain. He had some Dixieland records, and I remember 'Georgia on My Mind' was one of the early recordings that I listened to. There was a Spike Jones record that we listened to a lot. Incredible musicians, the Spike Jones band. I remember a rendition of *Carmen* that they did.

"On some of the high holidays, such as Christmas and Easter, my parents would drive us to Manhattan to attend the Armenian church service. These first forays into the city were when I was eight, nine, ten years old. There's an Armenian church on 184th Street in Washington Heights that my parents were married in and also my uncle was married in, and my grandfather was on the founding board of that church. I remember as a child the sound of the Armenian liturgy and it sounded very strange to me. I think I probably had an adverse reaction to it because I was going to school and growing up in a community where most of my classmates were either Italian or Jewish and there were a lot of Catholics. I was the only one of Middle Eastern descent. This is a very sensitive issue for me, my ethnic identity. I mean, to what extent do I see myself as Armenian versus American or as a jazz man, a jazz person?

"When we visited my uncle, who lived in Hackensack, New Jersey, my father's brother—we called him Uncle Don and he was a big fan of Armenian music—he used to play Armenian records, what you'd call belly-dance music, with the sound of the clarinet and the oud, a Middle East stringed instrument somewhat similar to a lute but without the frets, and the dumbeg, which is a round hand drum shaped like an hour glass.

"Also we had some friends of my mother on Long Island that we would visit occasionally, and I remember going to Armenian dances where they had an Armenian band playing. The thing that struck me most about that music was the odd time signatures, as well as the instrumentation that I mentioned before. This music was not in 4/4 and was difficult for me to feel, but you'd see a whole group of people standing up and dancing in *seven* and *five*.

"My first piano teacher was Mrs. Waldron, the school music teacher at our elementary school, the Whippoorwill School, in Armonk. This was in 1958. The following year my parents enrolled me at the Westchester Conservatory of Music in White Plains and I started studying the classical repertoire, the Bach *Inventions*, for example. The conservatory was founded in the late 1920s by cellist Pablo Casals and a number of other people, and the faculty comprised some of the top concert artists in the New York area, many of them émigrés from Germany and Austria who had left to get away from Hitler and the political environment in the world at the time.

"For the next nine years I studied with Michael Pollon. He was born in Austria, studied in Berlin, and was trained as an opera conductor and pianist. He was a great teacher and helped me uproot a lot of bad technical habits that I had fallen into. I remember telling Thomas Lishman, another of my teachers, who was British, that I wanted to play jazz more, because around ten, eleven years old I had started listening to my brother play clarinet and Pete Fountain and Al Hirt records. But Mr. Pollon wasn't even considering it; it was just out of the question. He wasn't going in that direction with me. My job with him was to learn how to play the classics and play them correctly. And, in a way, it was good, you know, 'cause I really made progress with him. He was very insistent that certain things had to be a certain way. He was very big on cleanliness of articulation, paying attention to the dynamics, what should be staccato, what should be legato, really playing the rhythms correctly. He also pointed out a lot of things about the broad formal design of the music and how things develop. I learned a lot with him. We studied Bach, Beethoven, Mozart, Schumann, Debussy, Prokofiev. I got a really good background in classical music through him. I did a graduation recital at the end of high school and played a Chopin etude, a Beethoven piano sonata, and a piece by Debussy. It was very important training for me as a solo pianist.

"At the same time I was doing this, my brother was playing all these records, and I got involved with a guy named Art Ryerson who was a guitar player and arranger. He had worked with Louis Armstrong and with Jack Teagarden's band and Paul Whiteman in the 1930s and was a studio musician for CBS. His kids were my peers in school. Art, Jr., played trombone and piano, Rich and John were both trumpet players, and Ali played the flute. His wife, Chick, had been a chorus girl on Broadway and was involved in a lot of the school musicals and talent shows.

"At the end of every talent show at school was the Ryerson band. My brother was playing in this band when I was ten, eleven years old, and then a couple of years later I got to play piano in this band. This was around the time that our uncle Bart had given us this fake book with 'Georgia on My Mind' and 'Ain't She Sweet' and all the Duke Ellington tunes and Cole Porter, and I knew that I had to play jazz.

"From that point on I was on this kind of two-track path: one was classical, and I was getting really serious into that and loving it, and the other was jazz. I had a little trio in school and we were playing Ramsey Lewis kind of bluesy jazz things. In my senior year I heard my first Art Tatum record, and when I heard that I just like, you know, my jaw dropped," he says, chuckling. "At the conservatory there was a teacher there, a guy named Irwin Stahl who had known Art Tatum and hipped me to some of the harmonic devices that Tatum used, his use of a cycle of fifths as a way to fill up several bars of free time or to turn around in a progression. I heard my first Bud Powell records around this time. I had been playing organ in church in place of acolyte service at St. Stevens Episcopal Church and I was playing in jazz bands and rock bands."

In the fall of 1968 Armen enrolled at Columbia University and majored in music, studying with Vladimir Ussachevsky and other professors of renown. He met alto saxophonist Marc Cohen—who later switched to piano and changed his name to Marc Copland—and did jazz workshops with him, playing Horace Silver charts and other "hard bop meaty repertoire." During his college years he began checking out, for example, B. B. King and Muddy Waters, McCoy Tyner at Slugs, Bill Evans at the Village Gate, and Albert King at a concert on campus.

Graduating in 1972, Armen found work accompanying jazz dance classes and took piano lessons with Richie Beirach, whom he credits as an important influence on his development. From 1975 to '77 Armen went on the road with Mongo Santamaria's band, sometimes two months at a time, and "got to hang out with a lot of really top musicians." He looks back on the tours as lessons in stamina and professionalism. "I mean, you get on a plane, you fly for six hours, get off the plane, go to the concert hall, do a concert. Next day you get on a bus and go here, go there. I was twenty-five years old and on my first real road experience and it was great. Living out of a suitcase, being away from home, away from all the familiar surroundings, really seeing parts of the country that I'd always wanted to see."

Free-lance work in the New York area, stints with Ray Barretto, Lionel Hampton, Ted Curson, Sonny Rollins, and Billy Harper took Armen into the mid-'80s. With Harper he made his first visits to Europe. Armen had cut his first album in 1980, a trio session with Eddie

Gomez and Billy Hart. More combo and solo albums followed over the years, including a 3-CD set, *Grand Ideas*, that he recorded at his home in 1998 over the course of three weeks and sixty hours of tape.

"Through a friend who's an Armenian I met a saxophone player named Arnie Lawrence and by hanging out with him at his gigs I met an Armenian clarinetist and saxophonist whose name is Souren Baronian, who has had a group called Taksim for about thirty years now. And he, being about twenty years older than me, grew up during the bebop era and was very influenced by Lester Young and Charlie Parker. In his compositions and his group, I found a way to combine Armenian rhythms and melodies with jazz improvisation. His music was coming out of that belly-dance music tradition. Of course, growing up in that time, he played in all those types of bands. But in his jazz compositions he had spaces where he opened up and actually improvised in a linear way similar to bebop. So that was, I guess, my first insight, or inkling, into how Armenian music could be combined with jazz. I started hanging out with him and we did some jamming together. But I never pursued working with his group, although he invited me to, because I was still uncomfortable playing a chordal instrument tuned in the Western twelve-tone scale with this music that had quarter tones and strange melodic twists for which I wasn't able to find the proper chords. Rather than make a fool of myself or make a mess of the music, I just said, 'I'm not ready for this now.'

"The oud player in Souren's band was a guy named Ara Dinkjian. He had a four-thousand-record collection in his house and is an amazing scholar of not only Armenian and Middle Eastern music but jazz and all kinds of pop music as well. And he's more or less my age. We found a connection with each other. He had started a band called Night Ark. The symbol of Armenia is Mount Ararat, the mountain in eastern Turkey, which used to be Armenian territory. Of course Mount Ararat was the resting place of Noah's Ark. So his calling the band Night Ark was an allusion to this vessel of rescue. Night? Who knows? I guess because music is played at night.

"The instrumentation of Night Ark was clarinet, soprano saxophone, a small flute called the kaval, oud, dumbeg, and electric bass. He also had a female percussionist who sang and was a belly dancer, a very talented girl named Shamira Shahinian who sang in Armenian.

She would scat some of the lines and play some percussion and dance in front of the band.

"Around 1987, after Shamira had left the band, I joined Night Ark. They had already made one album for RCA Novus and then we made a second album. Ara was playing oud, I was on piano, the bassist was Ed Schuller, Gunther Schuller's son, and the percussionist was Arto Tuncboyaçiyan, an Armenian from Turkey. I had met Arto in 1980 when I was touring with Billy Harper's quintet on a State Department-sponsored tour of Poland, Romania, Portugal, and Turkey. The next year Arto came to New York to live and he played in my band for a while—my quintet with Bill Stewart on drums, Anthony Cox on bass, Dick Oatts on tenor saxophone, and Barry Danielian on trumpet.

"The point of all this is that in the Night Ark group I had an opportunity to really explore the connection between Armenian music and jazz and to find new ways of developing that influence. Ara and Arto, being real masters in the field of Armenian music, showed me a lot of things about Armenian music and Armenian artists, about playing in different time signatures, about the instrumentation, about what kinds of chords to play, and how to play the right notes and avoid those other notes that were kind of impossible to play because they were quarter tones. I was a member of Night Ark until 2000 and made three albums with the group.

"Night Ark played around the New York area in several places, for instance, Fat Tuesdays and the Washington Square Church; we did a double billing in Boston with George Schuller and his group Orange Then Blue; we performed in Switzerland and in Athens and in the Istanbul and Jerusalem festivals; and we played in Armenia in the Yerevan Jazz Festival.

"When I was fifteen or so I had kind of made a break and didn't want to listen to Armenian music. It wasn't until after I graduated from college that I started getting more interested in the Armenian music and trying to find a way to connect my ethnic character to jazz. After all, American music is connecting the African tradition and the European tradition, and so I felt like why not connect the Armenian tradition to *both* of those traditions in some way? After all, there are definite synchronicities in certain ways, especially around improvisation. On the other hand, Armenian music has a very different sound. It's a more or less monophonic music. In other words, harmony is not really part of the development of traditional Armenian music. It's melody, maybe one melody, maybe two melodies, and rhythm. I think there is a definite sympathetic connection between Armenian music and, say, Slavic music and Russian and Gypsy music, and Arab music, as well. There's also a relationship to Turkish music, odd as it may seem. Armenians have always lived in Turkey, or the area that is now called Turkey, for centuries, and those populations have lived side by side.

"So, from my earliest days, it's been a progression: my listening to Armenian records, going to some of these social dances and listening to Armenian bands and hearing the different time signatures, listening to the Taksim group and hearing Armenian music combined with bebop, and then in the Night Ark group, where I was really free to open up to the sound of Armenian music, and using my personal musical ethos."

Armen's first visit to Armenia, as a member of Night Ark when it was booked at the Yerevan International Jazz Festival, was in 1998. "It was a lifelong dream come true, to go to Armenia and perform with Armenian musicians in the land of my ancestors," he says. While there he conducted a master class in jazz at the city's conservatory. He returned for a month-long visit in 1999 and in 2002 was granted a Fulbright fellowship for a three-month stay as jazz professor at the conservatory.

"Having been there, having met some of their musicians, I could hear that there is a lot of potential for development of the music and of jazz education. They need more contact with Western artists and they need more listening materials and books. So what I'm trying to do with the conservatory is build up their library.

"There are two jazz venues in Yerevan, the capital city. One is a place called Paplovok and, basically, it's run by the Mafia. It's a very nice place in a park in front of a little pond with café tables and there are glass doors and then inside there are more tables and chairs and a bandstand. And they have jazz music there pretty much five nights a week. But the people that go there are really not going for the music; they're going to be seen and noticed, because it's very expensive by local standards and the musicians are there to provide background music for whatever social events go on. The other place is much more of a jazz club and reminds me a little bit of the Vanguard. It's called Subway and people go there for the music; they really listen, they applaud. It's smoky, it's noisy, but it's a *jazz* club. How they survive, you never know. Do they survive on door receipts or sales of meals? Not in a jazz club, and if they do it's a very meager living.

"Now my interest is in two things: original composition, which I've always been interested in, and learning more about Armenian folk music and folk melodies and trying to expand my repertoire of those, such as the piece I played last night at the embassy. Then, hopefully, maybe I can do an album of solo piano where I can play some of these melodies in solo adaptations, open them up, play on them in the jazz way. There's a certain melancholy and sadness in the melodies of Armenian music. I hope to bring that feeling into my music so that I can develop it in a way that represents something for myself. I don't think about jazz and Armenian music as having boundaries. It's all music to me, and I guess the challenge of my life has been to try to integrate it all into a seamless style where you don't hear any boundaries."

I caught a boiling set of the Indonesian group Bhaskara at the 1991 North Sea Jazz Festival. Saxophonist and flutist Udin Zach was the ten-member band's leader and Luluk Purwanto—a guest, not a regular member of Bhaskara—was on electric violin. Luluk describes the band's style as "fusion jazz with a West Coast flavor" and "very groovy."

More than a decade went by before I caught up with the very talented Ms. Purwanto again and that came about on the spur of the moment. A fellow jazz writer, Paul Blair, had become a friend of Luluk and her husband, pianist René van Helsdingen, while living in Jakarta during the 1980s and '90s. He called me from New York early one late-summer evening a couple of years ago and urged me to get down to the Embassy of the Republic of Indonesia in Washington, D.C., only twenty minutes on Metro Rail from my home in Silver Spring, Maryland. Luluk and René were performing there at 7:30 P.M., Paul informed me. Bolting my dinner, I headed for the train station a mile down my street.

When I arrived, the first thing that caught my eye was a mammoth bus by the side of the embassy's driveway. The vehicle's side sported a stage with a canopy. Luluk Purwanto and René Helsdingen have traveled in and performed from this Stage Bus, as it has been dubbed, on their global tours for more than a decade.

The audience for the embassy performance was drawn mostly from the South Asian diplomatic community and sat on folding chairs while children played on the lawn behind them. Nearby, a five-year-old, with two sticks, mimicked the violinist. After the ambassador welcomed us to "the Indonesian parking lot," René kicked off the evening with a contemplative solo. Luluk took a seat on the front edge of the stage, her foot propped on the top stair. A tiny voice microphone was suspended from her head. Wearing the traditional garb of her culture, she tucked her wired violin under her chin and simultaneously scatted and played. Bassist Essiet Okon Essiet and drummer Marcello Pellitteri entered the fray and the quartet cooked, which they continued to do for an hour-and-a-half, blending exotic Indonesian melodies and straight-ahead jazz.

At the concert's conclusion, Luluk and René said their good-byes to the embassy staff and others and autographed purchased CDs. They then turned to me for fifteen minutes or so of conversation. This is all the time they could spare since they had to get on the road for an overnight drive, René at the wheel, as they continued their tour of seventy concerts at forty-five universities in twenty-four states. Their next stop was a college in New England. We discussed interview options and elected to do it in cyberspace.

A month or so later, when they had returned to their home base in Amsterdam, the exchange began. I initiated it with general queries and then, after their first e-missive arrived, asked more specific questions so that gaps would be filled and details provided. René began our e-correspondence.

* * *

Dear Royal,

My father, Carel Christian van Helsdingen, was a businessman and a mechanical engineer who built trains and agricultural equipment for companies in Indonesia. I was born in 1957 in Indonesia and stayed there for two years before the family moved to Holland.

My mother, Viviane van Helsdingen Fraikin, was French and was the one who stimulated me to study piano. When I was five she took me to a private teacher, Mrs. Komter Loeber. This was a tough mission which I really didn't like and my mother had to drag me there. I took lessons for ten years from Mrs. Loeber. She noticed that I would never play the stuff that was written. During home concerts by her pupils, Mrs. Loeber let me play whatever I liked—improvisations.

My brother, Robert van Helsdingen, had an album of Oscar Peterson, Ray Brown, and Herb Ellis. I never tried to copy exact lines of Oscar Peterson but I wanted to have his freedom and speed. My left hand would play a chord of unknown nature and the right hand would then improvise. As long as I would include the same notes in the right hand as the left hand, nothing would go wrong and it would sound like the correct way of improvisation. I learned scales the same way, by recognizing black and white keys. I called this "playing by sight."

I loved playing the piano—only my way, of course. When there were family gatherings and reunions I played for everybody, and also at performances at school. I would play congas with one hand and piano with the other in the same way that Herb Ellis would hit the rhythms on his guitar. I tried to develop my own techniques by moving my fingers very fast up and down the piano keys randomly. I did this all day long. Everybody around me would go nuts. But I knew somehow that if you would repeat doing these movements something had to grow out of it.

I remember asking my father to bring jazz records from America when I was ten. He went to the states almost every month. One day he walked into an American record store and asked the shop owner to give him the best jazz records for his son. My father did not know much about jazz. He brought me the Milestone recordings of John Coltrane, Bill Evans, Sonny Rollins, McCoy Tyner, Cannonball Adderley, Wes Montgomery, Duke Pearson, and Oscar Peterson. I loved those albums

My mother was an alcoholic, a very sad illness, and this is why my parents divorced when I was twelve. I stayed with my father. My mother died in 1973 of yellow fever. She was a great pianist and played a lot of Chopin. From the age of twelve I had to live with several nannies and aunties who had to take care of me because my dad was always on a business trip. The aunties didn't really like all that piano playing I did and therefore the piano was moved into a basement. I would spend days and days in the basement just playing and playing and listening to records. My father died of a stroke in 1975 during the great oil crisis. He lost almost everything he owned because of this crisis.

My first nonpaying gigs took place at high school, playing at school parties. There was no way people could request anything because I just didn't know any standards. In 1974 I formed a trio and made my first appearance at a jazz competition during the Singer Jazz Festival in the Netherlands. I saw Bill Evans perform during that festival. In 1975 I played a Jazz Festival in Delft. I remember this very clearly because it was that night when I met Ben Webster.

I moved to Delft in 1977 to study mining engineering. In this year I also started to play my first paid gigs. A father of a student friend of mine, Mr. Ten Have, offered to pay for a demo recording for a record company called Munich Records. This company, based in Holland, was owned by Job Zomer, whom I see as my second father. Up to now, 2002, Job has been the greatest support in my crazy career as a jazz pianist. My first album was released in 1978. All the song titles were related to my mining studies.

I used to visit a dentist who was a pianist. Every visit he would play a half hour of Debussy and Ravel, and then he would have me play some jazz. After the playing we would go up to his office and he would fix my teeth. This man one day told me that he was a good dentist and a good pianist but had never succeeded to be great in either of those professions. So he advised me to choose one profession. This is when I quit my mining studies and left for America to study music.

I lived in California from 1979 to 1981. After two months there I got a little apartment in Van Nuys and met Joy Hunter in the music department at Van Nuys College. She helped me with getting a piano from the school. Of course I promised to return it one day, which I did. I met bassist Essiet Essiet at Club 88 in Los Angeles and he moved in with me. At that time Essiet worked several jobs, one of which was as a taxi dispatcher. I worked as a telephone salesman for a company called Diversified Dentals.

We would go around to clubs like the Parisian Room and the after-hours Social Club. The sessions there would start at 2 A.M. and last until eight in the morning. Jimmy Smith and George Benson were among some of the guests. There was a lot of gambling and drugs and police raids. There were great jam sessions at a club called Pippy's on Sunset Boulevard. The session leader was pianist Kirk Lightsey. The club was always filled with prostitutes and a police raid ended it.

During this time I met many musicians. I met bassist Brian Batie and pianist Paul Holman and drummer Steve Jacobs. We moved into a house in Hollywood on Fountain Avenue. Nine people lived in this four-bedroom house and every time a musician would move in I built a new room with two-by-fours. This house was visited by many musicians.

My first professional gig was with saxophonist Charles Owens and bassist Leroy Vinegar. Another great session was at a recording with Billy Higgins and Obie Jessie. The album was never released. I remember sitting in the studio with headphones and playing with Mr. Higgins. I learned from these great musicians by experience.

In 1979 and 1980 I used to record material at a studio in Hermosa Beach. The technician, Spot, gave me free recording time in the middle of the night. The studio was near the famous Lighthouse jazz club. I took the tapes to Holland, and Munich Records released the material. I would have huge suitcases with no clothing and only tapes. These recordings would include most of the musicians I met at that time and who lived in the house in Hollywood.

In the following years my main goal was to produce a record every year. To finance these productions I would sell space on the album covers for advertisements. Organizing tours and getting sponsors, in 1982 I bought my first touring bus. This bus had a stage on its side. I'll tell more about the Stage Bus in a later e-mail.

In 1984 I was twenty seven-years old. An uncle in America called me and said that he had $13,000 for me which my father had left me. My father had told my uncle to give it to me when I was twenty-seven. I picked up the money and bought a round-the-world ticket, one of those special deals where you can fly and stop as many times as you want. I had a book with all the record companies listed and so I flew from one city to another and called the record companies from the airport for appointments. If I couldn't make an appointment I would go on to the next city. In eight months I traveled to forty major cities around the world. I managed to sign a contract with a Chinese record company in Hong Kong to record two albums and transform original Chinese folk songs. One of the stops was Jakarta, Indonesia. Mr. Indra Malaon, from the Jazz Lovers Association, picked up the call from the airport. He took me to a jam session in Hotel Mandarin and there I met Luluk Purwanto and played two songs. She gave me her business card. We only talked for five minutes.

A year later I was sitting at home looking through all the cards of people I had met during this world trip. The phone rang and when I picked up, it was Luluk. I was just reading her card and she asked me if I remembered her. I shocked her by reading her address out loud. She was in Holland to perform at the North Sea Jazz Festival and I was the only Dutch contact in her address book. We started working, recording, and playing together, traveling back and forth between Indonesia and Holland many times, until we finally married in 1987. The wedding was held according to traditional Javanese customs and took three days. We were really meant for each other.

We moved to Amsterdam in October 1987. At that time a company invited us for a special presentation. This firm was a sort of school for directors and professors where they had to learn to solve problems in unconventional ways. During one of the lectures Luluk and I were invited to give a problem. Our problem was how to stay productive playing jazz music without changing our music. During this lecture forty directors of big companies and professors at several universities had to give us fifty solutions within five minutes. We then had to pick one of the solutions. We picked "Music Shares." In 1988 we started our own company and sold over five hundred shares to finance a new production, "The Walz." In 1988 we started our group called Luluk Purwanto and the Helsdingen Trio. In 2003 we celebrated fifteen years of travel, performances, tours, and recordings in this format.

The great thing is that every time we make a new recording, we notice changes in our playing and composing. We are always trying to learn and compose new things. Together we have traveled millions of miles, organized many tours, and are planning to do this until the end of our lives, together.

Every year we spend time in Indonesia. In 1993 we started working with a Greek visual artist, Mikhail David. He had a restaurant and performance venue called the Stage. This was a venue where many different art disciplines were combined. With him we worked out the concept of the Stage Bus. Since that time we have performed more than five hundred concerts with the Stage Bus all over the world. In 2001 Mr. David set up an international festival in Jakarta that shared the same concept as the Stage Bus, "to bring art to the people." This festival was called JakArt @ 2001 and lasted the whole month of June.

Hundreds of artists from all over the world were invited to come to Jakarta to perform at hundreds of locations all over the city free of charge to the public. Luluk and I were appointed as management. We identified the locations and arranged for funding, signed the contracts, and invited the artists.

Mikhail David pursued his concept and organized JakArt @ 2002. The festival funded our Stage Bus tour, Born Free USA—seventy concerts at forty-five universities in twenty-four states. During this tour we met you, Royal Stokes, in Washington, D.C.

René Helsdingen
Amsterdam
October 2002

* * *

Dear Royal,

Thanks for being so patient with us. Luluk is calling her family to find out more about her great-grandparents. They were artists, too.

The last two months have been very hectic. We were involved in several projects. In November 2002, after the U.S. tour, we traveled to Paris and Italy.

Here is finally some information about the Stage Bus.

There have been three stage buses, the first in 1982. I remember buying it for $10,000, and spending another $10,000 on rebuilding and painting it. This was all paid for by Philip Morris, who sponsored a tour by our group, Superlights Quintet, with Obie Jessie, vocals; Don Mumford, drums; Essiet Essiet, bass; and Peter Guidi, saxophone. Bose supplied us with sound equipment. The repertoire was all originals by Obie and me. We did eighty concerts in two months, forty indoor and forty outdoor on the bus. People stood in long lines to see and hear Obie. The following year, 1983, Smirnoff agreed to sponsor a tour.

The next Stage Bus was purchased in 1994 with the support of the Stage, the restaurant and performance venue in Jakarta. This time the concept was really to bring art to the people. Visual artist Aart Marcus, of Amsterdam, did the rebuilding of the bus and its art work. The total cost was about $50,000.

In 1994, 1995, and 1996 we traveled all over Europe and participated in a lot of major festivals, racing from one country to the other.

Sometimes we would cross three borders in one day. In December 1996 the Stage Bus was shipped to Australia. This was an incredible adventure—crossing the desert, driving through wilderness, and performing in mining towns in the middle of nowhere.

The tour ended in Darwin and the musicians, Belinda Moody, bass, and Victor de Boo, drums, went home. Luluk and I were stuck in Darwin with the bus. What to do next? We found a shipping company that had a ship leaving for Sumatra Island with 1,500 cows on board. On the top deck, above all these cattle, there were thirty square meters for the bus. It took five hours to lift the bus with a crane onto the deck.

We flew to Jakarta and then took a ferry to Sumatra. The ship was there but the beams and cables that would be used to move the bus looked like matchsticks. We were really worried that they would break, so I tried to convince the workers to get different beams. There was no cooperation, especially because I was a foreigner. So I lost my patience and started saying Arabic prayers from the deck. Suddenly the attitude changed. They were all Muslims and therefore respected my knowledge of Arabic prayers. Suddenly the beams were a little bigger. Then the bus was still on deck and nobody was around. So we waited. After one hour a thirteen-year-old boy climbed into the crane and, without warning, he lifted the bus and crashed it on the dock front first. Luluk hurried to take some pictures of the event. Fortunately the bus was OK.

We are probably leaving for Indonesia on January 26. We will be performing with Dwiki Dharmawan, an Indonesian arranger and pianist, at the Prambanan temple in Yogyakarta. The performance is supported by the Indonesian Foreign Ministry to raise the image of Indonesia. It is also supported by the Sultan Hamengkubuwono X of Yogyakarta. Luluk and her parents have a good relationship with the Sultan. Luluk's father was the first person to organize classical performances at the Kraton Palace, in 1980, and in 1997 our band, with the Stage Bus, was the first to perform jazz at the palace. That evening, August 11, 1997, the doors were open for the public, which is very rare.

Yesterday I just returned from the International Association for Jazz Education (IAJE) convention in Toronto where I had the opportunity to meet with Oscar Peterson for the first time. He signed my agenda. I knelt in front of him. In between many other fans I told him that I became a pianist because of him. I was emotionally very moved and walked away with tears in my eyes.

OK, Royal, I am getting a little tired. It is 3:00 in the morning and we have a lot of stuff to do.

René
Amsterdam
January 2003

* * *

Greetings, Royal,

Luluk's story

The Sunan and his Queen knew René's grandfather, who was in the Indonesian government in the 1930s. His picture with Sunan is in the palace library. René's father used to work with president Soekarno and René was named after the president's doctor, Mr. Rubiono, who was also head of intelligence and colonel of the Army. René's name is René Peter Onno Rubiono van Helsdingen.

One day I met René, we got married, and we have been together ever since. Our parents set it all up for us without even trying.

I was born on the 25th of June, 1959, in Solo (also called Surakarta), on the Island of Jawa, Indonesia, but was raised in Yogyakarta, sixty kilometers south of Solo.

My mother, Aysha Gani Purwanto, is a coloratura soprano and in the 1950s she performed a lot at the Mangkunegaran Palace (Sunan's Palace). My dad was a tenor and a piano tuner.

My mother comes from a royal background (Kutianyir) in the village Lintau in the province of West Sumatra. The people in Lintau were called Minangkabau, an ethnic group. It is the only place in Indonesia where the people are matriarchal. Aysha's mother was an only child and from royal descent (Tuanku Lare from Rao Rao), and very smart, artistic, and cultural. After she got married, she wanted to leave all the royal tradition and so she brought her family to the Island of Jawa, to the city of Solo and this is where my mother was born.

In those days, every new arrival in the town of Solo had to report to the Sunan, the king of Solo. The King gave my grandfather a royal statue (Penewu) and a Javanese name, Projosukismo. The normal tradition was that every person to visit the King of Solo had to sit on the floor and the king would sit in a chair. Only my grandfather was also allowed to sit in a chair.

My mom had her own band called Sriwedani in 1937 when she was sixteen years old. She was the singer and also played Hawaiian guitar. They performed ragtime music and Indonesian evergreens in a Hawaiian style. She was very popular in that time.

Solo and Yogyakarta, where I grew up, have two completely different cultures, different dialects of the Javanese language, and different traditions, and they both have a palace.

At that time the King of the Palace (Kraton Yogyakarta) in Yogyakarta was called the Sultan (Sri Sultan Hamengkubuono IX), but the King of the Palace (Kraton Solo) in Solo was called the Sunan (HH Paku Buwono XI, Susuhunan of Surakarta, 1939–1945). The music in both cities is gamelan but in different styles. Yogyakarta was never really touched by outside influences and stayed very Javanese.

The Kraton Solo was much influenced by the Dutch during the colonial era. In their library you can even find pictures of the Sunan next to a Dutchman called van Helsdingen, a member of the Indonesian Council and one of René's great uncles. You can find European statues in Solo. The Kraton Solo hosted many classical chamber music concerts. The Queen, wife of the Sunan Ratu Pakubuono, was a classical pianist, and my mother, Aysha Gani, was one of the king's and queen's favorite—one of the very few—classical opera singers. She performed for President Sukarno in the 1950s. That's why, when I was born, I got a huge bouquet from the queen—lucky me.

In the 1940s a Russian cellist, conductor, and arranger, Nicolay Varfolomeyef, arrived in Indonesia. He had escaped from White Russia and traveled with his Hungarian friend, viola player Robert Pickler, all the way by foot, bus, train, and ship via Japan and Singapore. Nicolay, who didn't have status as a fugitive, stayed in Indonesia and Robert went to Australia.

Mom decided to study in the School of Music in Yogya, as an opera singer, coloratura, and pianist. All the teachers in that school were foreigners and Nicolay was the founder of the school and the first man who arranged many Indonesian folk songs for orchestra, including the national anthem. My mother traveled with the orchestra all over Indonesia. My dad was also a member and the only tenor in the choir. So, my mom and my dad fell in love and got married in 1958.

My mornings always started listening to vocal practice by my mom in the bathroom before she went to work; everybody in the house could hear it. At noon I listened to gamelan music from the batik factory on the other side of the river from our house. I had piano lessons in the early evenings, about four o'clock, which is the time in the tropics when the afternoon is just cooling down and the mosquitoes haven't arrived yet. I was five years old and would sing all the notes of my mother's students playing the piano—and also sing the wrong notes just to bug them.

In 1964 when I was five years old, my father, Julian Purwanto, went to Germany to study with Steinway & Sons in Hamburg to learn how to build, repair, and tune pianos. That's why my mom always had a regular job while my dad worked whenever he wanted to. Whenever he needed money he would just go out and tune pianos.

When I was nine I went to see an orchestra concert at my mom's school. That was the first time I saw somebody play the violin, so I asked my parents if I could study that instrument. We went to Mr. Karnaji Kristanto, also called Mr. Tan, and he lent me a quarter-size violin. I refused to accept this because I wanted to learn violin only on the professional-size violin which I had seen at the concert. My parents had to pay a lot of money to buy a violin for me, so they paid it bit by bit. Today, I am still playing the same German violin; it was the best of all presents from my parents.

In the meantime I had lessons with Mr. Tan once a week. Because my parents had to pay so much money for the lessons, I was not allowed to give up. The lessons were always at four o'clock. Always at that time a lady stopped by selling her Javanese cookies. Since I was always very bored learning the violin, the cookies kept me going.

My parents listened mainly to classical music, but my father also listened to some jazz from Australian radio broadcasts late at night, and I would sneakily listen to it, too. Ever since I was little girl, I've had trouble sleeping at night. My father also had some recordings of Astrud Gilberto, Stan Getz, and Carlos Jobim.

As a teacher for my parents and myself, Nicolay Varfolomeyef moved into our house in 1968. My lessons with Nicolay were just me and him sitting on chairs. I would pretend to read but actually I was playing by ear and memory. When I sounded good, he would fall asleep with a smile. But when I played bad then his asthma would get heavy. He was like my granddad. Every day at four o'clock he would call my name, "Lunatska, where is Lunatska?" I would hide at first, but then I would come and have lesson with him.

His health wasn't good at all and he died in 1970 when I was eleven years old. I was very sad because it was then that I realized how important he was in my life. It was in 1995 that he officially received Indonesian Citizenship and was recognized by the government as a great musician who had done a lot for the arts in Indonesia.

I continued studying and in 1970 I went back to my first teacher, Pak Tan, and performed with his string orchestra at the radio station on live broadcasts as a soloist. Later I studied with another teacher, Mr. Fauzan. But again, I was so naughty; they could not tell me anything, I created my own style of playing and they just accepted it as it was. They were all really sweet people.

With my sister Mya, who was a great classical pianist, we would go through violin and piano pieces together almost every day. This would also be without reading and by my just guessing the right and wrong notes. Of course, my sister was reading the music. Mya loved the Beatles, so we would play Beatles songs together.

Sometimes, guest violinists from abroad would be invited to visit my mother's school and I would get violin lessons from them, and most of them wanted to take me to their countries and teach me some more, but my parents would not let me go. I was too young then.

When I was thirteen, my mother was chosen to become the director of the School of Music in Medan, in North Sumatra, so we all moved there. That's when I found a lot of new friends and started listening to the incredible music of the Batak people. Instead of the very slow and polite Javanese traditions, the Batak people of North Sumatra had a completely different temperament. Hot blooded. They just sing out loud and have beautiful voices!

I still didn't have a steady violin teacher at that time, but I joined the orchestra in Medan and they practiced once a week. The orchestra consisted mainly of very sweet and old people, but I learned a lot. I listened to bossa nova, classical, rock, pop, anything. There was so much music around me, I didn't even bother to purchase any records at that age.

Both my parents were working really hard for this school. They were arranging with the government to invite a lot of musicians from abroad to come to the school for master classes and performances. One day the Australian Chamber Orchestra came to Medan. The conductor was Robert Pickler, the friend of Nicolay. At that time he didn't know anything about what had happened to his friend Nicolay or my connection with him. With the help of Robert Pickler I was chosen to get a scholarship to study violin at the Sydney Conservatorium of Music in Australia. This was the first scholarship they had ever given to an Indonesian student. This was like a dream for me. I couldn't even speak English.

When I arrived in Sydney in 1974, I was living with professional classical musicians. During my scholarship I had to stay with a family chosen by the Conservatorium. The husband was a violinist, the wife was a cellist. The daughter was fourteen; her room was opposite mine and she only listened to David Bowie. The son was a true Frank Zappa fan. They didn't speak Indonesian or Javanese, so I just had to guess all the time.

After six months, I moved out and lived with friends from the conservatory and for the first time started buying my own records, like John McLaughlin with Billy Cobham. I was amazed at violinist Jerry Goodman. I still couldn't read or write music so I created my own music writing and tried to copy his playing. I could not understand how Stephane Grappelli played all those notes. Jean-Luc Ponty I copied straightaway, memorized his lines. I was in love with "Matchbook," performed by Ralph Towner and Gary Burton. I started buying records of Bessie Smith, Charlie Parker. Wow! The recordings were so old but they were still too advanced for me to understand.

I stayed for three years, studying violin from Harry Curby, first violinist of the Sydney String Quartet. Again, with him, he just let me do whatever I wanted, playing clarinet sonatas and flute concertos on the violin by ear. I always asked him to play the pieces first. With classical music, I used to buy the records and the books and learned everything by listening. I really started to learn how to read music after one year with him. This happened when he didn't bring his violin to the lessons and asked me to play a certain part. Then he found out that I couldn't read shit!

When I was studying at the conservatorium in Sydney I met with Robert Pickler again. He was one of my teachers at the time. I told him the whole story about how I had a private Russian teacher when

I was nine. He asked me for his name and when I mentioned the name Nicolay, he started crying. All that time he had never known what had happened to his friend. So I had met them both and they had both taught me music, but they hadn't known anything about each other since they left White Russia in the 1940s.

So, I was growing up in Sydney, living with musicians not from my school, playing rock music, listening to Bessie Smith, Frank Zappa, Carla Bley, Gentle Giant, and Mahavisnu Orchestra. I saw Jean-Luc Ponty in concert.

In 1975, I had my first band, ALO, playing Gentle Giant tunes and gigging. This was a ten-piece band including painters and dancers. Our first gig was at Melbourne University after a performance of the Phil Manning Band; Manning was a famous Australian guitarist. For this gig we got $200 and on the way back home after the gig our van lost a sliding door, which hit the side of a taxi cab. Repairing that damage cost $100 so we actually made $10 each. The director of the Conservatory found out about the band and told my parents, but since I was a very good student, always doing my homework, they let me continue to play in the band.

My violin teacher, Harry Curby, was a sweetheart. He let me play all the non-violin tunes on the violin for exams and stuff. I shocked his wife once. She's also a violinist and sometimes when my Harry would have a gig in Europe she would take his place as teacher. I told her that I had bought a new violin and she was curious. But when I said the color was green, she screamed and refused to ever see it!

When we were in Australia twenty years later in 1997, I called Harry up. He still remembered me. "Luna," he asked me, "do you still play the violin?" After I told him that I only played jazz he was not surprised because in 1974 I was the only student he had that only wanted to play *Sonata for Clarinet* or *Concerto for Flute* on the violin.

In 1976 I was playing with the Australian Youth Orchestra, one of the best youth orchestras in Australia. That orchestra took me touring all over the United States in 1976, attending youth music camps. We went to the Fiji Islands, Hawaii, Fort Worth, Dallas, Berkeley, San Francisco, Denver, Chicago, Iowa, Michigan, Connecticut, and some more cities and states. The repertoire included Dvořák's *New World Symphony* and compositions of John Cage.

From then on I attended many more music camps and went to Hong Kong, the Philippines, Singapore, and Indonesia. These music camps were usually organized by the Conservatorium and governments—a lot of fun. In Hong Kong I had the honor of performing with Yehudi Menuhin. I was in the orchestra when he played the Beethoven concerto.

I returned home from Australia in 1977 and started listening to a lot of jazz. I began buying bootleg jazz cassettes and listening to anything that had a jazz label.

In 1980 I had my first opportunity to play with the jazz guys in Jakarta—Benny Likumahuwa, bass; Ireng Maulana, guitar; Abadi Soesman, keyboard; Benny Moustafa, drums; and many others. My first concert was at Taman Ismail Marzuki, the cultural center of Jakarta. I just played one tune and from then on, since there aren't many jazz musicians in Indonesia, I kept getting jazz gigs in Jakarta, Bandung, Surabaya, and Yogya.

In 1981 and 1982 I was in an "all girls" rock fusion band called the Pretty Sisters, a very famous group in Indonesia at that time, playing almost five gigs a week. In 1982 I went to the Singapore Jazz Festival with the band of Ireng Maulana; he was the person who helped me the most to get jazz gigs. Even today, whenever I go to Indonesia, I still jam with his band. In 1986 I went to Jazz Yatra in Bombay and New Dehli with René; Brian Batie, bass; and Rodney Mecks, drums. In 1985, a week before the Bhaskara band went to the North Sea Jazz Festival, I was invited to join the group.

In 1987 I got married to René in a traditional Javanese wedding that is supposed to take forty days. During those days I was not allowed to leave the house. Getting ready meant becoming beautiful by taking many yellow baths, a traditional Javanese herbal bath. One of the ingredients is turmeric, which causes the yellow color. The family also spoils me. During those forty days I am not allowed to see René, my future husband. My parents are very modern and understanding, and since we had recordings and performances to do, they allowed the wedding to take place in three days rather than the traditional forty days.

Then we moved to Amsterdam.

My surroundings were always music and, for sure, I learned from the beginning that any kind of music is interesting and serious. My parents really taught me how to listen and respect music in general, you know, not talking, being quiet.

Luluk
Jakarta
April 2003

* * *

Dear Royal,

Hope everything is OK.

We finished organizing the JakArt @ 2003 Festival in July this year and returned to Amsterdam. It was a big job. We managed 600 events at 200 locations in 30 days.

I am writing you this e-mail also to let you know that we are leaving again for Jakarta this coming Sunday, September 21st, this time to do another tour with our Indonesian Stage Bus. It is a very interesting project in which we will combine Indonesian shadow puppets with jazz. Our bus will be rebuilt and have a second stage for the shadow puppets. So in the next two months we will be organizing, building, and writing the music in cooperation with the puppet players. The tour will take place November 29 until December 24, 2003.

Another thing we wanted to inform you about is that a tour in the United States is a possibility for the summer of 2004.

OK, that's all for now.

Luluk and René
Amsterdam
September 2003

Over a few years, singer Nora York had sent me several of her CDs that convinced me she was an extraordinary and unique artist. I had the opportunity to see her in performance and to interview her while visiting New York a couple of years ago.

The gig was at Symphony Space on the Upper West Side. Nora's was one of many sets in the fifteen-hour *Wall to Wall Joni Mitchell*, a program that started at eleven o'clock in the morning. It was the thirty-third event in this annual series that celebrates classical composers and American songwriters.

York's contribution to the tribute fell in the early evening. She was accompanied by Claire Daly, baritone saxophone; Steve Tarshis, guitar; Dave Hofstra, bass; and Allison Miller at the drums. Of the several Joni Mitchell songs she offered, I was especially moved by her idiosyncratic and stunning rendition of "Both Sides Now." Nora's presentation of this classic piece was not only a showcase for her flawless technique and emotive delivery, but it also demonstrated her theatrical talents, a phenomenon that no doubt occurs whenever she mounts a stage.

Our two-hour discussion took place the next day at noon in Lower Manhattan. After making my way up several flights of stairs, stepping over paint buckets and squeezing by stepladders on the landings and in the hallways, I was welcomed into the one-room efficiency apartment by York.

Checking out the view from the window, I was startled to see that we were not far from where the World Trade Center had stood little over a year before.

"I saw the first plane hit, too disoriented to realize what had really happened," Nora began. "I came back to my studio to work 'cause I had to work. I was standing looking out my window when the first tower fell. The towers were about, I'd say, a half a mile away. It was really intense. We had a concert scheduled in ten days and decided to go ahead and do it. But I completely rethought the concert. I put together a sound and word journey that was a love letter to New York, a love note and a cautionary tale as well. There was such saber rattling going on outside New York. Here we were just sad, so very sad. It was a beautiful evening. No one clapped. We all just played, listened, sat together, and went home. I still feel proud about that night.

"I moved into this apartment in 1978. It was my first apartment out of school and it's the same apartment I'm in still, although they're working their hardest to get me out," said York, her laugh a wry commentary on the building's general disarray because of repairs in progress.

"I grew up outside of Chicago. My mother, Betsy Schwartz, is from a very small town in central Ontario and my father, John Schwartz, was born and raised in Chicago, the son of an appellate court judge. My father is also a judge. So I come from a lawyer family, a legal family. My original name is Nora Schwartz.

"In my house we listened to classical music. I have a brother, Andrew Schwartz, who is a year-and-a-half older than me, and a sister,

Sara Schwartz, who is three years older. My brother, in fifth grade, decided that he was going to be a bassoon player and he's *still* a bassoonist to this day. He saw *Peter and the Wolf* and he fell in love with the grandfather sound, which is the bassoon. So I grew up with the sound of a dying cow in the next room, my brother learning to play the bassoon. But it's a beautiful, beautiful instrument, and sometimes I think that my sound, my singing voice, actually resembles a bassoon because I spent so many years—I'm really very close with my brother—listening very carefully. I would always try and find the bassoon in the orchestra.

"The first musical training I had was when I was two. I was a very precocious young child. I walked very young. When I was two years old they took me to Carl Orff classes—early musical training for very, very young children. We played the glockenspiel and the triangle and the rhythm sticks and various things. I *loved* it, I absolutely loved it. And then I insisted on taking piano lessons, which I did, and in sixth grade I joined a little rock band in my school. I was going to sing. That didn't work out very well—that's another story—and then, in seventh grade, I started studying cello. I still studied piano and I was also interested in classical guitar. I was kind of a multi-tasker.

"My parents listened to Barbra Streisand and Ella Fitzgerald, and I saw Ella a couple of times when I was a kid. I also saw Louis Armstrong. My father was into Louis Armstrong, as I think most middle-class white families were at that time in the 1950s; he was very popular. My parents were very cultural people in Chicago and very involved with what was going on. I lived near Ravinia, which has a jazz festival and also had a pop festival, so I saw Janis Joplin when I was very young, and I was in love with her. I went to hear Sly and the Family Stone.

"I was very into soul music, the Philadelphia sound, that's what I was listening to, and Earth, Wind and Fire, a little bit of Crosby, Stills, Nash and Young, sort of hippie music. But when puberty happened I got more into African-American music, I was much more interested in what was going on there, *pre*-disco. I listened to the Ohio Players, and I was just *madly* in love with Jimi Hendrix when I was in high school. I liked Funkadelic but it was more Sly and the Family Stone. I couldn't stand the Rolling Stones at that time although I've come to embrace them and really enjoy them. I got very interested in Miles Davis's *Bitches Brew*. That was one of those cross-over records where it was the first time instrumental music got to me. I've always been a word person; I love to read, I've always read a lot. I studied philosophy in college 'cause I thought, as an artist, I didn't want to have to study arts; I wanted to have *ideas*; it was all about the concept of what I was doing, much less about the craft of what I was doing.

"And *then*, when I was about fourteen years old, 1970, I stopped *every*thing, totally stopped all musical training, and got very, very withdrawn and very interested in alternative social movements and political ideas. When I graduated from high school, at seventeen, I moved down to South America and worked in a literacy program in southern Colombia and northern Ecuador. I became very much, you know, a good person. It was fascinating, actually. They sing a lot, the Indians in northern Ecuador. When they get together, they sing.

"And then I came back from South America a year later. So I'm just now eighteen, graduated from high school a year early, and I was very interested in visual arts. I sort of switched, in terms of my art interest. I became really interested in drawing and painting and printmaking. I channeled all my creativity into the visual arts and ended up going to a school that was based on an international studies program, a small hippie school that no longer exists, Callison College, in Stockton, California.

"I already spoke Spanish at that point, but I really wanted to go to India. Callison College was a free-for-all; it was all independent study. I dropped out of school at one point and went with an anthropology teacher to Borneo. I was so into it over there that I decided I would take a year of absence from college and spend a year in Asia. And it was there I got re-interested in music, in a very strange way. I'd been making paintings in Bali; I'd been there for about three or four months, and my visa ran out, so I went to Bangkok.

"I arrived and walked into a bar and there was a woman on the stage—she sort of looked like Wayne Newton—and she was singing these really hokey songs. I started singing along with her in the audience and she called me up on stage. I ended up staying in Bangkok for a couple of months with these two women who were lesbians, one a cake decorator and one a Wayne Newton–like impersonator. And I sang in this bar, and I *really* enjoyed it; it was really, really fun!

"I was singing whatever tunes I was called on to sing. I was singing 'Tie a Yellow Ribbon 'Round the Old Oak Tree' and pop songs, but pop songs like Roberta Flack did, what I was listening to at that time. But the good part was the idea of channeling my creative energies in a formative way rather than being in my studio, making a piece of art and then bringing it out into the world. I started to feel this rift in my desire as a creative person. I had gotten off the track of being a musician and more on the track of being a wild person who had interests in the visual arts. I was sort of in a freefall—let's put it that way—kind of like a creative freefall.

"I finished college with a degree in humanities, but basically I was an artist. I got out of college and I didn't know *what* to do. I'd been singing in people's bands but it was a just a lark, you know, just like kind of country pop bands, rock bands. I came to jazz by mistake, Royal. I didn't come to jazz as a lover of jazz; I came to jazz knowing nothing about jazz. I was almost guided by the musicians I started working with. I didn't come to it by being a listener, thinking, 'I want to be like that.' I *totally* didn't do it that way, which is a little embarrassing. Claire Daly is one of my biggest musical teachers because I always say to her, 'What record should I be listening to?'

"I moved to New York in 1978, to *this* apartment. In1978, '79, '80 I was involved in the arts scene because I lived in this neighborhood. I was tending bar in the corner bar here, Spring and Mulberry. All the artists, people like Eric Bogosian, who is now quite a successful performance artist, Laurie Anderson, they were all hangin' out in my bar. I was making these paintings and things; they were very apocalyptic. I would do these huge things of the assassination of Sadat. I was really politically interested, but I was much more interested when people would come over to my studio and I would tell them about it.

"Simultaneous to all this, in 1980, after I'd gotten on my feet in New York, I thought, I really liked singing, I want to sing. Coming from my background, which is classical training, I thought, I want to be a *singer*. I found a teacher with whom I still study today, David Jones. He's great; he's one of the great maestros. He's in Europe now teaching a bunch of tenors. So I started to study voice seriously, and every day I would practice and once a week I would go to my lesson, which I still do. I started to develop my technique, having no idea what I was gonna do with my voice.

"At the same time, I'm on the arts scene and I'm making these paintings and I start hooking up with dancers and I start working in the performance arts scene, which was at that time places like the Kitchen, which was on Broome Street at the time. That's where all these performance artists were merging. It was sort of when these earlier avant-garde musicians that come from the New York Downtown scene were starting to percolate in the East Village and I started to go and watch and listen to the Microscopic Septet. That's pianist Joel Forrester's and saxophonist Philip Johnston's first band together. It was a small big band. And it was hilarious and it was *brilliant* musically.

"Someone took me to see the Art Ensemble of Chicago and I got my mind blown! I had never had that kind of musical experience before. I think it was probably 1979. They used to play in funny places all over the Lower East Side. And I became Joel Forrester's babysitter, for his son Max Forrester, who's now at Cornell.

"So, anyway, I'm working on the performance art circuit, I'm singing with dancers, we're doing this whole thing on Barbie Doll, and I'm starting to listen, more and more, to the radio. I'm listening to WBGO, to whatever the deejays were playing. I'm listening to it all the time in my little hovel here, looking out on the landscape of New York, and feeling like, 'I'm here, I *am*,' and it's a beautiful, beautiful view, and the World Trade Center was right out there. I could lie in my bathtub and look at the World Trade Center and listen to music, and it was, like, really fantastic.

"Then around 1984 I thought, I don't want to be in this performance arts scene; it's the same one hundred white people. I was very arrogant. So I joined a rock band again. I answered an ad, and there were all these off-duty cops and it was a heavy-metal band and I was the lead singer and I hated it, but I wanted to have experience in what I thought was the real world. I said, 'No, I'm going to start my own band.' I knew bass player Dave Hofstra from the Microscopic and I also knew a drummer named Billy Ficca, who was the drummer from an early '80s, very pivotal New Wave band called Television. They were *really* big in the '80s. I did not like their music, at all. But I liked Billy Ficca, and he lived right here over the Raven Nite Social Club, John Giotti's club, where Giotti got busted. Billy was a great rock 'n' roll drummer.

"At the time, I had stopped being a bartender and was driving a bread delivery truck. I started picking songs. The first song I picked that I wanted to sing was Jimi Hendrix's 'Manic Depression,' which is on my first album. I wanted to sing Donna Summer's 'Hot Stuff,' 'cause I thought it was funny. Hendrix, in my mind, is the closest rock 'n' roll musician to being a jazz musician that there is.

"So I put this band together and I would pick one song at a time, and pretty soon, under Dave's influence it was, 'Well, hey, have you ever thought of doing this standard?' He would pick a standard and we would deconstruct it. I'd say, 'What about "My Sharona"'"—she scats it. "'That bass line. And I'll sing, "I've got you under my"'"—she scats the melody—"'"skin."' We could take that music from the '50s and bring it right up *here*, where people could identify with it.

"I was playing on the Lower East Side. I never played in bars that had music. I would approach people and I'd say, 'Can I on Thursday nights play in the corner?' of some hip little restaurant. Eventually I added Dave Sewelson, a baritone saxophone player from the Micros, and I worked with Philip Johnston for maybe five years, singing a lot of his songs. We did soundtracks for a very successful filmmaker in Germany who was a very close friend of mine, Doris Dorrie. Then I wanted to start writing my own songs.

"In 1987, when the Knitting Factory opened I went up to Michael Dorf"—co-founder of the cutting-edge music club on East Houston Street—"and I said, 'Michael, I'm from the Midwest, too. Can I play here?' And he said, 'No problem.' That's where I really started developing my career.

"In '91—this is after I'm working at the Knitting Factory quite consistently—I'm actually starting to sing more and more jazz. By this time, I'm listening to *all* the horn players. The only singers I really listened to were Abbey Lincoln and Irene Kral; Kral blew my mind, with her emotional economy and the idea of just simply stating a melody. And then, when Shirley Horn came on the scene, I used go and hear her at the Vanguard around '86. There was something in their emotional simplicity and in their honesty of approach to a song. I've worked so hard on my instrument, and I also work *really* hard on what I'm doing conceptually. I feel like there's plenty of songs I don't want to sing because Ella sang them better or Sarah gave the definitive interpretation, so there's no need for a Nora York interpretation.

"And then, in '92, I got my first record contract. Once again, the left door swung open and it came in from the field of who knows where. I was doing the craziest stuff; I was making these insane juxtapositions and I was always on stage reading the *New York Times* or I'd bring a television and I'd talk about current events or I'd wear these wild outfits. They wanted people that were dressed in black evening gowns and singing. And then I'd do this whole thing where I was the extremo jazz singer where I'd wear these huge long gloves—I'm almost six feet tall—and these outrageous giant falls and stuff. I'd take it to the extreme because I was sort of playing against image, playing against type.

"I said to my lawyer, Marc Jacobson, 'Check out Japan; I know they're gonna like me.' I just made it up one day, just had this idea. And he went to the MIDEM festival, the music business thing they hold in Cannes every winter [Marche International de la Musique]. And he came back with a $35,000 record deal, sight unseen, from a Japanese label called Polystar. They gave me thirty-five grand and I sent them the art work and the record. They didn't tell me what I had to record, they didn't tell me who I had to record with. I could use anybody, do anything I wanted. I started writing in 1991 and I put everything on it I could *think* of, because I thought it was gonna be the only record I would every make. I recorded in this great studio, I paid everyone ridiculous amounts of money, I made no money on the record." She laughs. "I was just, like, 'Here, everybody, let's have a good time.' It was really great, it was a really cool time. Richie Beirach played on that record, *To Dream the World.*

"For the second record, I hired Maria Schneider to do the copy work. After Maria and I worked together on that I thought, 'You're so great!' So we spent two years meeting every Tuesday and we started writing songs. And then I made the next album and Polystar sent me even more money the second time. My first record did *very* well in Japan, and then, as we were recording the second record they gave me the money for, Japan kinda went belly-up just before I was going to go there on tour and I had no record company at that point. They'd dissolved their international division.

"I don't know if you want me to talk about sexism or not. Do you want me to talk about that? You do. It's hard to know the difference between sexism and your own experience of sexism and sour grapes, especially for a singer, because singers, when they make money, they make much, much more money than an instrumentalist. So I think there's a lot of antagonism toward singers 'cause often they aren't very good musicians. I am a good musician, but often they're not. I've *worked* on my musicianship. Dave Hofstra, for instance, worked with me when I was *not* a good musician, and he was one of my great teachers. All the musicians I've worked with have been my teachers. I was always long on ideas, so I've always had a very strong point of view. Vocally and also conceptually, in my work, I'm very *word*-based.

"I'm sorry, I derailed there for a moment. Well, here's an experience that I had with sexism that I believe is true and not sour grapes. I helped build the Knitting Factory, I and Marty Erlich and John Zorn and Bill Frisell and the Jazz Passengers, and a few others—we were all part of this movement that came up. For the first jazz festival they had, called What Is Jazz? Michael Dorf and his booking people, out of 150 bands, they booked seven women musicians. Early '90s and there were *seven* women musicians! I think I was the only bandleader of the seven. And I said something to Michael at that point because I had also had lots of run-ins regarding when they would take Knitting Factory tours and this and that and they would never bring me along, and I kept thinking, 'Maybe it's 'cause I'm a singer,' and then I thought, 'No, it's 'cause I'm a *girl!*'" York laughs. "I don't know whether it's because I'm a female or because I'm a singer or perhaps both. I know that I was respected in that scene and I still am. But In terms of sexism, it's been my experience with the Knitting Factory that it is truly a boys' club. You feel it when you're there; there's a marginalization of women that is so strong in that scene.

"I've worked with Claire Daly now for a number of years. She's a brilliant, gifted musician, and I cannot tell you, Royal, how my audiences respond to having women on stage. 'Cause what I'm doing is not the fading flower, you know, and even if I'm singing a ballad, there's always something very, very powerful about the ideas I'm working with and the stuff I'm doing. It's kind of in your face. And to have a woman, a beautiful redhead, at my side playing the baritone saxophone, *it blows people away!*

"Claire is an astonishing performer, and there's something so powerful about a woman taking on a big idea, or a big instrument, or a big piece of music, that is so moving and so galvanizing that I think these guys have made a huge mistake. What's going to move people, what has lived longest, are the things that give people a sense of their humanity. I have a job teaching song interpretation at New York University and I say this to my students—that they don't have to stand a certain way and they don't have to sing like Bernadette Peters. 'Cause to me it's so ghastly boring. And it's not what's going to move your audience. I keep thinking, 'How can I be more luminous?'

"I didn't work in the Knitting Factory for a number of years. That was it for me for about five years." York laughs again. "I cornered him in a deli one day, and I said, 'Michael, you've got to look at your booking policy; it's outrageous.' I said, '*Seven women!? Seven women!?* We're doing better in the *Senate!*' And then five years later, after they built the new place and everything, I went down there and I said, 'I want to work here again.' So he booked me in. And I started working there again. Then Joe's Pub opened and Bill Bragin is coordinating a really brilliant music program there and I asked to work there and I have been, and also at the Public Theater, on Lafayette Street and Astor. I've been doing concerts. And I did the Newport Jazz Festival.

"I got a grant this year, a New York State Council on the Arts Composers Commission, which *totally* blew my mind. It was to write a song cycle, which has now evolved into a piece that I'm doing at the Brooklyn Academy of Music called *Power Play*. One of the things I've gotten into is this juxtaposition thing, how I'll take eight bars of this and sixteen bars of that—it's kind of a postmodern thing. It's about war. I just finished a concert for a series called New Sounds Live, which is at Merkin Hall. It was called *I Dreamed I Saw*, the songs of Jimi Hendrix and Stephen Foster put together.

"Stephen Foster was the first American pop star. When I thought to align Hendrix and Foster's work I was operating on a hunch. One thing I knew was that both composers were tremendously appealing to me. The direct and saturated quality of their melody attracted me. It was not until I sang the songs one alongside the other that I discovered the incredible synergy between the works. As I developed *I Dreamed I Saw* as a concert piece, some striking similarities between the two artists began to emerge.

"Foster and Hendrix were separated by a century, yet they both use fantastic, surreal, and psychedelic imagery. They were both responding to the horror and unrest of the times in which they lived by creating a wild world of images. Foster lived with the ravages and promise of post–Civil War America. Hendrix's tableaus were the Vietnam War, the civil rights movement, and the sexual revolution. Both men traversed racial boundaries in their lives and in the making of their music, drawing from their own traditions and also profoundly influenced by the other. Hendrix and Foster were prolific in their very short lives. Both were thought of as womanizers and both were very involved with inebriants, dying drug- and alcohol-related deaths at the height of their successes. The juxtaposition of the two composers' songs amplifies each one in profound ways while evoking and highlighting distinct nuances.

"So I sort of have two lanes that I travel in now. One is that I'm writing songs that are like songs, and then I'm doing much more kind of really getting underneath, doing interpretive work. It's kinda like what Don Byron's been doing, except I'm doing different people. Rethinking, in very, very profound and in-depth ways, the music of, for example, Foster and Hendrix, and then juxtaposing them.

"For this *Power Play* I'm working with an electronic sample artist, Blaise Dupuy, and a kind of rock and jazz hybrid band that consists of pop players Steve Tarshis, guitar, and Charlie Giordano, accordion; jazz players Dave Hofstra, bass, and Claire Daly, baritone saxophone; and two players who inhabit the cusp of jazz and pop, Jamie Lawrence piano, and Allison Miller, drums. They asked me to do two nights of concerts on the Vietnam War era. So I'm trying, of course, to make it pertinent to today, which I'm always trying to do—relevant to today."

I asked Nora to speak of her relationship to her performance and its connection to the visual arts, which have always been of such deep interest to her, and to say something about what she strives to convey to her audience.

"Well, actually, I think a lot about this because I teach this, and I've thought a lot about it in the last three years because of developing this new piece. My husband, Jerry Kearns, is a painter. We've been married now four years; we've been together eight. I used to go to all of his shows—he's a famous and brilliant painter—and he used to come and hear me sing. And getting involved with Jerry has kind of brought me back to the art world. I've done a number of concerts in arts spaces and I've done a lot of work that relates to art. I got into this Stephen Foster work because I did a bunch of concerts at Brooklyn Museum relating to turn-of-the-century painting and I started to rethink and do contemporary arrangements of Stephen Foster and various turn-of-the-century popular songs in New York galleries.

"I'm just telling you this because it's a big piece of my puzzle that I didn't want to leave out, so I will work into this theme. I'm a singer first, right? And as a singer my voice is the first access that I have to interpretation, right? So I find that working on my technical chops is hugely important, and that's why I still study and still work hard on the technical aspect of singing. If I have a palette, I have enormous nuances of color that I can play with in order to interpret the song, because the second thing that interests me the most about being a singer is words. Since I *came* to singing via performance, via the idea that I had these ideas I wanted to express and that the vehicle of singing is actually a seductive way of introducing ideas, there's a whole relationship already that, as you step on stage as a singer, the audience already has with you. They sexualize you and they sentimentalize you. Like I told you, I used to *play* with that but now I don't play with that image as much as I *utilize* it.

"My repertoire is in some ways limited. Like if I go to a jam session, there are very few songs I know that everybody knows, because unless I feel like a song is something that I can express from my own experience or from an experience that interests me, then I won't sing it; I'll leave it to somebody else who has that experience or has interest in that experience. I don't think I always have to sing songs that I have personally experienced, but I *do* feel that I have to know something about what it is I'm singing, or at least be curious to find it out.

"So, as a singer, I'm not trying to make anybody feel anything; all I'm trying to do is find out what *I* feel about it. If I can tell the story as honestly and authentically as possible, then 99 percent of the time you're going to feel something. But it's gonna give you permission to feel your *own* thing. I really feel strongly about that. That's why I was telling you that the singers I admire most have the most emotional economy, because then it allows me, as the audience, to go toward the singer with my own emotion instead of being kind of preached to or told what I have to feel. Often there's just so much coming at you that you feel like, 'Uh, oh!' From the first *bar*, you're sort of like plastered against the wall and you're, like, 'Whoa!' It's never been my taste, let's put it that way. I'm not trying to make anyone do anything.

"Especially since 9/11, I've been working really hard to not tell anyone the right or the wrong; all I'm gonna do is tell you what I think and what I feel as honestly as I can. And often, a song can have huge ambivalence. I can be inside a song and one time through the chorus it could be, 'I really love this person,' and the next time I'm in it I might be thinking, 'I don't know if I really love this person.' It's like the way it is to be alive, if I stay on my pins, really inside my own experience, or the experience that interests me. Everyone can imagine even being a killer; I mean, we have that range of experience as human beings. But if I keep it *really* grounded in my own experience, my own expression, then I'm gonna move people.

"Singing for me is an essentially spiritual act with very corporeal origins. The voice is mined deep inside the vessel of the body. Song has corporeal beginnings but the import is spirit. In singing I locate a place where body and soul hold together. Through song I examine both personal and collective meaning, a depth and dimension of our shared experiences. In my work I enjoy mixing metaphors from history, popular culture, and the political world. I'm exploring diverse archetypes and ideas while trying to remain specific in my emotion and intention. I want the audience to *see* what they are hearing, to engage their feelings and thoughts. Even though I am striving for specific objectives, I often linger in the twilight between heart and mind, where the known and unknown can collide, where conflicting points of view reside, where *what I think* and *what I feel* dance in that liminal territory."

Acknowledgments

As in my two previous books for Oxford University Press, which were also collections of profiles based on my interviews with musicians, my biggest debt by far is to those whose stories are told between these covers. I wish to express my appreciation for the time and effort they gave to the project.

Second, I extend my thanks to the photographers whose splendid art graces this volume.

Several individuals provided me assistance in achieving access to specific musicians. Paul Blair put me in touch with Luluk Purwanto and René Helsdingen and alerted me to their imminent performance in Washington, D.C. Giuseppe Ballaris sent Patrizia Scascitelli to me. Lara Pellegrinelli alerted Carol Sudhalter to my Italy connection and my long-time support of the cause of women instrumentalists in jazz.

I am much beholden to Carol Sudhalter for her application of speed-of-sound keying-up skills to the transcribing of seven of the taped interviews, a contribution without which this volume would not yet be seeing print. Jack Towers transferred my 1976 Art Blakey radio interview from reel-to-reel tape to cassette so that I could play it on my equipment and transcribe it. Applying his exemplary print-making skills, Don Peterson enhanced several of the photographs.

Sheldon Meyer, as always, lent his discerning insights and sympathetic encouragement at all stages, from the book's inception to its completion. His editorial expertise is, deservedly, legendary. Others at Oxford University Press were very helpful, especially Joellyn Ausanka, Peter Harper, Patterson Lamb, Woody Gilmartin, Eve Bachrach, Melissa Renee, Matthew Sollars, Mary Belibasakis, Anne Holmes, and Kim Robinson.

My sons, Sutton Royal Stokes and Neale Hartmann Stokes, continue to inspire me in my chosen vocation of wordsmith.

Finally, my deepest gratitude is to my wife, Erika Else Stokes, for her steadfast support of my writing for lo these three-plus decades since I first "took pen to paper" as a chronicler of the jazz scene.

Index